'The

GRILL

of

Victory

HOT COMPETITION
ON THE BARBECUE CIRCUIT

WILLIAM BROHAUGH

emmis
books

For further information, contact the publisher at

EMMIS BOOKS
1700 Madison Road
Cincinnati, OH 45206
www.emmisbooks.com

Library of Congress Cataloging-in-Publication Data

Brohaugh, William.
The grill of victory : hot competition on the barbecue circuit / by William Brohaugh.
p. cm.
ISBN-13: 978-1-57860-267-4
ISBN-10: 1-57860-267-X
1. Barbecue cookery--Competitions--United States. 2. Barbecue cookery. I. Title.
TX840.B3B747 2006
641.5'78407973--dc22

2006005599

Cover & interior designed by STEVE SULLIVAN
Edited by JACK HEFFRON
All interior photography by BILL BROHAUGH
Cover pig trophy provided by MARY BARNES CLARK

DISTRIBUTED BY PUBLISHERS GROUP WEST

DEDICATION

For my sons Chris and Kevin, and for the pride I take in them.

ACKNOWLEDGMENTS

For their willingness to put up with me the summer of 2005 and to teach me barbecue from the other side of the judge's chair at multiple competitions (in alphabetical order): team leaders Terry Black, Brad Cheatham, Rick Dalton, Winfred Geer, Gary Kerce, Richard Lackie, Myron Mixon, Clara Scarritt, John David Wheeler.

And my appreciation of friendship and my thanks, as well, to:
Annie Sisson, for leading the way.
Karen Emerson, for accepting me as a judge the first time.
Leroy and Randy Rieckenberg, for accepting me as a finals judge the first time.
Carbondale Eagles, for forgiving me after whatever mistakes I must have made judging them my first time out 'way back when (and whatever mistakes I've made since then judging them and others).
Walt Brown, for pointing me toward Galax.
Larry Ohrberg, who along with Walt put up with me during Galax and other competitions—the two of them kept us on our toes and kept us laughing.
Richard Hunt, Jack Heffron and Howard Cohen for their vision.
Lauren Shepard, for her support of this project.

For their help, for their support and friendship over the years, organizers and judges and pals, again in alphabetical order: John and Nanette Atherton, Roy and Jane Barber, Jaye J. and Chuck Doan, Charlie Hagene, Richard Layne, Randy and Cathy McGee, Dave and Lynn McClellan, Mike Mills, Tim...I mean, Joe and Lisa Melvin, Katherine and Steve Mistilis (operators of that fabulous Memphis-area B&B, The Bridgewater House), Larry Nance, Ed Richardson, Terry and Brenda Rider, Angie Roach, Susan and Richard Schmidt, Mack Walker, Hap and Becky Zook. And a bunch of others over the years whose names elude me.

And the teams: Brad, Willie, M.J., Daryl, Jimmy G and Paul of Carbondale Eagles; Tim of City Hogs; Daryl/"Sarge" and his Da-Nite Outback crew; Fuzzy, he of Fine Swine; Chris and all the Flying Pigs crew; Hal, Al, Rusty, Russell, Rick and Lance of Gwatney; Greg, Jimmy and Fran of Hogwizer/Bubbacue; Myron, Nick and David of Jack's Old South; Dave, Chris and Don of Late-Night Porkers; Scott and Teresa (and darling daughters) of Mad About Que; Mark, Mark, Joshua and Claudette of M&M Cookers (who changed their name to J&J Cookers in an apparent-but-futile attempt to get a higher position in this alphabetical order); John, Carmen, Mr. Bill, Miss June, Ken, Birm, Mark, Tango, Craig, Curt, Tall Matt and the rest of Natural Born Grillers; Mike and his The Other Side crew; Roger, Gary, Ricky and Miss Pat of Pig Pounda Kappa; Keith, Julie and Gary of Pigs in Paradise; Rudy/Randy, Joyce, Cliff and Wally of Pork 4 Skins; Jay and Mary Kay and the rest of the Pork Improvements crew; Charlie and his lovely family of Porky's IV; Winfred, Clara, Wes, Boyce and Henry of Porky's Pride; Wayne and Linda of Red Hot Smokers; Chris (and father Bill), John, David and David of Rib Ticklers; Terry, Skip, Neil and Ron (God rest his soul) of Super Smokers; Richard, Tony, Mark, Pat and Amy of Sweet Swine o' Mine; Pat, Tom and Merrill and family of Tower Rock. And a bunch of others over the years whose names elude me.

TABLE OF CONTENTS

FOREWORD

In 1998, after years of pulling chef-hosting duty on TBS's *Dinner and a Movie*, I landed a job with *Southern Living Presents* as their television food correspondent. My first assignment: Memphis in May, the legendary world championship barbecue cooking contest.

Our show's producer, a native Louisianan named Ed Richardson, was so giddy to snag the Memphis in May assignment you'd a thought his lucky Powerball numbers finally paid off. By the time my plane descended through the sweet blue smoke over Memphis, Ed had already been scouting the park for the better part of a week. He smelled of burnt hickory and obviously hadn't showered or eaten anything except smoked pork for days. He was in a barbecue-induced frenzy, unable to form complete sentences without blurting out words like "dry rub," "bark" or "brine injection." (I learned later that this is a fairly common syndrome after initial contact with world-class barbecue contests.) By the time we arrived at Tom Lee Park, the first round of on-site judging had already begun. Contestants were scrambling in all directions and the rising hum of anticipation was electric. Unfortunately, I had no clue as to what the heck was going on. I desperately needed a crash course in the world of professional barbecue.

Enter William Brohaugh, veteran Memphis in May judge, pork historian, barbecue philosopher and teacher of all things barbecue to annoying chef-TV hosts like myself. Somehow in the heat of the battle, he graciously found time to walk me through the subtleties of the contest and even provide introductions to some of the hardcore contenders. (Believe me, an introduction from Bill goes a long way.) These were some of the finest people I've ever met, a number of whom are immortalized here with fondness, humor and bull's-eye accuracy.

Even after two decades in the restaurant business, I've never witnessed anything like the passion and dedication demonstrated by this smoky brotherhood. These guys make NASCAR fanatics look anemic.

Mr. Brohaugh's commitment and devotion are also unmistakable—enough so that he's been allowed access deep inside the barbecue culture. In some ways, the competitive barbecue circuit borders on religion; faith, myth and superstition all play a part. You'll find blood, adversity, bravery, triumph, loss, heroes and comradeship. Bill tells their stories, teaches us their language and spares no details. And I promise the reader will be left with images never to be seen on Martha Stewart or The Food Network.

Keep the fire low, the beer icy and save some bark for me.

Claud Mann
Ojai, December 2005

INTRODUCTION

I began my association with competition barbecue as a player in a barbecue tall tale. My friend Bruce Hillman had been judging for a time. His start came when someone from Tennessee spotted Bruce's freelance magazine piece about South Carolina barbecue, and invited him to come judge barbecue, Memphis style. In 1990, Bruce invited me to go along with him on one of his barbecue jaunts, to a small town six hours away.

What would I do? I asked.

Have some fun. Relax. We'd taken a similar road trip once before, when we hopped in a car and drove from Cincinnati to his alma mater town, Columbia, South Carolina, so that I could taste a decent version of a bar food just then gathering awareness—"Buffalo chicken wings," they were called.

So I went along with Bruce to this barbecue thingie, and I hung around. Had a few beers on Friday night, gaped at the teams, listened to the street-dance band. The morning of competition judging, one of the scheduled judges didn't show. Bruce popped up to the contest organizer and explained that I had judged a sanctioned competition in Kennett, Missouri, the year before. The first I'd ever heard of Kennett, Missouri, was when Bruce came back and told me I'd judged there. And told me, to my shock, that I'd be out along Murphysboro team row judging in just a few minutes. With that little whopper on my barbecue "résumé," I was able to sit in the judge's chair, I got to know some proud and good-hearted folks, and I ate some of the most wonderful cooking I'd ever had in my life.

I'd grown up in Wisconsin, and here I was just one state south, being introduced to the South. Murphysboro, Illinois, only a couple of hours out of Memphis, welcomed me, and I didn't know how lucky I was. Murphy has one of the most respected contests on the Memphis in May circuit (now

Memphis Barbecue Association), and the area has spawned some of the most consistently successful barbecue teams. For Wisconsinite me, barbecue was synonymous with "sloppy joe." (I won't engage in any debate about what the word *barbecue* should really describe. Some words describe different things, which I discovered culinarily anew when I moved to Cincinnati and was introduced—by the same Bruce Hillman—to what the spaghetti-esque concoction southwestern Ohioans also call "chili." Hey, at least I discovered Thai food and sushi without his aid.)

I've been judging barbecue ever since that '90 Murphy. It took me fourteen years to finally get to Kennett to judge and make good on my friend's barbecue fib, and by that time my wife and I had been feasting in Indiana and Kentucky and Georgia and Mississippi—and of course, in Memphis itself. In those years, I even cooked in a couple of unsanctioned events, procuring a small trophy or two. All because of *two* tall tales told. "My friend judged in Kennett" was one; the other, I suspect, was "The primary reason I'm inviting you is to have a good time," when perhaps that was indeed a good reason, but one secondary to, "Hey, your car is more reliable than mine so let's take *it*."

Now, these many years later, I want to share with you what Bruce Hillman shared with me: A visit to an extraordinary event, the barbecue competition. (You're on your own, for the moment, with that Cincinnati chili thing and you've likely already done wings.) *The Grill of Victory* eavesdrops on one such event, the Smoke on the Mountain Barbecue Championship in Galax ("Gay-lax"), Virginia ("Virginy'all"). This is but one of many competitions on the Memphis Barbecue Association circuit, which in turn is one of several barbecue competition circuits operating today. The circuits vary, just as definitions of barbecue vary. When I described this project to a North Carolina friend, a colonel in the army, at an outdoor cookout, he dropped his professional nonaccent and blustered in solid North Carolinian, "You're wasting your time. You're barking up the wrong tree, boy."

Memphis barbecue, he pointed out, was misguided in its use of tomato in its sauce. He popped into his house and returned with a bottle of authentic North Carolina vinegar sauce—tart, hot and, I agreed, delicious. Vinegar and peppers and a few other ingredients. *And those philistines from South Carolina, my gawd they put mustard in their barbecue sauce* (his point, my words). His wife, from those far yonder regions of Kentucky, shook her head. Tomato and sweet, she pointed out.

Me, I love 'em all. So the type of barbecue contest and the way the meats are cooked as presented in this book are dictated not by tastes and not by regions, but by rules. Soon, I hope, I'll be writing in as much detail about the other circuits.

Please be aware that *The Grill of Victory* is not absolute reportage of a single event. There are, for example, tales herein told about pranks and stupid moves and even heroics occurring at other contests, and those tales are retold here with fiction technique and license. (After all, it's rare that the cameras are rolling and the voice recorders are activated at all moments during a competition.) Some anecdotes from the Galax contest itself have been recreated with similar license. And at times I will integrate into my narrative Galax participants' quotes, actions and procedures that took place at other competitions (especially in standardized briefings and presentations to judges), but know that they are within the spirit and practice of *this* competition and they mirror what took place in Galax. They are simply more easily reported because cameras and voice recorders and notebooks *were* at work at those moments at other events. If such compressing bothers you, please report me to the International Bureau of Absolute Veracity, and keep in mind that however they're presented, the incidents happened. Still, a tale-teller's gotta be a tale-teller. And so it is with the teller of the tale-teller's tales.

Every so often, a name has been changed to protect the guilty. A team name, a contest's location, a judge who unintentionally did something embarrassing and doesn't deserve further embarrassment.

And will you find me in this book? I'm lurking in the occasional yarn within, yes. I've been judging competitions for sixteen years now, and I have a story or two to tell. So if you read a story involving an unnamed judge who does something stupid, it's more than likely that...um, it was someone else! I swear! (The unnamed judge doing smart things is most likely my wife.)

My friend Bruce Hillman, unfortunately, does not appear in this book in any form. He hasn't been judging for some years now. Family, very successful professional career, other hobbies—the usual. You should come back, Mr. Bruce. It's as much fun as it ever was. I'll even spin a tale for you to get you back in. I'll tell 'em you judged in Galax last year...

PROLOGUE

Thursday, July 14, 2005. "Portable" backyards are gathering in the mountain town of Galax, Virginia. Industrial-strength backyards, rolling in from North Carolina, Kentucky, Maryland, Georgia, Mississippi, Tennessee, and cross-state Virginia and just down the road Virginia. Mobile backyards which, once they settle into their designated spots on Galax's Main Street, will feature slow grilling, and serving friends, and exchanging some bull, and enjoying a tall cool one, under an awning in the shade or out of the rain. Unlike your typical backyards, however, the cooks here will accept more than thank-yous as their rewards. If they cook well, they'll come away with trophies and prize money and bragging rights, the grill of victory.

"What better way than to spend a day with your family," says one of the cooks on the circuit, "slow-smoking meat and having something good to eat at the end of the day, whether it be in a contest or in the backyard."

On this Thursday, the backyards-on-steroids begin arriving in Galax for the first-ever Smoke on the Mountain Barbecue Championship. On Friday, the participants start cooking. On Saturday, they entertain judges—new friends and old. On Saturday night, some of them whoop and holler and feel the thrill of conquering the wild, as it were. Even one cook who places a disappointing (for him) fourth place feels the thrill. On Saturday, he grins ferociously when he takes the stage, turns to the crowd, and thrusts the fourth-place plaque high in the air with two hands like it was the Stanley Cup, the Vince Lombardi Trophy, Wimbledon.

1 ARRIVAL OF THE CRASH TEST DUMMIES

"You can learn a lot from a dummy."
– Ad Council seatbelt awareness slogan

Wednesday, July 13, 2005. Ron Passmore is quietly fretting as he drives the evening mountain highways down from Galax, Virginia, toward Winston-Salem and then on to Greensboro, just over the North Carolina border. He's running just on the edge of being late picking up his guests at the Piedmont Triad International Airport just east of Winston-Salem, and he's mildly unhappy about that.

Ron, one of the two primary organizers of the Smoke on the Mountain Barbecue Competition to be held in the city of Galax in three days, is concerned about doing it right. No matter what the "it" is, he wants to do it right. Being late picking up the reps from the contest's sanctioning organization is, to his mind, not doing it right.

Ron regards the road with the same precise look that he has used to regard almost everything related to the upcoming barbecue competition. He looks at you the way a benevolent hawk looks at you; he smiles the way you'd imagine a hawk to smile, though more brightly so.

Ron's salt-and-pepper hair has been laser-cut into a flat-top. Close-cropped sideburns dip far down along his jaw line and under his chin to meet the perfectly trimmed goatee. He wears black—black sandals, black shorts, the black uniform shirt of the Galax Smokehouse. The shirt identifies him as "Ron—General Manager—Big Pig." In the SUV's cup holder is a foam-plastic cup, large, of Pepsi, a straw sticking out of its plastic cover. He's seldom without it. Sometimes he writes his name on the side of the cup so he doesn't lose track of it. And, especially these days, he's never too distant from a smoke. As the contest draws near, he looks at the cigarette in his hand and says, "I'm just about eating these."

His voice is deep, his voice is steady. The people who know him know that he's wound tight and nervous about the contest. The people who don't know him see stability in his calm intensity.

Carlene Poole brings a big dollop of purple to the ride down to Greensboro. Bright and brash and energetic and wearing a loose purple blousy top that's equally bright and brash, Carlene is full of questions about the competition. How it works. How to make it good. How to pull it off without embarrassing anyone or committing a barbecue faux pas. Carlene was eager to join Ron on the airport run on this Wednesday night, so she could quiz the reps from the Memphis Barbecue Association. The MBA governs the Memphis in May barbecue circuit; it sanctions contests, dictates rules, provides advice, offers up volunteers like Walt Brown and Larry Ohrberg as official MBA reps.

Carlene and Ron talk of how judging should work, what the volunteers should be doing, who's doing what and "I don't know who's doing that." Ron can't and doesn't track every detail, though he assiduously maintains a binder (black cover, of course) with pages listing local volunteers' addresses and phone numbers, photocopies of barbecue rules manuals, lists of barbecue teams and judges who have committed to coming to Galax, and printouts of almost every email to and from teams, judges, Memphis Barbecue Association officials, barbecue aficionado Al Roker (no evidence that he even received the email or was able to reply), the folks who created the contest's promotional brochures, and, of course, Walt Brown and Larry Ohrberg. But the binder covers Ron's responsibilities; as for the other responsibilities, that's what committees are for. Carlene lists several of the people who have gotten involved, a couple of them to Ron's surprise. "The problem with so many committees is you don't know who's helping out."

At one point along the drive, Ron and Carlene discuss the hospitality area—where barbecue judges and local VIPs and members of the incoming teams themselves can stop in for snacks, for a Friday-night supper, for air conditioning and a chair.

"If you have a plethora of chairs…" Ron begins to say.

"What's a plethora?" Carlene says. "I don't know what a plethora is."

"A whole bunch," says Ron. "Or, as they say around here," and he chuckles, "right many."

Carlene frowns a bit. "I don't have a whole bunch."

Carlene's from "around here." Ron Passmore isn't. Originally from Florida, transplanted to be closer to his spouse's family, he doesn't say "right many"—though, for that matter, neither does Carlene.

Their soon-to-be passengers, Walt and Larry, are being flown in from Memphis. Their location in the Memphis area is not surprising—they got their start in barbecue because of all the activity in Memphis. But they don't work out of the Memphis in May offices. They are, after all, volunteers.

"Now," Carlene Poole says about halfway into the drive to the airport, "when we pick up the Crash Dummies . . ."

She catches herself.

Ron winces a bit.

Crash Dummies?

"That's what I call Walt and Larry," Carlene says with only a hint of sheepishness. "You know, like the guys in the commercials." Those guys, the Crash Test Dummies, were the talking frozen-smiled mannequins who advised viewers on buckling up. Carlene knows their names weren't Walt and Larry, but the MBA reps' names are close enough to recall the classic public service announcements featuring Dummies *Vince* and Larry. The public service announcements were retired six years previous, and now we know how the unemployed dummies are spending their retirement.

Carlene is not wearing her seat belt. The Dummies are going to be appalled.

This worries Carlene—the Crash Test nicknaming, not the seat belt. Ron and Carlene and other Galaxians have met Larry. Crash Test Dummy Larry O visited Galax back in March, in an unprecedented pre-event visit to a contest site by an MBA rep. This being Smoke on the Mountain's first year, Larry had agreed to being flown in then to meet with city officials, survey the territory, lend some advice for setting up the physical site and organize the contest. Ron and Carlene know in person Larry's sly just-put-one-over-on-you smile that never changes no matter what tornado is swirling around him. Walt is the unknown. Carlene and Ron are anticipating a dour Walt Brown, the Walt Brown who was all business on a long conference call with Ron and co-organizer Judy Brannock, finalizing timetables and such, just three weeks before. They anticipate a Walt Brown who will frown at being tagged a Crash Dummy. And now Carlene is embarrassedly aware that word of her nickname will reach Vince and…um, *Walt* and Larry.

As Ron swings through the lower-level passenger pickup area of Piedmont Triad International not long after 10 PM, Walt and Larry already stand curbside. They are flanked by luggage and computer bags, including a stuffed blue bag on wheels that carries their portable office. Carlene tempers her assessment of Walt on first sight. "He's wearing purple. He can't be all bad." (Perhaps Carlene was expecting Walt to be wearing a dour gray, since the nonLarry Crash Test Dummy wore gray . . .)

Carlene Poole doesn't meet the reps immediately—a quick facility-stop inside the terminal beckons first. When she returns curbside, the now-informed Larry hugs her in greeting. Then he leans back and says, smiling brightly, "I'm Larry the Crash Dummy." Sly grin. I-just-put-one-over-on-you grin.

Walt carries it off deadpan, matter-of-fact: "They call us the Crash Dummies because all our contests crater."

Larry doesn't have to say it, but later on the drive back up the mountain to Galax, Virginia, he does. Larry says, "We're gonna have some fun."

2 BARBECUE ARRIVES UNDER THE CHRISTMAS TREES

"We're blessed to be doing this."
– Lance Freemon of Gwatney Championship Barbecue Team

Wednesday near midnight, July 13. Ron Passmore is showing Walt Brown and Larry Ohrberg how the Smoke on the Mountain Barbecue competition will lay out. It's close to midnight Wednesday night, Carlene Poole has gone on home, and the threesome are standing in downtown small-town Galax on the intersection of Main and Grayson. Not *at* the intersection. *On* the intersection. Traffic is nonexistent at midnight. Yet the traffic lights overhead change on their schedule, accenting the trio in green then yellow then red then green as Ron points out where the teams will set up, where the hospitality room will be set up, where vendors will be stationed.

Near the end of this consultation, Ron asks Walt and Larry, "You guys need a golf cart to get around during the competition?"

"No," says Larry dryly. "The limo will do just fine."

Larry just might need his joking limo: At Smoke on the Mountain, the teams will cook in the city of Galax, in Grayson County. To find the nearest services, such as the portable johns

Ron Passmore, Larry Ohrberg and Walt Brown conferring near the contest site on Thursday.

brought in for the competition, they must travel to nearby Carroll County.

And have only to cross the street to do it.

Galax is in what is known as the Twin County area. In fact, Galax straddles the border of the two counties. The border runs down the middle of Main Street, the street on which the teams will be situated north of the Grayson Street intersection. Team areas will be in the southbound lane of Main, facing east toward Carroll County a few feet off yonder. Soda machines and portable toilets and the flow of foot traffic will be in the northbound lane of Main. A few vendors, the "bungee jump" trampoline attraction for the kiddies, and the amateur division barbecuers (the "Patio Porkers") will set up on Main, as well, south of Grayson Street. Grayson itself will be the dedicated to festival business—food and crafts vendors, the beer garden, the Grayson Street stage.

In two days, a gazebo selling T-shirts and other memorabilia will occupy the intersectional real estate now lorded over by Ron, Walt and Larry.

The Crash Dummies consider the layout, picturing team needs. The northernmost part of Main will be given over to the biggest rigs. The street is wider there than it is down near Grayson. 220 electrical is available there, which will satisfy one team's request. Another team is bringing in a semi-tractor cab to pull one of its cookers; the public parking behind the cozy Farmer's Market at the corner of Washington and Main will accommodate that. Electricity seems to have been taken care of. Water, too. The city has invested in extra hoses to provide onstreet water hookups.

Walt and Larry are also picturing team complaints—not enough space, this team not wanting to be next to that team…."Space is limited," Walt says, "so there's not a lot of room for whinage."

Walt is a gentle soul whose sleepy eyes disguise sharp observation. One of the head cooks on the circuit calls him "Can't-See Walt" because of those drooping eyelids. Both Walt and Larry are themselves cooks on the Mile High Barbecue Cooking Team, though as MBA rep volunteers they are disallowed from competing on the MBA circuit. With Mile High, Walt is the rib cook and is something of a supervisor. Teammate Jim Johnson identifies one of Walt's qualities that make him a respected rep. "Walt," Jim says, "has the strongest pointy finger on the circuit." (Before joining Mile High, Larry was on a team called Two Fat Larrys. Despite lacking the sleek look of a well-exercised Crash Test Dummy, despite having a belly that stretches his polo shirt a bit around the beltline, it's hard to picture Larry Ohrberg being termed a Fat Larry. "There are people in this world," Larry says, "who should not be wearing hip huggers. Walt and I are two of them. We're actually wearing hip huggers right now, but you can't see them under these bellies.")

Ron is getting to know Walt better on this late-night tour. Galax's only contact with Walt thus far has been that phone call, the hour-plus mid-June conference call with Ron and co-organizer Judy Brannock. The phone is a perfect venue for advice and firm direction, and a crappy venue for pointy-fingering. On the phone, Walt doesn't crack wise with people as often as he does in person. On the phone, his low-key sense of humor can get lost in layers of perceived seriousness. Especially when details dominate a business conversation. Mostly the conference call covered team recruitment: The need for it, and the fact that there will be a fair amount of activity the week before the competition. "You need to get on the horn and start talking to these teams personally," Walt had said.

And the conversation covered details of timing of ancillary contests and briefings. Ron proposed to hold the cooks' meeting on Thursday, but Walt pointed out that all the teams won't be in by then, and besides, they expect Friday briefings. So the meeting time gets moved around a couple of times, until they agree to 5:00 Friday. Walt said, "Do you know when your announcements will be?" Ron asked for guidance about timing the Saturday awards presentation. "You're very safe if you do it at 5:30," Walt said, and the three of them agreed to move the awards even further back to 6:00 for time to spare. "You're pushing it at 5," Walt said. "You could have a computer glitch." Experience speaking? Prescience?

The conversation did not cover whinage.

If there is "whinage," Larry says, now in Galax, "we'll just deal with it." With short hair graying on toward white, a close-clipped mustache, and an expression that's sometimes skeptical but usually more toward the look worn by doting grandfathers teasing doted-upon grandkids, Larry has the look of a moderately flamboyant French chef, though real estate is his game.

His game used to be in printing, and he and Walt are sporting "Galax Barbecue" buttons that Larry himself made. Walt's game is the construction business; he has once said, "I've started a couple of businesses in the past two years, and they're wrecking my retirement."

And for the moment, Walt and Larry's game, as Larry has said, is just Dealing With It in their role of Memphis Barbecue Association reps. Officially, reps attend competitions to conduct briefings, issue judging assignments, tally scores, make sure people understand the rules. Unofficially, as Walt would describe it to co-organizer Judy Brannock after the competition's conclusion, "We're Marines. We adapt, we improvise, we overcome."

"You rise to the occasion," Judy said.

"Not as often as we'd like," Walt deadpanned.

"Not as high as we'd like," Larry added.

Unofficially, reps are jitter defenses, especially for first-time competitions. "We're here to calm them," Larry says. "It's not part of our job description, but we can handle it." Walt and Larry's Wednesday arrival is further evidence of their calming role; this arrival, earlier than that of reps at other events, comes at special request of the contest coordinators. Which is fine with the two—they enjoy helping out the new contests, to get them going well right from the start. So, partly in practicality, partly in the spirit of jitter defense, Walt and Larry are walking about with tour guide Ron Passmore, crossing from Grayson County to Carroll, crossing from July 13 to July 14, surveying and making late-night plans and nodding comforting approvals about the contest site.

Such an in-city and on-street location has considerable precedent on the circuit. Mt. Carmel, Illinois, shuts down three blocks of its downtown for competing teams, as well as for vendors and a street stage. Butler, Alabama, gives its town square over to festival activities, with the barbecue teams situated close by on a couple of closed-off side streets. In Evansville, Indiana, Smoke on the Water shuts down several blocks of pleasant downtown Riverside Drive so teams and judges and the strolling public can enjoy the Ohio River views. Ribberfest in Madison, Indiana, does the same. Washington, D.C., closes down several blocks of Pennsylvania Avenue (yes, *the* Pennsylvania Avenue, running between *the* Capitol Building and the White House) between 9th and 14th for its National Barbecue Battle.

Ron talks of moving the competition to nearby Felts Park, where the annual Old Fiddler's Convention is held, if and when Smoke on the Mountain grows in coming years. Walt and Larry consider this idea; later in the event, they will recommend against it. Even though such facilities provide a way to "gate" the event—close it off and charge a public admission fee—parks are susceptible to mud; streets carry rainwater away efficiently. Parks move commercial activity away from local businesses. One year in Mt. Carmel, the Airpork Crew barbecue team had just swept the competition, grabbed every first place available to them, and they were partying, eyeing the tattoo parlor across the street and threatening to head over there en masse to get celebratory branding. They didn't follow through, but at least the opportunity was there.

There is no immediate tattoo opportunity for the barbecue teams in Galax. Their commercial opportunities run more toward the antiques and the crafts, in this town of about 6,800 that has adapted to a fair amount of visitor business. On one corner of Grayson and Main, the Place in Time antique shop. On the opposite corner, Ron's Galax Smokehouse restaurant. Down the way a bit, past Tom Barr's Fiddle Shop, is the Tastee-Freez co-owned by Judy Brannock. Within a couple minutes' walk (*total*), the independent Chapters Bookshop, the Framer's Daughter framing shop, the appropriately named Roof of

Virginia Craft Shop.

Galax doesn't scream tourism until it's hoarse the way a Gatlinburg or a Wisconsin Dells does. It nods tourism at you kinda friendly-like (its chief industry is not tourism at all; it's furniture—pull up a chair, y'all). Galax pleasantly greets visitors for its Leaf and String festival, now a couple of weeks past, and for the Old Fiddler's Convention ("the Woodstock of Mountain Music," as it has been unofficially dubbed), coming up for its seventieth incarnation in August. Back in the mid-nineties, Galax was a stage on bicycling's Tour DuPont. Some of the money in Galax city coffers raised in relation to that event feeds the new festivity: The barbecue competition—the Smoke on the Mountain Barbecue Championship. Slogan: "Barbecue with Altitude."

Earlier in the evening, returning from the airport in the Piedmont Triad—named for the region in which the cities of Greensboro, Winston-Salem, and High Point are clustered—Ron, Carlene and the Crash Test Dummies drive on toward both barbecue and altitude past beautiful mountain scenery that you can't see at 10:30 PM in the fog. Still, Ron gives something of a travelogue as the SUV climbs back up into the mountains—he *is* the president-elect of the Galax-Carroll-Grayson Chamber of Commerce, after all. (And Judy Brannock, by the way, is its executive director.)

Over there on the right, you can sorta see the lights from Mt. Airy. That, Ron explains, was Andy Griffith's hometown, fictionally depicted on the classic television comedy *The Andy Griffith Show*. The TV show was set in the copyright-freely named town of Mayberry, which has hints of "Mt. Airy" in it. Ron and Carlene and the Crash Test's have already noted and passed Pilot Mountain, inspiration of the also copyright-freely named town of Mt. Pilot in the series.

Heading back into Virginia, Ron says that Grayson County

to the west is home to Mt. Rogers, the highest peak in Virginia (elevation 5,720 feet). The chief crop of Grayson County is Christmas trees, and perhaps the darkness is helpful here because you shouldn't be seeing Christmas trees in July anyway. The chief crop of Carroll County, Ron notes, is cabbage.

Had the city of Galax been named within the last decade or so, it perhaps would have named Christmas Tree. (Or Cabbage.) The Galax name came from a once-important area crop: The leaves of the galax plant, also known as a wand plant. Waxy galax leaves remain green long after they have been picked, and once served as pre-plastic, pre-silk "artificial" greenery. Perhaps an entrepreneurial botanist could create a pine-galax hybrid and grow natural artificial Christmas trees.

Galax has a charm deeper than its festivals and its shops and its mountain air and its evergreen crops. It's a city that seems to like itself. There's something to be said for a town that stages a lawnmower race and a demolition derby pitting the fire department against the EMS team against the police department.

The Galax Fire Department Demolition Derby is promoted as an unusual spectator attraction. That's not an observation. That's stated specifically in the rules. "The Galax Fire Department Demolition Derby is promoted as an unusual spectator attraction." And, hey, rules are rules. Among the other rules: No hearses. During or, one would hope, *after* the event. Actually, hearses are just one type of vehicle covered by an entire list of disallowed entries, including Jeeps, taxis, imports, and trucks. That latter ban is a shame—wouldn't you like to see a couple of fire engines going head to head? (For some reason, Chrysler Imperials are also singled out as a no-no.) In previous years, the Galax Volunteer Fire & Rescue had run other July events, including a tractor pull and a gospel music festival called Fire on the Mountain. Where there used to be Fire, there's soon to be Smoke.

The lawnmower race, held the week before Smoke on the Mountain, is part of a circuit sanctioned by the Alleghany Lawnmower Racing Association. The Lawnmower Racing Association has thirteen classes of mowers, from modified stock models (no blade in that deck, thank you very much), to twin-cylinder supermowers 46.6 cubic inches and above. And then there's the "Legends" class (rules: Driver must be fifty-five or older, vehicle must be a rotary-blade push mower, pit areas must include hammock and beer/lemonade for ease of mid-race napping.... OK, so the last two are made up). On the surface, it seems that competition regulated by an official sanctioning body governing something normally done in your backyard on a Sunday afternoon is a little silly, but the event that is about to take place in Galax involves competition regulated by an official sanctioning body governing something normally done in your backyard on a Sunday afternoon, as well. One man's backyard activity is another man's barbecue competition addiction.

The vehicles that will begin rolling into town the next day will not be gathering for the Demolition Derby, though barbecue rigs aren't specifically banned from the derby rules. These rigs are smokers, some big enough to cook entire pigs. They ride on trailers pulled by pickup trucks and, in one case at least, a diesel cab. They aren't backyard units by any stretch—in fact, if a typical one sat in your backyard, you wouldn't have much lawn left over to practice your lawnmower-racing skills.

Now in the initial minutes of Thursday, July 14, Walt and Larry and Ron wrap up their tour of where those rigs will be stationed later in this newborn day—later, after the Crash Dummies and *maybe* Ron get some sleep.

3 THE LONG HELLOOOO

"It's close to T-minus piggy."
– Brad Cheatham, head cook of Carbondale Eagles, about to prep his hog in Caruthersville, Missouri

Monday, June 27. Sixteen days before the entrance of the Crash Dummies and seventeen days before it would normally come to Galax, the first barbecue rig arrives. Gary Kerce of the Pig Pounda Kappa barbecue team is taking advantage of a fuss-saver that teams occasionally employ. Gary and his team are returning to their home in Loganville, Georgia, after participating in the National Barbecue Battle in Washington, D.C., concluded the day before. Galax is more or less on the way home for Pig Pounda, so bringing the rig into Galax will save time and gas they would otherwise spend dragging it down mountains to Loganville and back up mountains to Galax.

Approaching town, Gary uses his cell phone to call Ron Passmore at the Galax Smokehouse. Ron in turn calls Judy down at the Chamber of Commerce to alert her to the arrival. Ron then drives out to meet Pig Pounda Kappa, so he can lead them to the parking lot of the Galax Volunteer Fire & Rescue, which has offered the lot as a temporary location for Pig Pounda's cooker.

By the time Ron Passmore's SUV turns the corner onto the street adjoining the Fire Department, a greeting party has assembled: Among them, on-duty volunteer firefighter Zeke Morton; businessman Brian Funk (co-owner of Artifax Art & Office Supplies), also a reporter for *The Galax Gazette*; and Judy Brannock.

Judy, executive director of the Galax-Carroll-Grayson Chamber of Commerce for the past two years, is a short Southern woman with long Southern vowels. Earlier that day, she had explained, "My mother's best friend is from Pennsylvania, and she has very fast speech, don't you know, and she comes down here and she'll say 'Helllooooo,'" stretching the word comically. "I even took a speech class and my professor, one day he said, 'Judy, forget it. It's here, and it's never leaving.'"

Behind Ron's SUV, a black pickup hauls the Pig Pounda trailer (fire-engine red, so at least it won't clash with its new host).

Zeke Morton says only, "Holy mackerel." This from a man who, between fire trucks and being the winner of the 2005 Galax Fire Department Demolition Derby, knows his rigs. The fire department hasn't realized just how much space parking lot space they'd be giving up. The Pig Pounda trailer containing three grills and a kitchen is forty-four feet long.

"It's bigger than the home Larry and I had when we were first married," Judy says in something of an awed whisper.

As Gary Kerce swings onto the parking lot and begins to position his rig, the occasional passing car drives by...not particularly fast.

"It's already got people slowing down," Ron says as he nods toward one of the passing onlookers.

"Holy mackerel," Zeke says again. "That's a cooker."

When its trailer is parked, the Pig Pounda team—Gary, wife Pat and brother Roger—greet their hosts, and start talking barbecue. Gary is a bright-faced, short-gray-bearded Southern leprechaun. He's energetic in his contest presentations, and just plain loves to talk barbecue—to the point that he and his teammates appear in an instructional barbecue-cooking video. Roger, beardless but a little scruffy after the drive from D.C., is lighter-haired, quieter, more serious-looking, but just as open. And Pat Kerce, Miss Pat, is a quiet dark-haired lady who smiles easily yet sometimes looks a little sheepish about smiling.

Gary doesn't hesitate a second when asked to show off his holy-mackerel-that's-a-cooker. He and Roger open up the trailer by swinging open two sidedoors left and right to reveal three huge black grills—one for ribs, one for pork shoulders, one for a whole hog—resting on a black-and-white checkered linoleum floor. It looks like the stage set of a barbecue cooking show. To the left, a door leads to an air-conditioned kitchen.

Judy Brannock is reveling in innocent excitement (she is, after all, a woman who has on occasion exclaimed "Golly dingers!"). The first evidence of months of hard work has just arrived in her city. And she's starved for information. "Now, do you have a secret-recipe sauce?" she asks Gary. "They're educating me on this."

"We are now in the process at this moment of having our sauce bottled and marketed," Gary says. "We've been out here so many years cooking all the time that we need to start doing something with our sauce, get it out on the market."

"Are you allowed at these competitions, like if you have a bottle of your sauce, to let people have a sample?"

"Well," Gary says, "you're asking me that. Actually, *you're* supposed to be making that rule."

"You're allowed to do it," Ron quickly injects.

Judy says, "Do you do a big presentation on the on-site judging?"

"Yes, ma'am." Gary's answer has pride in it.

She leans in like she's asking for gossip. "What do you tell them?" She's heard of tall tales told. She laughs as she says, "I fell for some *awful* whoppers. Larry Ohrberg was telling me something about 'They'll tell you that they only serve ribs from the left side of the hog.'" Gary starts cackling—he knows what's coming—as Judy continues: "And he says, 'There's a reason for that. If you ever drive by a farm and you look at the hog pens, the hogs are always lying on their right side. Well, these are all tough and callous.'" (The hogs aren't the only ones lying on the side.) "And I was thinking, 'How do you tell at a grocery store if it's a right- or a left-sided rib?' And I said, 'Is that true?' 'No, it's a lie.' And I said, 'Oh.' I'm a real klutz at this... So..."

"I try my best to be real informational out here," Gary says. "I'm not giving them everything. But I'm going to give them enough that they know I know what I'm talking about. I bring 'em in here," and he turns and walks over to the "here" he has mentioned, an area just to the front of built-in steps leading down from the cookers. Gary's on stage now. It's not competition, but he's got an attentive audience and a chance to talk about his passion. "I show 'em what kind of wood—we cook with hickory wood—and I explain to 'em why I cook with a certain kind of hickory. You can cook with all kinds, but if you get like a shaved bark here you got thick bark on it. You got to cut that thick bark off because impurities in the bark cause bitterness in your meat. If you got a thin bark, that's fine. That's why some teams like to cook with fruitwood trees."

"Do they peel that bark?"

"Mm-hmm. Then you talk about your cooker"—he indicates the big grills he and brother Roger built themselves—"explain to 'em how your cooker works. Then you tell them how you took a raw piece of meat and bring it to a finished product. I tell them where the meat comes from, what you did to prepare it, what kind of seasons you put on it, at what temperature you cooked that, how long did you cook it. And once I run through all that, I've got a nice table set up"—he walks over to the other side of the trailer stairs and all probably see the table Gary's visualizing—"I'll bring a shoulder down here…"

"You put it on a big platter?"

"Yup. Then what I do is carefully dissect that shoulder. Take every muscle out of that shoulder."

"In front of the judge."

"Right in front of the judge," he says, almost delighted that he'd been asked that question. "He gets to check each portion of that shoulder, to see how much moisture's in it, how tender it is, whether it's cooked done or overdone, the flavor of it. He'll taste that, and then he puts sauce on it to see if the sauce complements it."

"I didn't know anything about it. People have asked us a zillion questions."

Ron says, "This area is very ignorant of professional barbecue."

"We really are," says Judy. She confirms with Gary that the public will be able to watch the judging, because those that watch are "gonna go back and they're gonna tell somebody and that will make it even bigger and better" next time.

"How many people you expecting?" Gary asks.

Ron answers precisely. "We have no clue. Scientific wild-ass guess, a SWAG. We have no idea how many will show up."

No predictions are made, and therefore no promises to be broken. "I'll be honest with you," Judy had told a prospective sponsor earlier that day. "This is our first year we have done this." She believes there will be strong enough response to benefit sponsors, but she offers no guarantees.

Jim Davis, the volunteer in charge of acquiring vendors and managing site space, says of vendor inquiries, "I've had these people ask me, 'Well, what do you expect? What can we expect?'" Jim tells them, "It's my first year at this, I don't have any idea. Larry Ohrberg predicted ten to thirty thousand people; we may not get a thousand people." No guarantees on sales, no guarantees on the weather. "All I can do is, you send me your money and I'll guarantee you a space on the street."

Local businesspeople like Sharon Ritchie, owner of the Chapters Bookshop across Grayson from the Smokehouse, are cautious, as well. "We merchants really don't know what to expect." She will buy in some barbecue books to see how they do. And she hopes that the event might fire up some additional interest in local and regional titles—those books rival the bestsellers in sales when the Fiddler's Convention and other events hit town. But in Sharon's life, as in all booksellers' lives in 2005, the big event on Friday night, July 15, midnight, will not be barbecue but the release of *Harry Potter and the Half-Blood Prince*. Chapters sold fifty copies of the previous Potter book on release night; Sharon hopes for seventy this time. "If I do that, it'll make my weekend. If I sell a few barbecue books, it will be like Christmas."

"For most natives, this is their first look at professional barbecue," Ron is saying to the Kerces, "so I look at this as an opportunity to educate the area about what barbecue is all about."

Galax Fire Chief Dave Hankley had at another time extended the definition—not just what *barbecue* is about, but what *competitive barbecue* is about. "The real question that a lot of people have is just 'What is it?'" Barbecue competition does not mean "barbecue festival." Festivals are chowdown affairs, where you can get just about any variation on a theme. From the Waynesville, Ohio, Sauerkraut Festival (vendor items:

Sauerkraut pizza, mashed potatoes topped with kraut, sauer-kraut doughnuts) to the Salt Festival at Kentucky's Big Bone Lick State Park to Grayson County's own Whitetop Mountain Sorghum Molasses Festival, American food festivals are correctly interpreted as places where food is made available. Hankley had said, "When they hear barbecue festival, they think, 'Oh man, I'm gonna come down here and eat all this barbecue.... They're thinking, 'Great eats' just anywhere you go.' ...I think that's going to be the thing, educating the public as to 'What is this barbecue fest?'"

Chief Hankley himself had asked those questions when first hearing of the idea: "How," he had asked, "'How do they compete *and* how do they serve food?"

"Well, they don't sell."

"You mean you're going to bring in these thousands of people to Galax at a barbecue festival and they can't eat it?" Hankley had said. "Man, you're asking for problems. That's like having a carnival and not letting anybody ride."

On his June 27 arrival in Galax, Gary Kerce echoes Chief Hankley's concern without having heard it: "That's one thing that makes the public mad," he tells the folks gathered around him in front of his parked rig, Ron and Judy and Zeke and Brian Funk—and Tom Barr joining the group from his nearby Fiddle Shop. "Be careful about advertising this thing. You say 'Come down and eat world championship barbecue,' and they expect to come down and eat from every team down here. That makes 'em extra mad when they can't do that."

Ron and Judy assure their visitors that they're working hard to spread the word that Smoke on the Water is a competition and not a festival. The local media, they say, has been cooperative in making that point.

"Y'all doing a People's Choice?" Roger asks.

Ron says, "Not to my knowledge. How does that work?"

"Some people work it different. Some people will provide like butts for the teams to cook, and they'll have volunteers come around to pick them up Saturday morning."

Gary says, "If you can give the teams a couple of shoulders and have them cook that meat while they're cooking theirs, the next morning at 10 o'clock give it back to you guys with their own sauce. Then you charge the public x number of dollars and they get little numbered-cup samples, and let them vote." It is an opportunity for the public to not only sample barbecue cooked by the competitors, but also to judge the 'cue themselves.

"Like a wine-tasting thing," Roger says.

Gary adds, "That gives the public something to do—you see what I'm saying?"

Ron sees, but knows he's running out of time to set something like that up. There's much already to be done in the next few weeks. When later that day Judy asks him how he's coming with contacting teams, he says, "I haven't had a chance to call. I've finished 92 percent of my Smokehouse backlog today. Tomorrow I've got to finish July's schedule. Once that's done, I can spend the rest of the week on recruiting teams. But I had to get bills paid, I had to get end-of-month stuff done...."

Judy knows what he's up against. She had scheduled out this day's work before leaving the office last Friday, but when the phone began ringing shortly after she arrived at the Chamber at 7:30 am that schedule was just "blown out of the water." She's facing work until midnight this night, and she's pretty certain about the same schedule tomorrow. Time's moving.

Before Gary and crew leave to continue on to Loganville, Ron invites the Pig Pounda team to visit his restaurant...and the sample Smoke on the Mountain trophy displayed there. Gary has already seen pictures of the trophies, and he knows he wants one. But seeing the sample close up opens the dampers wide on his already burning interest. The trophies are unique on the barbecue circuit, and Pig Pounda is not the only team coming to Galax to try to snare one. "Boy," he says, beaming. "I'm excited. I can't wait. I wish it wasn't two weeks away."

"I wish it was a little longer," Ron says.

Judy shakes her head. "I don't. It's time to get on with it. It's time to get it done."

4
NON SEQUITURS
AND RON SEQUITURS

"That Murphy's Law thing is working right well."
– Ron Passmore

Tuesday, July 12. Judy Brannock is talking about Smoke on the Mountain as the event nears. "At times I think, 'What if they come in and this is a shambles? Oh god!' You know, public humiliation, worst of all. You worry about that."

During the week before the competition, the organizers are pressing hard to defend against the potential of shambles. In a small brick cottage-style former residential house on Main just a half block from the police department and only a full block from the contest site, the Galax-Carroll-Grayson Chamber of Commerce is enjoying a benign but intense swirl of activity.

Judy is still mostly on the phone; Chamber employee Roger Poole greets people as they come in. Roger looks like a relaxed former cowboy sidekick, with his boots and his drooping mustache. "Uncle Roger" was his radio name in a former career, and he leans more to the Will Rogers than the Hopalong Cassidy.

"We're closed for business, sir," he intones to a visitor he recognizes, hiding a smile under that mustache until the last

Ron Passmore and Judy Brannock go over contest details in Brannock's Chamber of Commerce office

moment. Roger is Carlene Poole's husband. Or, as he phrases it, "I'm Mr. Carlene."

Paper "goodie bags" of gifts for barbecue judges and teams are lined up on the floor outside Judy Brannock's office and on a table in the Chamber's kitchen, one door over from Judy's office. Contributions for the goodie bags from sponsors are still trickling in. A gross of Smoke on the Mountain logo T-shirts sits in the Chamber's central area, a former living room, where visitors can grab city maps and calendars of events and brochures on everything from the Tuck Me Inn to Old Cranks Motorcar Museum & Ice Cream Shop over on Railroad Avenue. Judy frets a bit about the number of T-shirts ordered— did they order an appropriate number of them? For a previous event, three hundred related T's had been ordered, and about a hundred went unsold. But that was an event the organizers knew. This event, as is pointed out again and again by organizers, merchants, and teams alike, has no precedent. Too many shirts? Not enough? Judy notes that MBA rep Larry Ohrberg had advised her to leave the public wanting more.

Jim Davis stops by to use the fax machine in the building's once-upon-a-dining room. His black hair pulled back into a long ponytail, Jim wears thin spectacles, denim shorts, purple toes and a cast—he's recently broken his right leg, and he props a walker nearby.

"I originally started off with fifty-eight spots that were available to me," he says, talking about vending participation. "I filled those up and went to Ron and said, 'I still have people wantin' space, what do you want me to do?' So he gave me that south Main Street spot where the Patio Porkers are going to be." That move bumped vendor site availability up to ninety-eight spots, and, he says, pressing out his gentle sideways smile, "I've got ninety-four of them booked right now." Some vendors have booked more than one space—there are about fifty vendors total.

Judy, cordless phone in hand, comes out of her office to ask Jim a question. A vendor has called in, wanting to set up early Friday instead of Thursday when set-up is scheduled.

"Fine," Jim says. "They'll set up on south Main."

Returning to her office, Judy says into the phone, in a voice that's assuring and caring, "Jonathan, that would be perfectly all right."

Jim says, "I'll tell you one gal that's been really putting in some time, and that's this one." He gestures toward Judy's office. "It's going to be an awesome event, but we never could have done it without that girl sitting in there. Ron and I, we done a lot of scufflin' and shufflin', but she's been the main backbone. She's had the leverage with the sponsors to get them to come on board with us, and without that sponsorship, it would make that prize money a hard thing to achieve. We're at that point of no return, I mean it."

Later, Judy the backbone will say with a nervous laugh, "We're scared to death."

Jim says, "We've been working full force on this thing for about a month." For Jim, gathering vendors and clearing health department permits. For Judy, gathering sponsors. Personal visits. Half-hour phone calls sometimes into the night. Hanging up the phone near the end of one long day, she was overheard saying, "That was the hundred-and-fourth call today."

Further down on Main Street Tuesday night, at the other organizational focal point for Smoke on the Mountain, the cockpit of Ron Passmore's figurative 747 is bustling. Wearing a headset to field phone calls on the main restaurant line, he sits at his office desk, which overlooks, through a paneless cockpit window reminiscent of the slit opening of a bunker, the customer floor of the Galax Smokehouse. It's especially hectic because he'd been called out of town on Monday; he has not moved from his chair since 7:00 Tuesday morning. Phones, cellular and otherwise, are ringing about him. The main restaurant line, Ron's cell, his employees' cells. A waitress pops up the stairs. "Call for you."

This call. How are Natural Born Grillers going to pay for the bread for the team's side vending operation—with the meat payment or separately? Where will they store the bread?

That call. A sponsor needs tables.

The other call. An outgoing call, made again. And again. Ron has thirteen teams committed to competing. "One more has called in," he says, "but is not returning my calls." He puts in a call to one of the organizers of the Kennett, Missouri, competition where the team has participated, looking for another number for the team. In Kennett, Jason Rhea says he has to look it up, and will get back to Ron.

Meanwhile, Ron's working on revising agendas—not for

the competition itself. Those timetables have been set for a while now. Tonight he's writing agendas for the cooks' briefing and the judges' briefing. In his make-sure-nothing-is-forgotten fashion, he is putting on paper (complete with a heading stating the name of the competition, its slogan, and its run dates) the items that most organizers would either play by ear or simply jot onto a sheet of scratch paper.

Item number one on both agendas: "Thank you for participating." (At the Friday cooks' meeting, Ron ends up going off script by improvising, "Thanks, everybody, for participating.")

Part of his motivation for having the agendas spelled out precisely is a demand by the commonwealth health department. When on July 4 *The Galax Gazette* published Brian Funk's story about Pig Pounda Kappa's arrival, "Full-size barbecue rig rolls into Galax," Ron Passmore got a call.

The commonwealth health department was not pleased.

"According to contest rules and the city's health code," the *Gazette* article read, "competitors are not allowed to sell their food at the same place they are competing, so Natural Born Grillers will have two separate sites." No problem.

"As for the other competitors, they're free to give away samples." Problem.

To allow distribution of samples sold or unsold, Ron is told by the health department, the teams must follow the same codes that vendors abide by. Therefore, the health department has stipulated that Ron announce to the teams the ground rules, and that that announcement appear *in writing*. Ron types in the wording into his computer. "Announce: Due to the laws of the Commonwealth of VA teams will not be permitted to sample their product to the general public. To provide samples to the general public you must adhere to standards required for food vendors. Do Not Serve The General Public!"

That revision in place, he prints the agenda, reviews it,

clomps the page with a three-hole punch, clicks open the big black binder that holds, well, everything—everything that has been his life the past few weeks. Removing the previous version, he slips new into the binder, old into the paper shredder on the floor to his right. With a couple of grinds, it's gone.

Judy calls. More details.

The computer chirps, "You've got mail."

Ron reads the incoming email from barbeque team Jack's Old South. One bed in the motel is fine, head cook Myron Mixon notes. No need to move him to another motel to get a second bed. "That's the quickest Myron has gotten back to me," Ron says. He'd emailed Myron about room needs just a few minutes previous. Ron's dependent on his computer, even though he admits that "I am not computer-savvy. I can take you apart and put you back together, but I don't know my way around Excel." *Put you back together* is from Ron's former career as a cardiopulmonary specialist with twenty years of trauma surgery experience. His partner, Dan Milby, Sr., dining room manager of the Smokehouse, had similar experience. Together with pit master Jon Jordan, a former truck driver, they are the three pigs of their company entity: 3 Pigs and a Lady. Lady Barbara Jordan is the business office manager.

Ron's cell rings.

The thought, unrelated, springs out of Ron's mouth: "We gotta have radios," he says. *Non sequitur.*

On the speakerphone, Judy says, "Chill. The worst is over."

The thought, unrelated, springs out of Ron's mouth: "I gotta go to the hotels." *Ron sequitur.*

Ron needs to deliver envelopes of instructions for getting from that particular motel to the judges' hospitality room, delivered to each judge by name when they check in. Ron is surprised to hear that this might be something of an innovation for barbecue. Apparently instructions awaiting incoming guests are common at the music festivals.

He tries again to reach the team that had called him on Monday night.

Tuesday night, and Ron is still in the scramble to get more teams. To him, it seems too late. But Walt had told him in that conference call that there's a fair amount of activity the week before the contest. Some of the traveling teams, for instance, try to keep money tied up in only one contest at a time. They wait to see how they do at one contest to see if they can afford to do the next. (Later in the year—a year of ballooning gas prices, recall—Chris Beller of the Rib Ticklers barbecue team took the stage to accept the trophy for winning grand champion of the Columbus, Mississippi, Roast n' Boast. He looked at prize check and joked, "I need to cash this right away so I can buy diesel to get us home.")

Jason from Kennett calls with another number for the team Ron's trying to reach. At that new number, the person answering the call curtly points out that they are on vacation. This puzzles Ron. If they were on vacation, why had they called about their participation the night before?

"I am not ready for this event," Ron says. "I need two more weeks." Trying to buy some portion of the two weeks he doesn't have, Ron won't leave his chair for another several hours.

On Wednesday morning, Police Chief Rick Clark stops into the Chamber of Commerce to say hello and to check on things. Chief Clark has a sleepily stern poker face, which nicely frames his soft jests. He's just come down from the Galax Smokehouse where he'd stopped in to talk to Ron. One of Ron's Smokehouse staffers had told the Chief, "We don't know where he is, and he's crazy." Where crazy Ron is, is on his way back from his WBRF radio interview.

WBRF, broadcasting from Galax, has considerable range to

its signal, reaching into North Carolina. Each Wednesday morning, local businessman Maurice Vaughan, owner of the Made in Galax furniture gallery, both hosts and serves as the only sponsor of the 8-9 AM slot. Normally during his hour, Maurice counts down the top country hits from #10, concluding with #1. This Wednesday, he starts with #1 and works down, knowing he's not going to make it through all ten. This Wednesday, he's giving much of his time over to Galax to be talking barbecue. Maurice wears crisp businesswear even on the air, including a classic blue tie. His white hair and white dress shirt is in yin/yang contrast to Ron's graying hair and black polo and shorts. His voice, his energy, is in yin/yang contrast to Ron's straightforward business delivery. Maurice is dynamic enough off the air, but when the microphone switch goes on, a kind of a calm excitement overcomes him.

"So tell me something, sir," says the animated Maurice, "tell me a little more about this event this weekend, Smoke on the Mountain."

"Well," says Ron, not as tongue-tied as he'll be on a live Friday-morning TV interview a couple of days hence, "Smoke on the Mountain is a competition—it's a professionally sanctioned competition by the Memphis Barbecue Association. It's not a festival, but it does have a festival atmosphere. There's a serious competition, in points and product. It's like NASCAR. These teams get points in addition to winning on their product." To modify Chief Hankley's analogy, *That's like having a NASCAR race and not letting anybody ride.* "The teams are not going to be providing food to the general public, but there will be two award-winners…right now, Natural Born Grillers is number one on the circuit in points and will be selling barbecue, so you can get some championship barbecue, as well as the Galax Smokehouse, who has won the Best of the Best Barbecue Restaurant two years consecutively."

"I'm just curious," Maurice says. "I know that an effort is really made to support all the local entities and the businesses and everything, and of course the Galax Foundation for Excellence in Education is one of the recipients. All of these profits are spent on local charities and local things, right?"

"Right," Ron replies. "The Smoke on the Mountain competition is to benefit the nonprofit Galax-Carroll-Grayson Chamber of Commerce. But we made a commitment to give something back from what we raised to our local community, and we chose the Galax Foundation for Excellence in Education. Ten percent of the sponsorships that we've raised goes to that foundation."

"And I should tell you folks, the Foundation for Excellence in Education awards scholarships to the graduates of the Galax City School Division and over the last ten, twelve, thirteen years that group has awarded over—are you ready for this?—over seven hundred *thousand* dollars in scholarships to the Galax City School Division who are going on to other opportunities of higher education, whether it's to junior college, trade school, four-year university. It's an exceedingly unique operation there, here in Galax, and folks, your participation in Smoke on the Mountain this week is one of the things." The charity is unique; the contribution of a portion of competition proceeds is not. Charities ranging from hospices for children with cancer (from Columbus, Mississippi's, Roast n' Boast) to Operation Home Front aiding the families of soldiers in Iraq (from St. Louis's Barbecue Fest) receive support from barbecue competitions.

Ron promotes the philanthropic; later that day Jim Davis sets down the practical. That afternoon, Jim supervises from his golf cart as his team lays down stripes of yellow duct tape on Grayson Street and Main Street curbs to designate the boundaries of team and vendor sites. They're working in the sunshine, but rain is predicted and they're hurrying to beat it.

There have been some issues of which electrical circuit is connected to which. "I had to juggle to get enough electricity," Jim says. "I mean, I got it; we just aren't going to get it from the side of the street I thought we were going to get it from. So I'm having to juggle to get that, and I've had to add on some more water supply and stuff like that. That's just part of the game." He's also juggled some of the vendor spaces. "It started off really like I was going to have five food vendors because we're concentrating on the barbecue.... I had a guy call me this morning, wants to do blooming onions, two spaces, ninety bucks a space—I can't turn that money down for the Chamber. I had to juggle things around because I'm going to keep all my food items together down on that one end of Grayson Street near the beer. I don't like to mix foods and crafts together." And he juggled the backyard teams—the Patio Porkers—down Main Street a bit to get them off a grade descending from its intersection with Grayson.

At one point, he says with sly eyes and pressed grin, "I thrive on this."

Back at the Chamber, local attorney Raquel Alderman Lyons pops in to report to Judy that setup of the VIP lounge is going well. Judy explains the difference between two ice barrels that are going up there, and which is to be used for what. Details. Millions of details. Raquel says, "You know what I'm going to ask Ron, if we can have a list of my staff at the door and not…"

"You don't have to ask Ron," Judy says. "This is your committee." Ron may be fretting, but he knows how to delegate.

Still, he's personally attending to any number of details. After 2:00, he meets with city employee Randy Butcher to get access to city electrical circuit breakers so he himself can restore power should hair dryers converge with microwaves sometime during the contest. He wants a backup plan in case power goes out in the middle of the night. The ice-vending machine needs to be on its own circuit, Ron says—if the power goes out and the ice melts, the competition will have to eat the cost. He'd like a connector with a light on it so he's assured the machine's circuit is live.

By 3:30, Ron and his Pepsi are back at the Chamber, going over more details with Judy Brannock. The two primary organizers. The woman in yellow and gray stripes and the man in black (and, as it turns out, one of the many men in black at the contest). The die-hard Republican and the die-hard Democrat. Miss Judy, as Ron calls her, and "Reginald," as Judy calls Ron when she wants to get under his skin a little bit. "Judy and I work well together," Ron says. "I think."

"I think you do very well," Judy says.

"She keeps me in line. I'm more outspoken and she's more politically reserved."

Together they know the potential rewards of their work— more visitors to their city, economic benefit to good causes and to the city, community spirit. And they know the dangers. "All the big players in this community have invested money," Ron has said, "and if we make this thing a flop, our name is mud. Bigtime. Because we'll have lost their money."

And Judy has said, "I have a sick feeling once in a while that we're gonna get to Friday evening and nobody's gonna come. And you think, OK, you can't make people come. I think they will."

Doesn't matter if they do or not, because Chief Clark tells Judy at the Chamber, "I'm shutting it down Saturday afternoon.... I'm going golfing." He regards her with that judiciously brightening poker face.

On the serious side, Chief Clark says, "This will happen.... From my end of it, I'm anticipating no problems at all.... We run a hundred thousand people through here every year for the

Fiddler's Convention, so we can do this standing on our heads."

This Wednesday, Judy doesn't need reassurance. She knows it will happen. She knows. "The people are good, we're gonna make it, it's going to be good. . . ."

"When this thing's over," Ron says, "I'm disconnecting the phone."

5 THE HOG AND THE FIDDLE (LEAVING OUT "HEY DIDDLE-DIDDLE")

"Announcing Auditions of the Galax Virginia Symphony Violin Section"
– Newspaper headline you will never see

Friday, March 25. Ron Passmore is out of uniform.

It's not that he's wearing long black pants instead of long black shorts—pants are more appropriate at the end of March in the mountains anyway. It's the pink suspenders. The pink suspenders adorned with a repeated black-outline illustration of a pig a-frolickin', doing a dance on two legs, "hands" in the air.

An outbreak of pink pig suspenders is usually a symptom of Larry Ohrberg being around. And indeed he is, touring the city of Galax in March 2005 along with Ron, Roger Poole, Jim Davis, Dr. Noah Malavolti, Judy Brannock, Brian Funk and other city representatives. Larry is known for making a gift of the piggy pink.

"It was so great for us, with this being a first-time event, for him to be here," Judy says in late June, a couple of weeks before Smoke on the Mountain gets underway. "It could be a one-on-one meeting, instead of part of a large organization.... It was a huge benefit for us to have Larry here to look over the city, to make the suggestions, to help us with our setup that will happen in July, to lay out some organization for us that is hard sometimes to pick up out of a book."

The book, one that Ron feels like he's memorized, is the manual for organizers that the MBA has prepared. It covers contest rules, describes obligations of the contest (for instance, you have to carry liability insurance, and you have to award the promised prize money), and offers strategies for getting sponsors and community involvement. It is a supplement to an MBA organizers' seminar, attendance for new contests required. However, the seminar had been delayed for various reasons during the time Smoke on the Mountain was seeking its sanctioning.

Instead, Mohammed in the form of Larry Ohrberg came to the Mountain comma Smoke on the.

In March, Larry and his hosts meet with city officials to answer questions. Fire Chief David Hankley, for instance, wonders about what would be done with ashes. Live-and-in-color Larry is able to recommend metal cans with covers labeled "Ashes Only." The covers ideally are metal, but even a plywood topper would help keep people from tossing flammable trash into them. And with such details and answers at hand, Larry delivers not only information, but also authority: Larry spreads the word that Judy is in charge of the competition budget. "If you do something without her permission, you just donated it."

He answers questions, but more important, Judy says, "He let us know it was very doable."

"It was cancelable at that point," Ron says.

Judy says, "He made it come alive."

Literally. And in more ways than one.

The doability of Smoke on the Mountain had been on edge for a long time preceding Larry's visit. The idea for the barbecue competition had gotten off the ground quickly, but had managed to clear only a few trees and glide back to earth where it stayed for a long time.

The competition was conceived as part of Ron's career change from cardiac specialist to purveyor of barbecue. (Says Judy: "He handled hearts. Now he handles hoofs.") But Ron's goal at first was to enter competitions himself, and he still harbors that dream.

"The goal was to compete," Ron says. "We'd be gone on weekends with the crew here running the restaurant. But our business has grown so consistently we're required on weekends to be here from a staffing standpoint. We decided we can't get away on weekends to go to them because we have to be here, so we'll host one here."

Ron and partner Jon Jordan attended a North Carolina competition and met Danny Sneed of Kings Cooking, one of the teams now scheduled to compete in Galax on July 16. Danny and his team talked about the different barbecue circuits, and Danny's enthusiasm for MBA in part convinced Ron to contact Memphis in May. The choice was between MBA and another major circuit, the Kansas City Barbecue Society (KCBS). MBA competitions cook only pork, and require their teams to make on-site presentations to judges in addition to "blind" judging where judges evaluate samples without knowing who cooked them. KCBS competitions cook chicken and beef brisket in addition to pork, and they require no on-site presentations; all judging is blind. Ron was looking for a public-complementary event, and he liked the "face" that teams presented with the more elaborate cook areas required by the on-site judging. And his own restaurant touts Memphis-style barbecue, so it was natural to lean toward Memphis in May.

Ron called Larry Gaschen of the organization. "Very infectious fellow," Ron says. "Whatever little spark I had, he fanned that fire big-time. And identified that we needed a nonprofit organization to benefit. Most of the nonprofit groups in this area have something big every year that's their big yearly fundraiser. Chamber was the only one that didn't have something. I went to Judy as our executive director and presented the idea. Of course, she didn't have a clue what I was talking about."

"It was very unique," Judy says. "It was very different for the area. He said, 'What do you think?' and I said 'Let's take it to the Executive Board,'" which they did. "Ron did a little explanation of what it was. Many of the Board had watched it on the Food Network channel, and were just blown away. So then, of course, we had to get permission from the city."

In front of City Council, Ron showed a video of an Al Roker special covering the Memphis in May championship. After some further explanation and a few questions, Council voted to approve. Unanimously.

Smoke on the Mountain first applied for MBA sanctioning in February 2004. "It was late October," Judy says, "that we found out that we were sanctioned. And from that we went to doing our research and we found out that Galax is now the second city in the commonwealth that is sanctioned by Memphis in May, the other one being Fredericksburg."

Ron and Judy had planned on attending the daylong MBA seminar for organizers originally scheduled for January '05, "and it just didn't happen," Ron says. At the time, Memphis in May was in transition to the Memphis Barbecue Association. Memphis in May actually is an organization that handles events over a four-weekend stretch (oddly enough in Memphis and, yes, in May). The Beale Street Music Festival takes the first weekend of the month; the International Family Festival, the second; the Sunset Symphony, the fourth. The World Championship Barbecue Cooking Contest (WCBCC) is the third-weekend event, just a part of the month's festivities, yet on the barbecue circuit both the championship and the barbecue organization itself were called Memphis in May. But with a change in name, some change in structure, and some shifts in staffing (including hiring a full-time administrator of the barbecue division), the Memphis Barbecue Association emerged.

But in this time of transition and rebuilding, Ron Passmore and Judy Brannock were getting frustrated. And worried about the timetable. In part, "We were getting antsy because it had already been in the paper that it could happen," says Judy.

"'We need a lot of hand-holding,' we thought," Ron says. "To me it's the same as you walking into an operating room tomorrow and trying to do a coronary bypass. You've never seen one, you've not been taught how to do it, but you gotta do it. That's where we were."

"I'd never seen one, except for the video," Judy says.

"I'd never seen a Memphis in May event, ever, in person," Ron says. "So we took the money we had budgeted for Judy and I to go to Memphis, and we flew Larry here. Which is what I would recommend for any first-year event. It makes better sense to send a rep to a locality and have him walk your streets, walk your area and tell you exactly what will work, what won't."

And now here he is, live and in color, your walking-talking-joking portable organizer's seminar.

The group visits the abandoned First National Bank building which will house several of the competition activities. Larry takes pictures.

They visit the store just down Main Street that Tom Barr has operated for twenty-five years, meet up with Tom and son Stevie, pose for a group photo, and begin the multistoried path toward the brainstorm about the unique Smoke on the Mountain trophies.

Now, like any good barbecue story, the tale of the conception of the Galax trophies has several versions, each with its embellishments and the vagaries of memory-challenged yarn-

Tom Barr of Barr's Fiddle Shop and Gary Kerce of Pig Pounda Kappa talk about the Galax fiddle trophies

spinners. And like any good barbecue story, it doesn't have to be the truth, but at least in spirit it is the truth.

Tom Barr's store is officially the "Fiddle Shop," but he sells other stringed instruments, like guitars (including a luscious-pink one), and banjos, and even…violins.

Sometimes folk will come in and say, "Now, I don't want a fiddle. I want a *violin*." Tom walks them over toward the back and points out the wall on the left displaying rows of instruments. "I carry violins, too," he says, and helps them pick out a symphony concert instrument.

Sometimes folk will come in and say, "Now, I don't want a violin. I want a *fiddle*." Tom walks them over toward the back and points out the wall on the left displaying rows of instruments. "I carry fiddles, too," he says, and helps them pick out a mountain-music instrument. Same wall. Same instruments.

Understand the importance of the fiddle in Grayson and

Carroll Counties, Virginia. The sign welcoming you into Galax announces the city as the "World's Capital of Old-Time Mountain Music." A figure on the sign plays the fiddle.

A police car passes you on the drive in. On the squad car's door, an outline of a fiddle. The two other major events in the Galax area are (well, after the lawnmower racing and the demolition derby, of course), the Old Fiddler's Convention and the Leaf and String Festival (galax leaf, fiddle string). The fiddler's convention that will follow the Smoke on the Mountain will be the seventieth in seventy-two years (World War II forcing a two-year hiatus because of blackouts—the electrical kind). And Tom Barr enjoys telling a brief genealogy of mountain music traced back to 1725. (Traced, one might add, with the aid of land records that escaped the genealogically inevitable "The courthouse burned down.")

In reflection of this heritage, ten of the Galax trophies (first through third in each of the three major categories, plus grand champion), are fiddles mounted on instrument stands. Not fiddle silhouette plaques. Not fiddle-shaped cutting boards. Working, playable fiddles. The fiddles come in different sizes; the third-place trophy has a fiddle made for kids just starting out, and as kids and barbecue scores get bigger, the fiddles do, too.

Engraved on each instrument—in the same gold-reflective lettering that's used on fire trucks—is the category and the place for which the award is given. The stands, like stock cars converted to racing, have been modified for speed. Two arms on the cradle normally wrap to the front of the vio...fiddle, to prevent it from falling forward. The tips of these arms have been trimmed off so that more vio...fiddle is displayed.

The bottom of the cradle has been modified to accept the mounting of a black walnut plaque scrollsawed by hand into a silhouette of the Sta...Commonwealth of Virginia. Similar plaques, fiddleless, will be awarded to fourth- and fifth-place winners in the primary categories, and to winners of the ancillary contests.

People *ooh* and *ahh* the trophies he has helped put together. *Ooh*. A few weeks before the contest, Lauren Shepard, Barbecue Program Administrator of Memphis in May, emailed Ron: "I showed the pictures of your trophies at a meeting last night and they went over HUGE! I'm going to use those pics in the PowerPoint presentation we're working on for the Organizers Seminar as an example of unique and special trophies." (The irony here is that the Organizers Seminar showing off the Galax fiddles is the one that Ron and Judy couldn't attend because it had been delayed, forcing them to request a personal visit by an MBA representative.) *Ahh*. In another email, this time from a judge known only as Arthur, "The trophies are absolutely *gorgeous*."

Tom Barr's response to the oohing and ahhing? Tom smiles. He's mustachioed, unassuming, a bit taller than Judy Brannock, wearing glasses that are well within modern style though—on him—they seem to ask to be called spectacles. He wears a ball cap with a banjo manufacturer's name on it and not the name of his own shop; the manufacturer had created a one-of-a-kind banjo worth four figures and, out of respect for Tom and his shop, had donated it for Tom to raffle off. The least he could do, he says, is wear their cap. His smile, it seems, is louder than his voice. Ooh and ahh? He says, "I think they'll be all right."

To appreciate the very-much-all-right scroll saw artistry involved in producing these trophies, picture Utah, for contrast. Utah. Box. Straight cut, straight cut, straight cut, straight cut. Now picture Virginia. Flat bottom (fortunate for mantel placement), borders flowing along the meandering rivers. A scroll saw blade might as well be a whitewater river raft navigating those curves and dips and plunges.

"I had to go through three or four different of my wood-workers to find the one that had the ability to do that scroll saw type work," says Jim Davis. Marvin McKinnon is the gentle-man's name, and he donated the intricate woodworking in exchange for free booth space to sell his wares. "I been work-ing with him since back the first of May on these trophies," Jim says. "He's good to work with…. I bet I could call him right now and get more cut if I need more by the end of the week."

The words of prophecy.

A couple of the Virginia cutouts get lost before they can be engraved. Replacements are ordered and Jim wins his bet. He gets more cut by the end of the week. They are engraved in time; and like all the other black walnut Virginias, a galax-leaf-shaped ornament is mounted to mark the city's location on the plaque, and delivered to the city that the ornament marks on the map—the trophy that Smoke on the Mountain organizers will help put Galax itself on the map.

Larry Ohrberg had of course had been told the stories of the importance of the fiddle to Galax. Judy Brannock says that while Larry was in Tom Barr's Fiddle Shop, he said, "Man, it's a shame we can't have a fiddle for a trophy."

In Judy's version, Tom replied, "We can." And, that quick-ly, the concept for the trophies appeared.

Tom Barr doesn't remember the story that way. Tom does-n't remember "a whole lot about exactly how it came to be." He's pretty sure it was "Ron or somebody come up with the idea of having a real instrument, a working instrument."

Jim Davis is pretty sure it wasn't Ron who came up with the working fiddles, though he recalls that Ron may have come up with the idea of a fiddle-shaped cutout, maybe even a plaque (oddly, the scroll saw work involved in creating such a shape would probably be less involved than the work required in making plaques in the shape of Virginia, even considering the fiddle's scroll, tuning pegs and curlicue body shapes). "When Larry was here," Jim says, "he said, 'You know, we all got a basement full of these pigs.' He said, 'Come up with something unique.' And one of the guys said, 'How about cutting out a fiddle out of wood?' I went home that night and laid around for the longest kinda time kicking that thought around. And then it hit me. Tom and I are friends. I knew he had all these different sizes, and I went in the next day and I grabbed two fiddles, and I took them up there and laid them on the table and I said, 'Here's our trophies.' And Larry just went into orbit. He said, 'That is awesome.'"

People who slip and refer to them as "working violins"—as Ron ("I'm from Florida") Passmore once did when reporting progress of festival plans to the Chamber of Commerce—earn scowls and a fair amount of gentle crap from Tom Barr.

Tom Barr got a bit of gentle crap about the naming convention in return. The Thursday of the competition, judge Arthur looked somberly at the awards, then at Tom. "You'll have to start over on these, Tom."

"What's wrong?"

"These are all violins. You'll have to rebuild these trophies with fiddles."

Not all of the trophies are Arthur's "violins"; on the grand champion trophy is a viola. Technically. On the mountain, at Smoke on the Mountain, it's still a fiddle. (And in case you were curious, the cello in a bluegrass band is, of course, a bass fiddle, or perhaps more appropriate to a barbecue tale, a "bull" fiddle.)

Luckily, there have been no "second-fiddle" jokes at Galax.

Not even from Larry O.

Until this one.

6 BLUE RIDGE MOUNTAIN BREAKDOWN

"Now my engine's running hot"
– lyric from "Grayson County Blues" by Steve Barr

Friday, July 15. The *Bluegrass Lullaby* CD from bluegrass band No Speed Limit was not in the stereo of an RV making a two-day trip for Thursday arrival in Galax Virginia, but it should have been. The lyrics of one of the songs, "The Hometown," extols the lyricist's roots, noting that if you wander, you'll soon plan to get back home and rediscover your soul "before it burns."

The lyrics to "The Hometown" were written by Galax native Steve Barr, No Speed Limit's banjo player and son of Tom Barr. Steve is closing in on thirty, though he looks like he's too young to make purchases in the Grayson Street beer garden. In many ways, Steve and Tom *are* Galax—its present, its history. "My grandparents moved here in nineteen and four," Tom tells a visitor. "And Galax become Galax in nineteen six…. Galax is known for the galax leaves. My grandparents used to collect them and sell them—that was their business, they sold these galax leaves. They're only found in this area. That's what people done for a living back then." That and the furniture economy—

Tom's grandparents sold chairs, too. Now Tom and Steve are important parts of Galax's present, the World's Capital of Old-Time Mountain Music; Tom used to be in a band himself—the Whitetop Mountain Band. He was apprentice to Albert Hash, who has been called "The Stradivarius of Southwest Virginia." Now Tom the luthier himself handcrafts mountain music instruments. And Steve plays the hell out of 'em.

On Friday evening, Steve demonstrates just how well he can play, nimbly plucking a passionate "Foggy Mountain Breakdown." Steve and the banjo careen fervently and confidently along those mountain curves, picking up speed, holding the road, thrilling the folks along for the ride—the cooks at the Galax Smoke on the Mountain Barbecue Championship. Steve has been invited to perform as the capper, the dessert, of the cooks' briefing—and he plays like an accomplished demon. To Steve's left, his father's trophies line one wall in display to the cooks. In front of Steve, the cooks are applauding vigorously as he completes the "Breakdown."

The briefing has been standard up to that point. There's considerable blah-blah-blah in the various barbecue briefings—for cooks, for judges, for judges' assistants, for the blind-room team. It's necessary blah-blah, fresh and eye-opening to newcomers like John Bennett of the So-Co Smokehouse team and Cody Cline of the local Nervous Wreck Cook'n Crew, an "I've-seen-it-a-billion-times" *M*A*S*H* rerun for vets like John David Wheeler of Natural Born Grillers and Pig Pounda's Roger Kerce. This blah changes from time to time, that blah sometimes is forgotten, and the other blah might cover a new rule or discussion of a problem, but in many spots the briefing might as well be on tape.

On Friday in Galax, Walt Brown calls team roll, to confirm that the teams are there and will indeed be cooking the categories they signed up for. Walt will enter this information into the computer shortly after the team meeting. He doesn't do it before, because if a team doesn't show, or elects to cook in more or fewer categories than Walt's records indicate, information will have to be reentered.

As Walt calls each team name, a representative names the categories his or her team will cook in. "All right," Walt says. "Pig Pounda Kappa."

Roger Kerce replies, "Here, all three." The "three" that Roger refers to are the three categories to be judged in the competition: whole hog (minimum weight eighty-five pounds, cooked in one piece), pork shoulders (including the butt and picnic sections intact), and ribs (generally loin backs but sometimes spareribs—country style ribs are not allowed). Pig Pounda cooks irregularly, not nearly as often as other teams whose names are about to be called, but they are among those being referred to when organizers tell sponsors and such that five of the best teams in the world are attending. Their second-place rib entry at this year's Memphis in May World Championship Barbecue Cooking Contest merits the accolade.

"Natural Born."

That's Natural Born Grillers, hailing from Southaven, Mississippi. Team leader John David Wheeler responds: "All three." At Caruthersville later in the season, Natural Born Grillers alerted contest officials that they wouldn't be sending a team member to the briefing because they were short-handed. During the briefing, rep Gary Countz called out "Natural Born Grillers?", and a member of another team deadpanned, "They dropped." Members of a couple of other teams believed the jest, and likely were relieved. Coming into the Galax competition, Natural Born Grillers lead the MBA circuit points race, with a slim lead over powerhouses Gwatney Championship Barbecue and Jack's Old South. Gwatney won the hog category and the overall WCBCC grand champion;

Jack's is two-time WCBCC grand champion, and has been top circuit points winner consistently over the last several years. These teams are also in the "five."

"Hawg Wild."

Jeff Holmes is head cook: "All three." Among the all three Jeff will cook will be one of the hogs that Jeff himself raised. Hawg Wild comes in from Corbin, Kentucky. Jeff looks almost gleeful to be sitting in the cooks meeting, getting ready to engage in his passion. It's the same look he'll sport when he serves food to the judges. Only the seriousness of the work of meat prep interrupts that smile.

"Kings Cooking."

Paul Goforth: "All three." And two of the all three will be cooked on grills Paul himself built. From relatively close Shelby, North Carolina, Kings is the only team Ron Passmore has met before any of them came to Galax, other than…

"Nervous Wreck Cook'n Crew."

Cody Cline supplies more information than is needed: "Anything But, shoulders and ribs. And sauce." The ancillary contest entries—Anything But and sauce—mean nothing to Walt, since the ancillaries are technically separate from the MBA competition, and therefore the responsibility of Smoke on the Mountain and not the MBA reps. But Cody understandably doesn't realize that. This is, after all, his first competition. He's local, from the neighboring community of Baywood, Virginia. He'd originally set his sights on entering the Patio Porkers, but allowed himself to be talked into, as Ron has phrased it, "running with the big dogs."

"The Pit Connection."

Jerry Dyer replies, "Shoulders." Jerry is the head of this family-run team out of Fredericksburg, Virginia. Though the team was begun many years ago (and even cooked in the Memphis in May championship very early in its history), they've been on hiatus, and have only recently begun cooking again. They'll start with a single category. "We're going to start branching out," Jerry noted shortly before the cooks' meeting began. "At this point we're not even looking at doing whole hogs, but we'll get into the ribs." But not this time.

"Gwatney."

Gwatney Championship Barbecue Team out of Memphis is one of the two teams on the heels of Natural Born in the points race. Al Norton makes sure he's heard when he replies: "All three." In the Butler, Alabama, cooks' briefing held about a month later, Al would change his reply to "We're here and we're cooking roadkill."

"So-Co Smokehouse."

John Bennett says, "Ribs." This is John's first contest; he's looking to test the barbecue contest waters not so much as a competitor but as a restaurateur. He's thinking of expanding the menu of his Arlington, Virginia, restaurant, the Boulevard Wood Grill. He'll take prizes, but he's looking for feedback. His business partner's activity as an MBA judge sparked John's idea, and it was fueled by "Kind of a do-what-you-like-and-like-what-you-do sort of thing," he says. He's quiet, perhaps being observant, perhaps just unused to being out front and not inside the kitchen where he usually is while at work.

"Sweet Swine o' Mine."

All three of the members of Sweet Swine who were able to come to Galax attend the cooks' briefing, one of the few teams that has dispatched more than one team member. Amy Milam says, "Whole hog and ribs." Sweet Swine would have cooked shoulders, as well, but shoulder cook Mark Lambert was unable to join the team in Galax. The team decided to compete in Galax the day after Mark had committed to a catering job. Sweet Swine is another WCBCC category champion, having won the shoulder category—they round out the "five."

"Pure and Sinful Barbecue."

Dan Puryear: "Ribs." Pure and Sinful would normally cook shoulders, as well. But they, like Sweet Swine, are short-handed this weekend. Along with Nervous Wreck and Pit Connection, Dan's team is the third Virginia team here in Virginia, hailing from Richmond.

"Smoked Encounters of the Third Swine."

Chris Carter has come in from a different Mt. Airy—Mt. Airy, Maryland—along with his father-in-law and his nine-year-old son Sean, to cook, as he responds to Walt, "Ribs and shoulder." D.C. is about the only other close competition for him, and he's come to Galax because of the proximity. It was a last-minute decision to participate; Chris had just returned from vacation, and called early in the week to see if there were still openings. Sean says, "It was my idea."

"Jack's Old South."

No one from Jack's Old South is there to answer the roll call. Larry responds "They're in all three" when Walt says the name. Jack's Old South is in Galax, but the team arrived late, and is now scrambling to set up. So no one from the team is around to hear the blah-blah-blah, the jokes, the sparkling "Foggy Mountain Breakdown."

Jack's Old South's breakdown wasn't in the fog and it wasn't on the mountain. It was on a freeway entrance ramp outside of Knoxville. Myron Mixon and his team had just fueled up, and were about to hop onto the freeway, when he noticed smoke coming out of the wheel area of his rig. At first he thought it might be something like water spray from hitting a puddle. No such luck. The axle chain had broken.

When Myron rolls into Galax at 3:30, two and a half hours after his hog should have hit the grill, Jack's Old South gets to work on setup.

Jack's is in Galax only about three minutes before Crash

*The cooks at Friday's cooks' briefing, listening to
the unseen Larry Ohrberg*

Test Larry O starts riding them. "David, you got that hog prepped yet?" he calls out to Jack's team member David Hair.

Mr. Bill—gruff Mr. Bill Wheeler of Natural Born Grillers, John David's daddy—stops by to welcome Myron. "Heard you had a little trouble, brother," Mr. Bill says.

"Always." Myron is a barbecue-circuit icon, no matter which of the circuits he's cooking in on any given weekend. He's getting more comfortable-looking as he's getting grayer—his graying beard and wavy, swept-back hair are providing accents to his usual black shirt, black pants. He's been called the Johnny Cash of barbecue, the man in black, though Ron Passmore is out-blacking Myron on this day, Myron in blue jeans and all.

Myron's running behind, but he's not concerned. "Anyone can cook in perfect weather," he says broadly. He teaches cooking, and he's got a reputation as one of barbecue's most polished presenters, and you can see it when he talks barbecue, even in earthier, less formal formats: "You got a perfect size of meat, you got a perfect quality cut of meat, you got the perfect fire, no wind blowing, the stars are aligned—anyone can cook like that. You give somebody turmoil, you give somebody aggravation, and then you separate the men from the boys and the women from the girls. Then you have to improvise. If you got any cooking talents, then you got to illustrate them and rely on them to get the job done.... If I ain't under pressure, I ain't cookin'." And he's proven that. The year before, Myron's truck broke down on his trip from hometown Vienna (that's "Vy-enna"), Georgia, to Evansville (that's "Evansville"), Indiana, for the Smoke on the Water competition. He was forced to rent a U-Haul, which also broke down. He arrived in Evansville at midnight Friday night, set up quickly, got his hog on at 1:00 AM. A full twelve hours lost. Only ten hours of cook time before him.

Myron's hog made finals that Saturday. As he says as he sets up in Galax, "We're seven hours, eight hours ahead of schedule" compared to Evansville.

Every competition, it seems, has its travel stories. It was vehicle problems that ultimately kept the third of the Memphis in May WCBCC category champions away from Galax, though indirectly so. Rib category champ Porkosaurus didn't make the trip. The Porkosaurians had talked about Galax, and were interested in going, but three weeks before, they experienced two breakdowns on their two-hour or so drive from Bartlett, Tennessee, in the Memphis area to the Show-Me State Championship Cook-Off in Kennett, Missouri. The breakdowns tempered their appetite for longer travel so soon after. Galax did attract the WCBCC rib runner-up, though—Pig Pounda Kappa.

Pig Pounda ran a little behind schedule themselves—twice,

on both trips into Galax. On the way to dropping off the rig in late June, the Kerces endured the obligatory flat and a vicious rainstorm that forced them to pull over for an hour. Gary says, "If I could hook my rig to an airplane . . ." The second slow-down, on the trip returning to Galax, wasn't vehicular. The hog that Gary Kerce had planned to pick up on Wednesday wasn't available until 10:30 Thursday morning, delaying his departure.

Gwatney's delay was vehicular, but for a change it wasn't their vehicle. They hit traffic from a bad accident near Knoxville on the way in. At least this delay didn't force them to drag the tire jack or the sledgehammer out of their supply trailer. Gwatney blew three tires in traveling to and from Washington D.C.'s Barbecue Battle the same weekend that Porkosaurus was suffering multiple breakdowns. And an axle broke on his support trailer on the way home from Caruthersville, Missouri—the cost of repairing it drained him of his Caruthersville prize-winnings. And on the road from Memphis to Butler, Alabama, on August 8, a tire blew on the Gwatney support trailer. Head cook Rick Dalton was driving lead of a three-rig caravan: support trailer, blind-hog cooker, main cooking rig. The tire-burst rocked his pickup truck, and sent a spray of treadlets onto the windshield of teammate Lance Freemon's vehicle—the third in the parade. The sound of the tire blowing was loud enough that even Lance heard it, despite being immersed in his trademark decibel-enhanced travel music.

The caravan pulled to the shoulder. "Time to sweat like hell," Rick said. Rick Dalton has a face formed of out of pure focus. His expression rarely varies. Even when he wins. When he took Grand Champion at the World Championship Barbecue Cooking Contest in May, by his own description, "Everybody's saying, 'Well, you didn't jump up and down, you don't yell, you very seldom smile, you don't let it out.' People say, 'Rick, you weren't excited.' Yes I was. I was very excited. I was happy. It was a very very special victory." The goal of one of the MBA judges with a photography bent is to catch Rick in a smile. Some shutter speeds can catch that smile and catch lightning, too. There, sharp and bright, gone.

That day on the way to Butler, Rick Dalton didn't realize how much sweating was going to be involved.

Shredded treads flailing counterclockwise had slapped and bent and in a sense "sucked in" the fender into the wheel well. Changing the tire was just one element of repair. Pounding the fender back into rough shape with a sledgehammer was another. At least the trailer still had a fender—a blowout on the way to another competition had blown the fender clean off, "like in NASCAR," as Rick described it. There would be further repairs later on—body shop work, paint, replacing the taillight that had sat on the fender.

Tires self-destruct, wheels fall off, hitches break. Perhaps such activity was the source of the team name "Kick the Tire, Light the Fire." In the land of barbecue legends, one team lost its trailer en route when the hitch broke off; they were sufficiently libation-enhanced, it is said, that they didn't notice that the cooker was AWOL until they arrived at the competition.

Natural Born's delay was short—sitting around a gas station for an hour waiting for propane.

Team Thirteen—the team whose name was not called in roll call despite its scheduled arrival after 5:00 on Thursday—is not delayed; it has cancelled, which Ron discovered in a harsh way pre-dawn Friday morning. "I waited up *all* night long thinking as soon as I laid down they would call from the interstate having left late or something." Or perhaps, like other teams, their cell phones had gone bar-less in the mountains. "I called them and did not get a response. Then a few minutes later the head cook called me and was very angry that I called that early in the morning." Ron explained that he had called to make sure they were OK.

The head cook said they couldn't make it because of an illness. Someone had called earlier in the week to inform the competition of that.

No one had called Ron's cell to say that. He'd not gotten the message.

Or so he thought.

It's likely that the message Ron had gotten during his absence Monday, the one without leaving a number, was the call from Team Thirteen, calling the Smokehouse instead of Ron's cell. The message had been somehow misinterpreted as being from a team interested in coming to the competition; thus Ron's Tuesday calls to a different team that ended in a curt response that the team being called was on vacation.

Had Ron been at the Smokehouse on Monday, he likely would have received the call from Team Thirteen. But the death of his son's father-in-law had taken him off to Concord, North Carolina, to deal with family matters.

On Sunday evening, Ron's daughter-in-law, Teresa Milby, called from the New Mexico air force base where she and Ron's son "Boone" were stationed. She was "hysterically upset," Ron said, because her father, Clifford, had collapsed. Emergency teams were at that moment trying to revive him. Ron and Dan were close; Ron and Dan had vast cardiopulmonary experience. "She was asking us to go down to be with her mother and help. To be with her."

Ron and Dan didn't get there in time. "They never got him back," Ron says. "He was D.O.A. So we spent the night with my daughter-in-law's mother, and her family started coming in on Monday." Boone and Teresa flew in on Sunday, as well; Ron and Dan picked them up with the airport, and eventually returned to Galax late Monday.

Years ago, Clifford owned a barbecue restaurant in Jessup, Georgia. "He was his own pit master there," Ron says, "and hired Deborah as the hostess. They ended up getting married. So they started their marriage off with barbecue. And the night he passed away, they had gone out to dinner." At a barbecue restaurant. "They started with barbecue and their last meal was barbecue. The irony."

The following November, Teresa and Boone, by that time out of the air force, would move to Galax.

Thursday, July 14. Galax is not precisely home for Ken Nottingham of Natural Born Grillers, but it's close. Ken's rich accent, spoken softly, is Mountain Tennessee, and though he's now in an RV on the two-day trip from his current home in Memphis, he grew up a couple of hours away from Galax in Kingsport, Tennessee. "I miss the mountains," he says. "It's cooler…. It's home. It's family," and in fact, his parents will come to Galax to meet up with Ken, and to see just what he's been doing so many weekends of late: cooking barbecue with Natural Born. And leaving Galax, he'll join his parents for a couple weeks' stay.

But for the moment this Thursday afternoon the 14th of July, he's part of a small caravan that pulled out of Natural Born's home in Southaven, Mississippi, on Wednesday, resting in Knoxville on Wednesday night before continuing on to Galax.

Terry "Tango" Downs leads the caravan, driving a red pick-up that hauls a smoker used only for cooking whole hogs on an equally red trailer. Looking like an oversized black safe, the hog cooker is mounted on the back of the trailer. Two smokestacks rise out of its back, then slant out until they clear the red metal tent that covers the trailer, and then up again. The poor hog to be cooked in the black safe is iced down in a large red built-in cooler at the front of the trailer—tucked into the cooler are the other meats to be cooked, as well as the greens and pineapples and vegetables that Grillers will use to decorate the grill minutes before judges arrive on Saturday. It is as if the hog were an Egyptian ruler entombed with foodstuffs so he has something to munch on during his journey to the great beyond. Between the cooler and the cooker are stacks of chairs and tables and tent poles and other paraphernalia.

Tango's a bit ahead of the other Natural Born vehicles, and he parks on Main Street to wait.

"I love this country," Tango says of his mountain drive into Galax. "If I didn't have to be somewhere, I'd still be driving."

But somewhere he must be. He just doesn't know where yet—at least, where he needs to position the cooker he's brought into town.

So he waits, waits until the Big Show enters stage west and begins stopping traffic.

OF COOKS AND COOKS AND COOKERS

Barbecue contests are often called "cooks." There are cooks and cookers at cooks. Consider that one of the cooks is named "Cook" and runs "Cook's Barbecue" and you can note that the Cook's cook Cook cooks at cooks, and doesn't "cook" look like a damn funny word 'long about now?

— Just thought you'd like to know

Thursday Afternoon, July 14. The Natural Born Grillers cavalcade of smoke is idling on Center Street just before Center intersects with Main. Looking like the advance scouts in a carny caravan, the other Griller rigs wait along with Tango until their drivers can get instructions on where to go to set up. Traffic begins to pile up behind them. It is 4:00 on this Thursday afternoon, an hour before streets are to be officially closed off with long knee-height orange-plastic barricades ("Jersey barricades," in the traffic-control lingo) given substantial weight by filling them with water. Police and firefighters are starting to erect those barricades; they're soon in place on Grayson, a block east of Main. Crews are working on other feeders into Main. They aim to have several blocks—four along Main, two along Grayson, and others along the north stretch

John Bennett of So-Co Cookers with his Backwoods grill.

that feed into Main—closed by 5:00, and the Big Show is unofficially helping get the street shutdowns underway. Judy Brannock goes to one of the stopped cars, explains what's going on, advises the driver to do a U-turn and find another way.

The Grillers bring three rigs into Galax, one more than usual. One cooker—the second in the procession—will be used in vending barbecue. The vending unit is a silver commercial box smoker on a trailer somewhat similar to the hog cooker's—black instead of red, a flatter roof. It's being pulled by the RV. Kitchen, shower, TV, air-conditioning. Stair steps that glide out when you open the door and retract when you close it. Attached retractable awning. The RV is new, bought to replace an older, smaller unit during the interval between this contest and a previous one, the Tennessee Funfest in the middle of June. At the Funfest, one of the Griller team members tried opening a non–twist-top beer with a late-night last-resort

The Big Show—the Natural Born Grillers cooker—arrives in Galax

technique: hooking the lip of the bottlecap over the edge of the counter and punching down on the bottle. This succeeded in removing more laminate from counter than cap from beer. The second and third attempts produced similar results. Seeing the new RV, people kid Griller chief John David Wheeler that he had to replace the old one because of those dings.

Behind the RV, big rig pulls big rig. A third of the wheels of an eighteen-wheeler, the red over-the-road cab pulling the Big Show is a mini RV in itself. TV. Comfy chairs. Sleeping berths. And, ah, air-conditioning. It pulls the flagship Natural Born Grillers cooker. And ship it is—long and squat and looking like the *Monitor* and/or the *Merrimac* equipped with air dampers, smokestacks and pig ornamentation.

The team has christened this rig (likely with most every alcohol other than champagne) the Big Show. A fair number of teams name their cookers. Porky's Pride (which is not cooking in Galax this weekend) began giving names to their cookers

when rib cook Clara Scarritt joined the team, so she and everyone else knew which cooker was being talked about. The grills
were given such names as Bertha, Boss Hog, Shine, T-Bone and
Chicken Cooker. The sources of the names? Says team chief
Winfred Geer, "Anywhere from their size to what they were best
at cooking, to a good-looking girl doing the honor of naming
one." Clara began cooking on T-Bone, but now cooks her ribs
on Bandit. Chris Carter of Smoked Encounters named one of
his earlier cookers "The Iron Lung." Elsewhere on the circuit,
the Da-Nite Outback cooking team has a little red cooker with
a happy face painted on one of its round ends. It started out as
a sponsor's round logo, but when sponsorship was withdrawn
the next year, head cook Daryl Haury stared at the logo a bit.
He could see eyes—at least the position of eyes—staring back
from within the logo, and with a few deletions with a paint-
brush, he "revealed" the happy face. How could he not tag it
"Happy Grill"? Especially since "eliminating" the former sponsor's logo so easily made him happy. "The Big Show" as a name
has a bit of haught and pretense to it; on the other end of the
spectrum is team Grills Gone Wild's cooker, humbly dubbed
"Steve."

The Big Show is a black metal unit, with more doors than
an Advent calendar—one set of grill doors on each side. Silver
sheet-metal cutouts of pigs race along the top of the unit, as
well as along the sides of its red trailer and the massive red
trailer tongue, taller than most human beings. At the back of
the trailer, behind the Big Show, are a pair of three-foot-deep
coolers and a boxy Backwoods smoker.

There's another competition later this summer of 2005, in
Caruthersville, Missouri. Along the back of the small park that
serves as the contest site, a tall concrete wall looms. A utilitar-
ianly tall concrete wall, seeing as Jefferson Park strolls along
the banks of the Mississippi. When Grillers arrive, the RV rides

along the city side of the floodwall toward the entrance. From the park, all that can be seen is the white, rounded HVAC unit on the RV's roof, looking at that angle like it is riding the surface of the wall, like it is a shark's fin gliding the surface.

"You know," a competing team member comments then, "I think they understand the importance of a big entrance."

The Griller caravan is given directions to the fire department parking lot, which has been designated as a holding area for the big rigs until they're all in town and downtown has been closed down. Gather all the pieces of the puzzle—or at least the cornerstone pieces—before beginning to put them together.

The people of Galax must by now be thinking that barbecue is the battle of the grills of the gods. Their first experience with a barbecue rig is Pig Pounda's trailer parked in the Galax Fire Department's parking lot, made all the more wondrous and mysterious by the fact that it is locked up tight, hiding its contents. Then the road show, the Big (road) Show, arrives.

And many teams do indeed use the grills of the gods.

And many teams use the grills of the mortals. At Kennett, Missouri, the cook who insists "just call me Guido") visited old friends and mentors the Carbondale Eagles. Guido is head cook of Porkosaurus. "These guys were our neighbors the first year we made it into finals," Guido is explaining. "We weren't even prepared for finals. We didn't have a table large enough for finals. And they helped us. They gave us a table, they gave us chairs, they offered to garnish." Guido indicates one of the Eagles' team members. "He was talking earlier, 'Be careful who you help; they might just end up beating you.' But that's the way it is." During the conversation, the Eagles continue work. Head cook Brad Cheatham sets to work on his hog cooker, an Oklahoma Joe's offset firebox unit. "Now there's a classic," Guido comments, with something of the tone of a car buff drawing his finger along the fins of a '57 Chev. The Eagles' other units are homemade former oil-tank jalopies with more than a few miles on them. The shoulder cooker has a metal patch welded over a spot that had broken through during the off-season. Before the hole was patched, Brad pointed out the hole to judges and extolled this unusual feature as his "turbo-powered ventilation system." These barbecue rigs of the mortals kept Eagles in the top ten most of the 2005 season.

In fact, barbecue competitions are where propane tanks and oil drums go to die. The purple behemoth Pork 4 Skins cooker was converted from a *thousand*-gallon tank; 500-gallon jobbies usually do the trick. (One of the companies that creates collectible figurines has a line featuring the Simpsons. One figurine depicts Homer, gasoline can in one hand, extinguished match in the other, a mushroom cloud rising from his backyard grill. His hair, his "Kiss the Chef" apron, even his eyeballs are singed. The fun detail is that his grill is a converted drum that obviously served a previous life storing radioactive waste.)

Other "things" can be and are converted into grills, too. The old Wildfire team (you can get barbecue sauce based on their recipe at Bob Evans) converted a refrigerator into a convection smoker. The Great Boars of Fire somehow found inspiration in dry-cleaning equipment. In Galax, one of Cody Cline's cookers is a converted truck hydraulic tank. It's a gleaming silver unit, with red detailing, and a truck exhaust pipe as the smokestack. Cody did the conversion himself—he's a mechanic for a truck body shop. "I done that small one initially to sell," Cody says. He looks down-home and at-home in his denim coveralls and straw cowboy hat. "Because Ron said, you know, you oughta make something flashy and show it and sell it. We thought it would go good…. And then I cooked on it. When I sell a grill, I want to cook on it, season it, make sure there's no hot spots. I was just impressed with the way it held heat, so I decided to hold onto it for a while." He built his shoulder cooker, as well. It's black and bigger than the silver unit, boxy instead of round, and weighs in by Cody's description at around 2,800 pounds—but it sports red handles and other details like its little brother. Atop the cooker is Cody's team logo. Not painted on. Welded on. A black plate rises out of the top. Red metal flame-shapes rise from the black plate. And written, in red-colored welding, on the plate itself: "Nervous Wreck."

The Kings Cooking shoulder and rib units are shining silver, as well—aluminum. Aluminum cookers are rare on the MBA circuit—and these particular ones are doubly rare within the MBA world, in that they are direct cookers. That is to say, the heat comes from fire directly below the meat; most cookers, and all the others at Galax, are indirect. They have offset fireboxes or chambered fireboxes underneath the meat, so that no flames ever touch meat. The Kings' smokers are, like Cody's, specially built; Kings team member Paul Goforth is a metal fabricator by trade. He also builds smokers for sale.

Roger Kerce at Pig Pounda is in both those lines of business, as well—metal fabricator who builds grills for sale. He and brother Gary built their current grills; other successful teams use the grills the Kerces previously competed with.

Winfred Geer designed his cooker using a computer-assisted design (CAD) program. Even though the program was intended for house design, and Winfred had to convert all measurements from feet to inches (Winfred's hog unit is a big cooker, but not quite as big as a house—even Judy Brannock's first house), Winfred made it work. Asked if he can share the resulting plan, Winfred says he doesn't have it anymore. "Plus, it's top secret."

There's plenty of show in some of the cookers you'll see on the circuit. Cookers shaped like pigs. Aerial-themed cookers: the Cessna, the B-52. The Bop-N-Qrs out of Memphis built a grill shaped and painted like a jukebox to match its "oldies" theme. The Bar-B-Q Bandits out of Kilroy, Texas, have a cooker shaped like a twenties-era truck, with diesel-truck-style exhaust pipes mounted on the back of the "cab" that serve as smoke stacks. And Old 97 is a legend, a double-decker cooker shaped like a train locomotive.

Sometimes the show is mandated: How can the Coors team *not* have a cooker shaped like a beer can and painted appropriately? How can the Jack Daniel's Team not have a bottle-shaped cooker? The Caterpillar team could very well not have a cooker shaped like a big ol' yellow dump truck. But they do.

Some teams use commercial units build and sold for restaurants and catering. This makes particular sense if you're a restaurant and a caterer, as Terry Black's Super Smokers team is. The Ole Hickory smokers, the Southern Prides—they cook good but they ain't cheap. The Great Boars of Fire moved up from homemade cookers to commercial units as part of their move to the catering business; a newspaper article about the team misquoted leader David Fombelle as saying he had "Southern-fried" pits instead of Southern Pride pits.

And because this is the twenty-first century, and the next set of NASA moon explorers are certain to be grilling on the Sea of Tranquility instead of showing off low-gravitation-enhanced golf drives, another source of cookers is, of course, eBay. That's where Sidney Garner of Jefferson Georgia found the Chew Chew Express, a locomotive-styled cooker. The barrel cooker serves as the locomotive's steam engine, the smoke stack exhibits the function and location you'd expect, and the rest of the unit is decked out with cowcatcher, piston-pumped train wheels and a locomotive cab ("Casey Bones" stuffed pig engineer and "Driving that train high on propane" jokes sold separately). It's about thirty feet long and a tad big for your basement HO model railroad layout.

In total, some thirty grills are brought into Galax by the twelve teams that will participate. So-Co Cookers and Pure and Sinful each have one cooker, while Gwatney has four (head cook Rick Dalton cooks a second hog on the fourth cooker). Generally, each team will cook each of the three competition categories on a separate grill because of the vast differences in meat size, from 200-pound hogs to two-pound slabs of ribs. The Kansas City Barbecue Society cooks different meats of more consistent sizes. The pork butts, chickens, ribs and beef briskets are within a certain range, at least, of sizes, and cooks on that circuit often work a single cooker during contests. (The Chew Chew Express would be particularly suited to KCBS and Texas competitions, with its cowcatcher and all….)

The grills of the gods and the grills of the mortals trickle into Galax. There are those that claim that money talks and, by implication, money cooks. The fancier the cooker, they complain, the better the chance of winning. For those with such claims, a story:

August 5, Caruthersville, Missouri. Three weeks after Galax and just about three states away, Scott Cutler is gesturing in the general direction of Natural Born Grillers and Gwatney. Scott's team is Mad About Que, a Mom-and-Pop team in the literal sense. Young Pop Scott and young Mom Teresa are the core of the team, assisted by Scott's Mom and Pop. They've just set up their site on this Friday of the Caruthersville competition: Two long white canopy tents, a couple of work tables, a plastic picnic table where judges will sit, one cooker not terribly larger than your typical backyard Brinkmann. "It's a little intimidating coming in here and seeing all these rigs," Scott says, standing next to the cooker. "They," he says, as he gestures toward the Grillers site a few yards away, "have a nice setup. And," gesturing at a trailer rig a fewer yards away, "they have a nice setup," even though the Rib Ticklers' rig is relatively modest.

"And we look like the Clampetts."

But TV's Clampetts made it to Beverly Hills.

The next day, so would Mad About Que.

"Doesn't matter how much money you have," Gwatney's Rick Dalton says. "Still gotta cook."

Mad About Que, the Beverly Grillbillies, took first place ribs in Caruthersville, beating two of the top then-current ribs points leaders—Grillers and Gwatney.

Still gotta cook.

8 THE RUN FOR PRIDE AND POINTS AND PROFITS...WELL, FORGET THE PROFITS

"We got the world-famous Vietnamese potbellied pigs gonna race at this time....Let 'em go! We got number 24 in the lead, followed by number 6, there goes number 8, and number 88 is in the rear! He's comin' down in the third turn. Let's get these old fat boys around the track, folks! Number 24's still got the lead! Now number 88's on top of him...he's coming up...number 88 is your winner!"

– Dennis Cook of Hogway Speedway calling a hog race at the Charlotte Blues, Brews & B.B.Q. cook

Friday noon, July 15, Galax. Richard Lackie and Pat Rooney of Sweet Swine o' Mine are waiting for Winston-Salem's WXII Channel 12 noon weather report to finish. They rest against their rig, Pat leaning back, Richard propping himself up with one hand against one of the black metal struts supporting the rig's roof and resting his other hand on his hip. Richard and Pat watch WXII meteorologist Austin Caviness not because they're interested in the weather (though the weather's about to take some interest in them). And they watch not because they're interested in current TV announcer fashions. (Pat already sports a pair of cool-guy sunglasses much like the pair Caviness is wearing, and

Austin Caviness of **WXII** *broadcasts his noon weathercast live Friday while Pat Rooney and Richard Lackie of Sweet Swine o' Mine watch; between Pat and Richard stands their first-place* **WCBCC** *shoulder trophy*

Richard's plain red apron is identical to Caviness's—Richard had supplied the apron to the meteorologist, after all). They watch because they are about to rock and roll.

Pat's sunglasses and close-cropped goatee are applying additional layers of cool to his typically stern look. Richard, on the other hand, is squinting a bit as he watches Caviness, and when he thusly squints or finds opportunity to peer at you over his glasses, he effects a slightly college-professorial owlish look. Standing between Richard and Pat is the big boy, the trophy all the MBA-circuit barbecue teams covet. It is the trophy Sweet Swine o' Mine took home for copping the first-place shoulder honors at the 2005 Memphis in May World Championship Barbecue Cooking Competition, overthrowing long-reigning shoulder king Big Bob Gibson.

People on the barbecue circuit—and on competition circuits of various ilk, one can imagine—refer to the trophies as "hardware." And the WCBCC big boy is not among the hardware-challenged. This trophy stands almost as tall as Pat, almost as tall as the Backwoods cooker it is being displayed next to. It is big, green, stately. And big. And—oh, yes—big. (But not as big as the Grand Champion trophy, which you have probably seen in smaller form as the Washington Monument.) Win four of these, and you could use them as the cornerstones of a commercial bank building not unlike the bank building that will house the Smoke on the Mountain judging facilities, just a half block from Sweet Swine o' Mine's site.

Hardware? The WCBCC trophy is constructed of weathered copper. It's hollow, but doesn't look hollow. A silver-colored bas relief of a pig's head stares out at you from the front of the trophy. A meat cleaver, gracefully suspended over two lolling silver pigs by an arc of polished metal, tops it.

Elsewhere on the circuit, the trophy of the St. Louis Barbecue Fest has true hardware credentials, as well. When the Gateway Arch was completed in 1965, one of the contractors spotted a roll of leftover inch-thick cable, and bought it. On the Barbecue Fest category first-place trophies and the grand champion trophy, a couple of feet of that cable is mounted in the shape of, of course, the Gateway Arch.

Hardware? The Blues, Brews & B.B.Q. competition in Charlotte, North Carolina, features about the only open loving cup trophies on the circuit—the first-place cup could more accurately be described as a basin. "You could wash a baby in that," judge Annie Sisson notes.

And more hardware? The trophies given by the Bowie BBQ Duel in Vidalia, Louisiana, are blocks of wood with, of course, Bowie knives imbedded in them (if you're able to remove any of the knives from the base, you're the next king of England).

In addition to hardware, there's glassware. The KCBS Annual Variety Barbeque Bash contest in Memphis presented its winners with trophies constructed of a glass gravy boat in the shape of a pig, and mounted on a solid wood base. Natural Born Grillers won one of those; at a competition not long after, team member Chris Birmingham was putting the pig, removed from the wooden base, to practical use as a giant whisky glass. (The trophy has since been respectfully returned to its intended use—when Birmingham thought that so employing the trophy might have been jinxing them.) Meridian, Mississippi, creates trophies with pottery pigs—the pig is unique to each year, as the mold it is made from is destroyed after each contest.

There's the woodware. For instance, totem-pole-esque pigs carved of wood. And cutting board plaques are common. Madison, Indiana, in 2005 presented a grand champion cutting board in the shape of the home state, as well as a pig-shaped cutting board for the pork categories, a cow-shaped board for the brisket, chicken-shaped for the chicken, and…um…sauce-shaped for the sauce (if you imagine spilled sauce pooling itself into the shape of a pizza board).

There's the plasticware. In addition to the plastic piggies (and chickens and cows and Winged Victories and loving cups and, in the case of Bowling Green, Kentucky, in honor of its local manufacturing plant, Corvettes), there are clear plastic plaques mounted on bases, in standard rectangle shapes, in the shape of Illinois, in the shape of guitars, in the shape of fish.

And there's the everyware, the Everything But. Like the Blues Brother-inspired blues pig figurines given in Charlotte. Like the iron cutout of a delightfully dancing pig presented by the Pickwick Pig Out.

In Caruthersville three weeks after Galax, Rib Ticklers displays its array of trophies outside their rig. The selection is particularly impressive given the mere two years Rib Ticklers have been competing. Impressive in a lesser sense is one of the second-place trophies the team had won the year before. Bite-size, wallet-size, hand-held (unlikely trophy slogan: "Melts in the South, not in your hand")—use whatever term you will. David Wilkins of Team Tickler holds the bite-size side by side with another piece of hardware, one considerably less height-challenged, and says that the ittybitty would make a good topper for a normal second-place trophy. (About twenty-four hours later, David and his fellow Rib Ticklers would be posing with piece of hardware just about big enough to entice Kong to scale it with Fae Wray/Jessica Lange/Naomi Watts in hand: the grand championship trophy for Caruthersville 2005, balancing the ittybitty quite nicely, stands about seven feet high.)

Even smaller than the handheld second place trophy is the one that doesn't exist at all. Occasionally, a competition gives out only plaques. Rarely, exceedingly rarely, the competition gives out only checks. That's fine if you have, as has been phrased, "a basement full of plastic pigs." But the newer teams crave the hardware. Plaques and uncashed checks framed on the wall are decorations; trophies are 3D, comin' atcha.

Even judges get trophies occasionally. The Steeleville, Illinois, Annual Bar-B-Que Cook-Off presented a "Judge Traveled the Farthest" award. The Steeleville cook was organized in large part by Leroy Rieckenberg and Randy Rieckenberg, whose own team was named the Ricky Rover Rooter Roasters, thus the travel award was called the "Rough, Rugged, Rocky Road Award" ("Rut-roh, Shaggy!"). Had Galax made such an award, it would have gone to Terry Jo Litchfield, who drove with family all the way from Manhattan, Kansas, on a vacation/barbecue jaunt.

In Galax, TV meteorologist Austin Caviness admires the Memphis in May trophy near the end of his live weathercast interview with Sweet Swine. This hunk of hardware is one of the few trophies on team display to the public in Galax. Pure and Sinful populates a table in a back corner of their tent with a handful of hardware. Gwatney displays a picture of the team clustered around the their Memphis in May grand championship trophy. And that's about it. In days gone by, teams as a matter of course displayed an array of their successes in their booths. Trophy display was such a booth-decoration convention that some teams, it's said, *bought* themselves trophies to show off. At that time, successful teams would plant veritable forests of trophies around the fronts of their booths, practically eliminating the need for fencing and other barriers. Natural Born once built such a hardware Oz with trophies; one strong award-toppling wind in St. Louis and several hundred dollars of repairs later, the size of the displays diminished and now consist of banners announcing the competitions the team has won. Such is the trend with most teams these days. In fact, several teams donate old trophies to church groups and community groups. Take the pig off, relabel it, and an organization puts it to good use instead of it cluttering up a successful team's basement. Besides, as proud of the awards as the teams are, after a while they become just one more piece of, yes, hardware to set up and haul around and take down. That's why Sweet Swine o' Mine is displaying just the one.

"That's bragworthy to me," Austin Caviness says of just-the-one on the air to Pat and Richard. "You guys travel all over the country. You're like rock and roll barbecue cookers, aren't you?"

"We *are* barbecue rock stars," Pat Rooney says. "You can see the trophy. That's world champion. That's barbecue rock-star status to us."

Now, not many rock stars are backed up by fiddles. That fact is salient only because this group of barbecue rock-and-roll stars is seeking a fiddle this weekend in Galax, Virginia. The Memphis in May trophy stands to their right while they talk to

Austin Caviness. To their left, propped up on a folding chair, a picture of the Galax fiddle trophies. In their presentation to judges on Saturday, Richard will say, "We do this for one thing and one thing only. We came here to get the fiddles."

Some teams came here for the fiddles *and* the points.

Like NASCAR and Alleghany-sanctioned lawnmower racing, teams on the MBA circuit accumulate points in their quest for team of the year. Getting one point is easy. You get a point for showing up. Gold star. Pat on the head. Not quite Miss Congeniality, but a bit of recognition nonetheless. (In fact, if you cooked in an MBA contest on *every* available weekend during a given year and took last place every time, you'd likely end up in the top twenty on pure Brownie points for good attendance.)

Barely missing finals in a category—taking fourth place— gets you another point. Making finals but losing out—taking third—gets you two points. Three points for second. Four for first. Three more if you take grand champion. Therefore, completely sucking will earn you a point. Completely dominating— that is, taking first place in all three categories and grand champion—will nab you 16 points. Such domination is called, as it is in other sports, a sweep. And, as in other sports, sweeps are rare.

Coming into Galax, the run for points on the MBA circuit is neck and neck, shoulder and shoulder, rib and rib. Natural Born Grillers leads by a snout with 62 points. Gwatney and Jack's are tied for second with 60 each. Fourth place is a distant 30 points, held by Roadside Grill Cooking Team. Of the other Galax teams—who don't cook nearly as often as the points leaders—Sweet Swine o' Mine has 8 points coming into the weekend; Pig Pounda Kappa, 7.

Like most teams, Sweet Swine and Pig Pounda know that they don't have a shot at the number-one slot overall, nor are they aiming for number one. They don't cook enough contests to accumulate the points. But they'll work toward another honor—top ten placement. It's a good team that hits the top ten, a great team that can hit top ten year after year. As Smoke on the Mountain convenes, the 16 points earned by a team called The Good, the Bad and the Swine mark the cut-off for the top ten.

Also being contested is the "Team of the Year" honor in each of the three cooking categories. The three overall points leaders—Natural Born, Jack's, Gwatney—are duking it out for category leadership, as well. In Hog, it's Jack's with 23, Natural Born with 19, Gwatney with 15, and Barnyard Roasters and Boggy Pond BBQ Brigade tied with 7. In shoulder, it's Gwatney and Natural Born tied with 19, Jack's with 16, Roadside Grill Cooking Team with 12, Rib Ticklers with 8. Slightly different faces in ribs, however: Parrothead Porkers with 15, Gwatney with 14, Barnyard Roasters with 10, and Boggy Pond and Natural Born tied with 8. This year, 2005, is one of the first years in several where Jack's Old South at this point in the schedule is not leading just about everything.

The competition leading into Galax has been, during the previous weeks, last-hog standing. One month previous to Galax, Jack's and Gwatney had been tied for first overall. A grand championship a week later at the Tennessee Funfest June 18 put Gwatney in the lead, two points ahead of Natural Born and four points ahead of Jack's. That weekend at the Funfest, the teams had gone head to head.

The next weekend, however, two contests were held half the country apart. Jack's Old South and Gwatney went to the National Barbecue Battle in Washington, D.C., while Natural Born Grillers went to the Show-Me State Championship Barbecue Cook-Off in Kennett, Missouri.

Kennett drew about fourteen other teams to a small fairground in back of a legion hall. A small carnival was set up adjacent to the teams—carny games and Tilt-a-Whirl and merry-go-round and chug-chug-little-toddle-trains. Country station doing live broadcasts. Karaoke contest on Friday night.

D.C., in contrast, was held on Pennsylvania Avenue. (D.C. is also the only contest to hold the cookoff on a Sunday, leaving Saturday open for a variety of public and ancillary events—from beef and chicken competition to chef's demonstrations to the appearance of the Oscar Mayer Wiener Wagon—and, importantly, leaving Pennsylvania Avenue open on Friday).

At Kennett, Natural Born took firsts in hog and shoulder, and the grand championship. At D.C., Jack's performed the same feat. Gwatney in D.C. took second in hog and thirds in shoulders and ribs. These results allowed Natural Born to leapfrog Gwatney into its tenuous position in first overall, and allowed Jack's to move into a tie with Gwatney for second just two points behind Natural Born.

Thus the hog race comes to Galax in near dead heat.

Not a single one of the teams came looking for profit from the prize money. They won't turn down whatever prize money they win—$750 for first place in a category, $350 for second, $200 for third, $100 for fourth, $1,000 for grand champion—but it's not enough to provide *profit* motive.

Says Myron Mixon of Jack's Old South: "Before you bought a motel room, before you bought anything to make sauces, before you bought decorations, before you eat, before you buy rooms and gas, before any of it, you got a thousand dollars tied up. And then you got teams around here taking fourths and fifths, and I'm not knocking that, I don't see how they do it. It ain't that Myron's gotta win so bad—Myron's gotta win, or I won't get to go."

Some of the teams do it, win or not, out of pocket. Some teams trim back expenses by cooking in fewer categories—skipping hog can save a chunk of change, between the cost of the hog and the expense of hauling another cooker to a site.

Some sell barbecue or cater. More than one team charges "dues" to become "team members"—for a price, you can come and party with the team.

Some are helped by sponsorship. A little money in exchange for signage, free charcoal in exchange for displaying their product, or, as is the case of Gwatney, a complete free ride in exchange for displaying the sponsor's name and the name of his Memphis-area car dealerships; the side of Rick Dalton's cooker rig fairly shouts Gwatney Chevrolet. "A lot of times over the years, and I'll say this, a lot of people have always been jealous of me—very jealous because of the money," head cook Rick Dalton says. Rick prides himself on speaking directly. "I call 'em as I see 'em," he's said. "If you don't like the way I call 'em, change the way I see 'em." The way he sees sponsorship money: "I always tell people that you have every bit of the same opportunity that I have to go out, promote yourself, and get sponsorship.... It's all about marketing."

Friday, July 22, Memphis. At a judging seminar the week after Galax, Wayne Booth and wife Linda—the two and only members of the Red Hot Smokers barbecue team—are addressing the judges-in-training from the teams' perspective. "Some people don't understand this sport," Wayne says. His heavily Southern smooth voice has comfort to it. Hair combed back, mustache trimmed precisely, he regards not only his judges but also his barbecue product with almost a nurturing look. "I tell people sometimes, 'This is a dumb sport.' To be honest with you, we take two days before we even get ready. We gotta wash our coolers, get our tents clean and everything."

"We start about Tuesday getting ready for a contest on Saturday," Linda says with the typical soft-edged intensity that she applies to her storytelling and to her smile.

"Then," Wayne says, "you gotta pick up your meat, then you make your dry rub up and your sauce up. You got like two, three days there. Then you go out in the hot sun and set that tent up. Then you stay up all night long fighting that heat off your cooker…"

"And the rain…"

"And you give this stuff away for free."

Dumb sport.

"So why do you do it?" a student asks.

Linda says, soft-edged, intent, "You have to love it."

"We do it to have a great time," Wayne says. "You can't do this for the money. You've gotta do this for the love that's in your heart. And that's why we do it."

"We have made lifelong friends with our barbecuing," Linda says. "That's why when we don't cook, we judge. We're both certified judges. Any contest we're not there cooking, we're there judging. It becomes a family."

The fun, the fiddles, friendship, the points, the family—all are callings. But no one has come to lose. The teams have come to Galax, Virginia, for the triumph. They've come to rock and roll. The victory of the grill, the grill of victory. Says Myron Mixon of Jack's Old South: "I'm intense. I'm intense about winning. I love to win. You show me somebody that don't like to win, I'll show you somebody who ain't never won."

Rick Dalton sees the love of winning in teammate Hal Berry. "He cares about one thing and one thing only. Walking to that stage. The last time of the day."

BUILDING THE INDUSTRIAL-STRENGTH BACKYARD

"Hog on. Shirts on. Leg on."
— Verbal checklist just before judges arrive, from the leader of a team whose presenter has a prosthetic leg

Thursday afternoon, July 14, Galax. On Washington where it crosses Main, Chris Birmingham stops the Natural Born RV and steps out to survey where he is to park it, where the Natural Born cooksite is to be arranged. He doesn't like what he sees. Too cramped. Too difficult to maneuver big rigs.

He swears. "I'll be damned if I'm ever coming back here." And he pops back into the RV.

Ron Passmore is shocked. The first team in, the first few minutes of setup, and already people are ticked-off, threatening to boycott. Already. In the first few minutes.

Ron Passmore has not yet met Birm—the outspoken Mr. Birmingham.

Birm is the Natural Born Griller's hog and shoulder cook and sometimes big-rig chauffeur. At a previous contest—the Tennessee Funfest in the Memphis area the weekend of June 17—Birm had been setting up the Big Show on Thursday, and noting aloud how only one other person was at that moment at the cooksite and helping him. "It's obvious who does all the work around here," he grumbled to Glen "G.T." Tubbs (G.T. being that one other person). Birm fished inside the belly of the Big Show, lifted a grate that he wanted to place on a higher rack. Birm wanted to, the grate didn't. Birm clanged the grate against the side of the Big Show as he tried to angle it so he could move it. Failed. "If they think I'm going all the way to Galax and do all this without any help, they're crazy." He banged at the grate again, dropped it to where it had been in the first place. The final frustration. "I quit." He slammed the cooker door shut. "I'm done." Birm grabbed his shirt, donned it, and stalked off, beer in hand.

G.T. swung the cooker door back open, began fighting the out-of-position grate, raised it and popped it into its new place. "Either you're in trouble," an onlooker said to G.T. "Or he does this every cook."

G.T. smiled and replied, "What do you think?"

Chris ("If I ain't raising hell, they know something's wrong") Birmingham, yet a Natural Born Griller in Galax, backs the RV into place, curbside, facing north. Ken Nottingham directs him to back up until the RV's tail is about a foot away from the trailer carrying the hog cooker, parked facing east at the southern boundary of the cooksite. Or more specifically, in the northernmost boundary of Gwatney's cook-site, by about three inches.

Larry Ohrberg is playing traffic cop, but mostly he's just playing. Earlier that day when someone asked him the best place along Main to put a portable toilet, he took the it-does-n't-matter-and-we-can-fix-it-if-it-eventually-does-matter tack: Put it down for now, and move it to the right place later. "Just make sure no one is in it when you move it," he says. "They'll come out with a blue butt and they won't like that."

He's now working to make sure someone's butt is blue as

he helps the Gwatney team back its supply trailer into place—facing east, just south of the Griller hog cooker. "You can come as close as you want," he says while helpfully directing. "He's encroaching by three inches. You can shave his hubcaps off."

Natural Born Grillers do a bit more encroaching when they maneuver the Big Show into the cooksite. When the trailered grill is in place, it will form the northern boundary of the contest site, even more definitively than the water-filled Jersey barriers on the grill's north side. The Big Show will sit perpendicular to the team's RV, facing east, facing the cozy structure—Galax's Farmer's Market—on the corner of Central and Main. The Farmer's Market is a green-painted carport-sort-of construction covering a widened stretch of street-corner concrete. It houses built-in benches and counters where farmers and farmees can ply their business, where festival-goers can duck out of the rain.

Tango backs the Big Show up with the pickup while teammate's George Nicely and Ken Nottingham direct. Then Tango pulls forward, looking for maneuvering room, backs up, pulls forward, encroaches one of the Farmer's Market benches with a crunch. One of the boards pops out of the bench's front a couple of inches on the right; the pickup's bumper had encroached the board inward a couple of inches on the left.

In the center of the little marketplace is a sign announcing its purpose. "Downtown Farmer's Market," it says under a rustic yet elegant illustration of carrots, berries and corn. "Please help keep clean and beautiful. Report any loitering or vandalism." Then it displays the local Crimestoppers number, a number that no one with tattletale inclination has to call, because a Galax police officer has been watching the load-in of the Big Show and the pickup's rather physical encroachment all along.

When Tango and the Show back up again, the officer walks

over to the slightly disfigured bench, pops the protruding end of the board back into place with a smack of the fleshy part of his fist. The bench is again sittable. No problems. Everything back to normal. Apparently more out of curiosity than concern, the officer resumes watching the load-in.

"Load-in" is barbecue jargon for getting set up. "Load-out" is the antonym with the meaning you'd expect. The jargon is not exclusive to barbecue, of course. Most every pursuit that involves hauling around and setting up a lot of crap uses the slang, from Broadway road shows to cartoon-costumed ice-skating extravaganzas to convention-center trade shows. And Sweet Swine o' Mine may be rock-and-roll barbecue stars, but they, like all the other teams, are also their own rock-and-roll barbecue roadies.

On the return-to-Galax leg of the Piedmont Triad International Airport run the night before, Larry had teased Carlene, "Are the teams loaded in?" Tough to do, considering that on Wednesday night, no teams were even in town yet.

"I'm not familiar with the terminology," Carlene said. "Loaded in?"

"In their spots and all set up."

"Oh hell no." Carlene, in her vocation as a children's librarian, doesn't have a lot of experience hauling around and setting up a lot of crap, though as the week progresses she will get to meet load-in firsthand.

With the rigs situated on Thursday, site setup begins. From the inside of the back door of the Gwatney support trailer, Rick takes down coils of electrical cords—a half-dozen or more cords in colors matching those of the Christmas tree lights they would otherwise be powering...yellow, orange, and red...and then the purple cord with black striping and the pink cord with green striping.

Rick and Lance lay out the cords in a neat line extending

from the support trailer to the back of the site, and then over to the stack of power outlets several teams will connect to. They neatly zip-tie the cords together, and the effect is as if a kid with pastel chalks had outlined the back of their site for them.

Pig Pounda lays down hoses, and Crash Test Larry O lays down crap. "Why did you use that white hose?" he jibes Gary Kerce. "It clashes with the building behind it."

Silver tent poles clatter here and there along the row of teams. Corner fittings get laid out, looking like a huge game of jacks. Then the poles are laid onto the concrete, in a formation approximating their eventual positions when the tent is complete. Lying on the ground, the poles look like an extremely organized game of pickup-sticks in progress. Jacks and pickup-sticks. Big boys about to play their big boy games.

Popup tents go up like mushrooms after a rain. They're designed to go up fast—one person on each corner, a few shakes to get the cross-hatched bracing to begin extending, an arm under the tent pushing up, a few poles within poles at the corners sliding out and locking into place, and these tents are up. In this case, the mushrooms are popping up not after a shower but in anticipation of showers. They would go up no matter the forecast, but today the forecast suggests that they will be used.

Down the way, just up from Grayson, Cody Cline and his Nervous Wreck Cook'n Crew have erected a 10x20 white carport canopy, its tarp lashed to the metal frame with ball ties, and are fighting a second tent into place *under* the south half of the canopy. Once the green 10x10 is erected, Cody will put up its mosquito-netting walls, forming a room where the judges' table and storage closet-full of other items will be housed. His cookers will go into the north end of the canopy.

Kings and Pig Pounda have no tents; with the trailers they have brought in, retractable awnings (and the trailers themselves) will serve for shade and shelter.

It looks like the work is just beginning, but for the teams it actually began earlier in the week. "I probably got a minimum of eight hours in stuff that I do *before* I go to a contest," says Rick Dalton of Gwatney. "Dumb sport" stuff like cleaning the cookers and anything else that needs cleaning. Prepping the rub. Picking up the meat. Restocking supplies.

In fact, with its coils of electrical cords, bags of charcoal, refrigerator, tarps, chairs, two-wheeler, chairs, row upon row of plastic or organizing drawers, and the mandatory fire extinguisher, the Gwatney supply trailer looks like a rolling bomb shelter.

At the Madison, Indiana, Ribberfest KCBS competition in August later that year, Joyce Lindenberg of team Rub 'n' Que was fussing with her chicken blind box. Joyce opened the foam-plastic box, closed it. Opened it. Revealed the lettuce bed that garnished the box. Closed it.

"What's wrong?" said teammate Dave Sickmeyer.

Joyce said, "The lid is broken."

Dave nodded. He knew how to fix it: "Duct tape."

Problem solved, though with only a jest. (Joyce did not plan to repair the box with duct tape. The roll of her eyes told Dave that.)

Later, Rub 'n' Que's Wally Wathen was himself fussing over blind-box prep. Wally was slicing pork butt and wasn't happy with the way the slices were holding together. He weathered the joked solution: Duct tape.

Duct tape has already served Rub 'n' Que, when one of the team members took off the Ribberfest festival's entry wrist band and tried to put it back on though the original stickum was gone. The answer? Well, of course.

Do you need to disguise the brand name of your spray-on cooking oil so it doesn't get inadvertent advertising on national television during a cooking competition? You'd better believe that the answer in the case of the Food Network's *Tricked Out Tailgating* special was, for participant Gwatney, duct tape.

The lesson driven home by Rub 'n' Que and the Tricked Out Tailgaters is the very Boy-Scout-ish "Be (um, where's the duct tape?) prepared." Quein' is a lot like testosterone-overbalanced camping, and like camping (testosterone-overbalanced or not), you'd better be able to 1) have the proper gear, 2) make do with what you do/don't got, and 3) know which side of the tree that mold grows on. It helps if you know that the mold does not grow on the north sides of trees, especially since it's *moss* that grows northward on trees. A judge once interrupted John David Wheeler's presentation to point out the mold/moss distinction to him. Explaining why Natural Born Grillers cook with barkless wood, John David had been for months saying, "You heard how mold grows on the bark on the north sides of trees? You want to eat that? Neither do I." When going through that presentation at the judges' seminar, the judge, new to competition barbecue but not new to the world, said "moss" about three seconds after John had said "mold."

This revelation stymied non-camping Wheeler (he of the nice RV) for a moment, but he dove straight back into his presentation, showing off shoulder that sported neither mold nor moss. (At one later competition, he changed his presentation slightly, asking "You know what grows on the north side of trees?" And waited for the judge to supply the answer. Just in case.)

Gary Kerce of Pig Pounda agrees with the camping analogy, perhaps more vigorously than his wife would like. "My passion is fishing, and camping," the outdoors, says Miss Pat. Gary tries to convince her that she already is camping every time they stop at that campsite-that-oh-my-goodness-also-happens-to-have-a-barbecue-competition-attached-to-it-so-why-don't-I-fire-up-a-hog-a-long-as-we're-here,dear? "He says, 'You're campin'," Miss Pat says. "Yeah, but I work myself half to death. It's not quite the same…. He says, 'You got a fire going, you're grilling out, what else do you want?' I said I got a kitchen in there that's got everything but an ironing board…. I'm afraid he's gonna put one of those in."

To make sure they are prepared, Sweet Swine o' Mine organizes its gear, in part, with plastic tubs and indelible ink markers. The cook's name is prominently markered and permanently markered on the lid of the hog box: "ROONEY" (underlined once). This is followed by "HOG BOX—COOKS ONLY!" (underlined twice). Followed by a list—a numbered list, at that—of the tub's contents:

Hog Prep Knives
Latex Gloves
RAGS
Spritz Bottles
Sharpies
Xtra AAA Batteries
Digital Thermometers
Can Opener
BASTE Spoon
Knife Sharpener
Injection Needles
STRAINER
Pastry Brushes

Some of the individual contents of such boxes are labeled, as well. For example, the handle of the rib knife is clearly markered and permanently markered "Ribs."

Not on this list of hog items, but on at least one other team's list: disposable razors. Sometimes you have to shave wayward hairs off your hog. It's an odd sight seeing someone shaving a dead hog's behind.

From their supply trailer, Rick and crew slide out several plastic-top folding tables. They'll use six of them, but pull the spares out anyway, to get them out of the way of other items that will be unloaded. Two tables will be devoted to meat prep on Friday and blind-box prep on Saturday, one will stand sink-side for dish patrol, two will provide a staging area for judging (holding hot plates for warming sauces and plates and glasses and water bottles), the final one will hold the stereo. Rick and crew turn the spares top-side down and heft them up to the top of the supply trailer, where they slide them to rest atop the trailer. The hefting is relatively easy; the tables are sturdy but lightweight, unlike the big sturdy but anchorweight veneered plywood monsters that you might find in old school lunchrooms…or in abandoned bank buildings like the one just down the street.

Layers of old folding tables stacked sideways line one side of the First National Bank lobby, opposite the row of teller windows. Carlene and volunteer coworkers begin to load in, to haul and set up the heavy crap. They drag, one-by-one, four cumbersome plywood tables into a hall leading from the lobby to business rooms at the back. In one of these rooms, Walt and Larry will conduct the cooks' meeting on Friday. In another—actually two others accessible from a single hallway door but linked by a door between them—the contest will stage the blind judging. At the table that the volunteers set up in the hallway itself, teams will deliver their blind boxes full of meat ready for judging on Saturday. They'll come in through the bank's rear entrance, and give the boxes and foam-plastic cups of any accompanying sauce to the volunteers seated at the table. The entries will be logged, the labels with the team names stripped off, the boxes numbered, and the samples placed anonymously on one of the two tables in the blind rooms.

Now that the rigs are largely in place, Larry O has wandered over to traffic-cop this activity, as well. He points to the blind check-in table, and asks a volunteer nearby, "Do you have some Magic Markers to mark the carpet where the table is so we know where it was if we move it?"

The volunteer looks at him like she'd like to make his butt blue with a swift kick.

Load-in is just as vigorous inside the bank as it is on Main Street outside. Upstairs, the VIP lounge has already been set up. There, sponsors, organizers, community leaders and invited guests only will enjoy an open bar and canapes and goodies. On a table against a row of windows overlooking the bank lobby are empty silver serving trays, salsa boats, a fondue pot, a chafer, serving plates, and enough fancy toothpicks to keep the colored cellophane industry going for at least another week. On the other side, a serving bar has been covered with an oddly black tablecloth…oddly black because it was left over from the *wedding* of one of the volunteer's daughters. Ice bucket, drink garnish tray, empty glasses…the usual items await filling for Friday's VIP festivities.

The bank has been cleaned; it will be returned to its donor owners in better condition than the contest found it—and in cooler condition as well. A local HVAC firm donated the labor to get the broken air-conditioning up and running again before the bank is put to its contest use.

Walt and Larry have completed their setup in the bank, as well.

As a Memphis Barbecue Association rep, "You have to be able to react to changes," Walt has said. And you have to be able to react to the opposite of change—you have to react to the reactionary—and what could be more reactionary than a scoring software program that requires DOS?

As wacky cartoon inventor Clyde Crashcup would say on the old *Alvin and the Chipmunks* show, that's "D for D and OS for OS, DOS."

If you remember either Clyde Crashcup or DOS, you're…um…youth-challenged. Or an MBA rep.

One of the primary challenges facing MBA organization of a competition is getting the organizers to supply a computer that 1) allows you to find a DOS prompt and 2) does *not* have a USB printer port, and we won't get into the technical (or nontechnical) reasoning behind requirement #2.

Galax has met that challenge, setting up in a back room in the bank building an ancient-computer-history-compatible combination of computer, monitor and printer. The printer is even dutifully labeled "BBQ" on a strip of masking tape. On the two folding tables set up in this room, Walt and Larry do their own load-in, unpacking the blue suitcase on wheels: the spare computer and printer, copies of the program they'll load into the competition's computer, the manuals, the spare score-card and blind box labels in case the competition couldn't find the right Avery 5161s the MBA reps need. Among the other things unpacked: Briefing agendas and notes, a list of all the judges who had served as finals judges up to this point this year, and samples to help educate contest participants. These samples include scorecards for the volunteers, sample completed finals scorecards for the finals briefing, and pictures of open blind boxes from previous competitions so that anyone who hadn't experienced blind judging before would have an idea of what's involved.

Scoring will be done here in the rep room, as will any consultations about problems or issues arising in the contest. A typewriter will eventually be brought in—typing the winners' checks will be done here, too.

This rep room, though a bit tight, is a relatively nice one. Over the years, reps have been set up in tents and under canopies, in small motor homes, on fraternal-organization-hall stages, in small rooms that are little more than glorified closets. On Saturday, Walt will be seeing a lot of this room as the scores flow in and results are calculated.

Back through the hall in the main bank lobby, the remaining lumber on legs that some have called folding tables are being set up, and surrounded by the metal folding chairs with that indescribable color that seems to have resulted from mixing gray paint, chocolate milk and mud. The chairs are scuffed, the tops of the seatbacks worn. These *are* your father's folding chairs.

Each table is covered with white plastic, then adorned with a square red paper table covering, set at a rakish angle so its corners point toward the ends of the table. In the center of the red paper, a white napkin, upon which is placed two galax leaves.

The teller windows have been draped with black crepe streamers layered on gray paper napkins layered on white cloth, all covering the FDIC signs posted next to each teller window as well as the windows themselves. By judging time Saturday morning, red and green balloons will populate the teller portals, one each.

Balloons and not judges.

At one point Ron had considered seating the blind judges at the teller stations to tie into the "theme" of the surroundings. This is the sort of creativity Ron applied when first thinking about getting into the restaurant business. He and his three partners (dining room manager Dan Milby, Sr., pit master Jon Jordan, and business office manager Barbara Jordan) had looked into setting up a restaurant in an abandoned jailhouse built in 1936. Servers would wear guard uniforms, customers would eat in the cells, and after processing the proper paperwork (i.e., paying the bill), customers would be escorted by guards to the front door to be "released."

When the jailhouse was subsequently made unavailable to

the four, they moved to plan B. Plan BB. Plan BBQ. A barbecue joint. The inspiration came from Ron's business travel. He'd stopped for a meal at a restaurant in Johnson City, Tennessee. In the restaurant was posted a guide to regional barbecue sauces:

Tennessee…tomato-based
North Carolina…vinegar-based
South Carolina…mustard-based
Virginia…ain't no such thing

Ain't no such thing meant opportunity to Ron Passmore and company. They brought Memphis-style barbecue to Virginia.

Now, just as Ron Passmore's customers do not now dine in jail cells (obviating the need for signs saying, "No Shoes, No Stripes, No Service"), judges will not sit at teller windows, for reasons of pure practicality. First of all, the numbers don't work out: eight blind judges for each category (groups of four seated at two tables); seven teller windows. More important, the mechanics of blind judging demand grouping. The first step in judging blind is opening up all the samples on the table, and marking scores for appearance. Does the entry look appetizing? This requires clustering about. When each judge is done marking appearance scores, he or she sits. When all four are seated, the eating begins. Like a family dinner, there are requests of *pass that sauce* and *I need another napkin* and *can I have some more water, please*…all things that diners do and tellers do not.

The blind judges, therefore, will be seated at the awkward monstrosities that Carlene and her cohort have loaded into the blind judging rooms.

Outside, work on team tables continues as Natural Born Grillers empty a bag of white PVC tubing. The inch-and-a-half-diameter tubing has been cut into two-foot lengths, which Ken and Birm slip onto the legs of the folding tables, one to a corner. This extends the table legs, bringing the tabletop up to more comfortable workstation height. It's a common trick used by other teams, as well. Gwatney lifts their tables this way. Jack's, too. Pig Pounda Kappa, on the other hand, does not.

At Galax, team setups are modest, aside from the RVs and trailers—generally variations of tent(s) aside cooker(s), with a serving table and chairs for the judges. The food prep and cleanup areas are blocked off by tent walls from public/judging view. Most teams have mounted fences of one sort or another: plastic white picket, in the case of both Grillers and Pig Pounda (the latter featuring a gate monogrammed with "PPK" in wrought iron), wood picket for Pit Connection, chain link for Hawg Wild, simple poles and plastic chain for Jack's and Smoked Encounters, wrought iron for Kings. Gwatney sets off its area with Tensabarrier posts with adjustable, retractable cloth tapes, like you see in banks and airports for traffic control. So-Co marks its perimeter with tiki torches mounted in five-gallon plastic buckets of sand. The Nervous Wreck area is a bit looser, but a couple of large ferns help define it.

About the fanciest setup decoration is the Kings scarepig— a scarecrow type of stuffed clothing (including a Smoke on the Mountain T-shirt) wearing a pig mask and lounging on a folding chair just inside the Kings Cooking area. Above their gate, a neon "Kings Cooking" sign—the words in white, a three-pointed outline of a crown between the words in red.

At competitions that sponsor best booth contests, the setups can get more elaborate. Teams competing in Murphysboro, Illinois, for instance, often take it up a notch. One year, the theme of Murphy's cook was "Good Old Days Reunion Tour," and the best booth award-winner featured a classic black-and-white Chev convertible (and that competition gave great credence to the observation that one of the prettiest hogs you'll see on a barbecue competition-site is a Harley). Booth contests, though, seem to be waning. Disappearing, too, are the "Showmanship" competitions. Judges would travel from team to team, to be entertained with skits and parodies and, in the case of a team called the Bop-N-Qrs, oldies stage shows. Back when the Pigs in Paradise team were the New Pigs on the Block, they entertained with what they called "The New Pig Rap." They began by singing along, not to a New Kids song (about which many spectators were likely grateful), but to Queen's "We Will Rock You."

New Pigs!
New Pigs!
On the Block!

One verse of the rap:
We raise it from a baby,
give it love and affection.
Then we shoot it in the head
and we cook it to perfection.

It's unlikely that Steve Barr will use these lyrics to write his next bluegrass tune. The Memphis in May World Championship Barbecue Cooking Contest has a showmanship contest for the best "Ms. Piggie" (carefully spelled so as to not be confused with the trademark-protected name of one similarly named Muppet), that involves skits and dance routines, and of course such frivolity is the darling of the media. The frightening thought is that the WCBCC is not the only place where you can see robust men with beards sporting plastic hog snouts, tutus and falsies, but it definitely is one of the few. The booths themselves are literally over the top at Memphis in May, with some two- and three-story structures costing tens of thousands of dollars. Some teams go full-tilt: Above the Super Smokers booth floats a yellow balloon bearing the restaurant's logo, a balloon big enough to eclipse sun or moon depending on planetary positioning. One Memphis competitor, Pig Nation, built a wall at the front of their site. A stone wall, with stones large enough to frighten hernias everywhere, held together with masonry, and topped with slate slabs. Packing up your site is sometimes called "tear-down"; packing up this site may have involved "demolition." Walt's Mile High Barbecue team has airport connections among its members (and Airpork Crew connections, as cook Jimmy Johnson once captained that team). Lounge chairs for its guests, spread around the outside of its area, are airliner seats (first-class and coach, though the drinks seem to be free in both classes, and unlike modern-day airlines, all flights are smoking flights).

Occasional competitions have "themes," and teams are welcome to dress their booths and themselves according to the themes. This leads to sights like former military men wearing coconut bras and hula skirts, and it's all good, silly fun.

Smoke on the Mountain has no booth competition, no showmanship competition, no theme. It's just as well. There's not a cook in Galax that you could consider a boppin' kinda guy. And none of the male competitors could bring off coconuts or a tutu.

Except maybe with a little duct tape.

10 HAPPY HOG GETS HIS RUDE AWAKENING

"I'm just a ~~love~~ rib machine."

— lyric change suggested by rib cook Clara Scarritt for a toy pig that lip-synchs "Love Machine"

Saturday, September 17, Bowling Green, Kentucky. At the Balloons, Tunes and BBQ competition, Birm and John David of Natural Born Grillers evaluate the hog they've just smoked. Lying on its back inside the cooker, the mouth-open hog is clearly revealing its upper row of teeth in a kind of death grin. No apple.

"He's smiling—look at 'im," Birm says. "He's got a happy smile on his face."

John David jokes in reply, "It's important to have a happy pig right before you kill and cook him."

Thursday, July 14, Galax. Volunteers are setting up the hospitality room for teams and judges in the abandoned First National Bank building. One of the first decorations to be mounted on the wall opposite the row of teller stations is a hand-lettered pink-paper sign announcing "Welcome to Galax." The hand-drawn pig next to the lettering looks distressed. As well he should, given the culinary activities that are about to ensue. The half-panicked, half-dazed pig is unlike the happy hogs you see on team logos and on barbecue restaurant menus and on judges' business cards (yes, some carry "BBQ Judge" business cards) and as piggy knickknacks…

…And on posters touting barbecue competitions. The pig on the Smoke on the Mountain logo is a chipper little beast, wearing naught but a chef's hat, and posed like he's doing the boogaloo in front of mountains in the distance. On the chef's hat, a first-place ribbon. That's appropriate, because this festive logo was in itself a first-place winner. The Chamber of Commerce held a contest to create a Smoke on the Mountain logo. Becky Guynn's design was selected from among about fifty entries.

Happy pigs are strutting up and down the Galax contest site the way they do every contest, from the Kings Cooking scarepig on the south end to the Natural Born piggy chef (apron, red shirt, red shoes, just like the Grillers themselves) triumphantly brandishing spatula and grill fork on the north. In between, Hawg Wild's sly-winkin' coveralled butcher pig and the rarely encountered green-snouted antennaed alien porker at Smoked Encounters of the Third Swine.

The stylin' pig with sunglasses, the cocky grin and the blade of grass sticking out of his mouth at Pit Connection—he's new. "We didn't start out with the pig that we have right now," says Pit Connector Mary Dyer. "We had an ugly pig, so we had to change it, 'cause this one looks cool." Pig Pounda Kappa's bright-eyed piggy professor (with mortarboard and bow tie) was drawn by Roger Kerce, though teammate/brother Gary has encouraged Roger to come up with something more "animated."

Why are these pigs so gleeful? Why are they as happy as shigs in pit (to borrow one of the KCBS circuit team names)? Wouldn't you think that *running away* would be the kind of "more animated" that the pigs would be aspiring to? They're gonna die! Sweet Swine's logo pig is a fairly natural illustration of a hog; it seems neutral about the whole affair. The pig illustrated in outline on the back of the Jack's Old South rig seems at least mildly wary.

Yet, all along the circuit, the anthropomorphic pig is celebrating the gobbling-down of its brethren in all manner of get-ups. Flying pigs, hillbilly pigs, pigs in U.S. military garb. Pigs on pogo sticks, pigs with mouth harps, cardplaying pigs. Pirate pigs, blues-crooning pigs, pigs making happy homes in backyard grills and lolling about on them like they're on tanning beds. The suave tuxedo-garbed pig of the Q-2-U team (as least the happy pigs depicted on the Q-2-U chair back covers wear "Please eat beef" aprons). Elvis pigs, Marilyn pigs, and the Loin Ranger ("Hi-Hog Silver!"). Fat pigs, skinny pigs, pigs who climb on rocks. Tough pigs, sissy pigs, even pigs with chicken pox.

Speaking of chicken…poultry and moo-cows get their exercise on the non-MBA circuits. Like the scared-eggless chicken on the back of the Chicago Smoke Competition Team. Or the cow and chicken running away from home with hobo kerchief packs on the Ulcer Acres BBQ logo. Or the cow, chicken and pig with chefs hats on the 3 Men With Nothing Better to Do logo (the pig, by the way, is the smart one—chicken and cow hoist fork and spatula, respectively, while pig hoists a full beer stein).

And the booth decorations—figurines and stuffed piggies, from porcine salt-and-pepper shakers to battery-operated walking-oinking pigs to pigs in dominatrix outfits to the Hogs on Harleys. And, oh yes, the pinkish coffee cup that, when you tip it up to take a drink, makes you look like you have a snout.

In Columbus, Mississippi, rib cook Clara Scarritt of Porky's Pride shows off one cute-little-bastard pig—a battery-operated stuffed animal wearing a red tie. Activate him, and he lipsynchs a piggy-playful snippet of "Love Machine."

All these porkers are obviously in a different frame of mind than the scared little devil on the Galax hospitality room wall. And obviously in a different frame of mind than another pig that appears on the Smoke on the Mountain poster. Standing on a reversed-out text block saying "Memphis in May Sanctioned Contest Network" is a woodcuttish illustration of a hog, branded with a big letter Q, and sporting butcher-shop dotted lines outlining the various cuts. The hog looks a little dazed.

Madison, Indiana, in 2005 conducted a "decorate the pig statue" contest. Local businesses painted, dressed and otherwise embellished two-foot-high pig figurines. Entries ranged from John "Deere" Pig to Batpig to Dragon Pig. One statue was accompanied by a hoof-painted "Eat More Chicken" Sign, playing off the Chick-Fil-A promotion in which cow figurines painted the Don't-Eat-Cow sentiment on billboards in childish ("bovinish"?) scrawl. The eat-more-chicken pig in Madison was cute. Clever. Until you thought about it a moment. This pig statue was wearing a chicken mask. Accompanied by an "Eat More Chicken" sign. This smacks of cross-species suicide. At least the pigs are better spellers than the cows, who scrawl "Eat More Chiken."

A couple hundred yards away from Clara's Love Machine in Columbus, Mississippi, a first-time team displays *its* stuffed-animal pigs in appropriate fashion. Team Hog Wild (not to be confused with the *Hawg* Wild cooking in Galax) displays its name on a banner about six feet wide hanging from the front of their booth roof. Tied to grommets at each side of the banner's bottom are long white cords holding anchor weights. Those weights are a pair of cute pink stuffed-animal pigs about the size of a couple of fistfuls. Like Clara's Love Machine, they wear neckties, too—these once-happy hogs anchor the banner by hanging at the end of little nooses.

11 THE PRIMAL URGE TO HUNT AND ROAST AND GIVE EACH OTHER CRAP

"Thanks for the ashes, Ashhole!"

– a call overheard after a fellow team member clapped a firebox door shut too hard, stirring ashes in the cooker

Friday, July 14, Galax. Smoked Encounters of the Third Swine's Chris Carter—dark-haired, with a dark, neat clump of goatee under his chin—is enjoying shooting the breeze with a couple of judges, talkin' barbecue, talking about his team, talking about how the team started.

He says, "A friend of mine…"

Judge Gregg Snyder jumps in. "It always starts with 'a friend of mine,'…and a beer."

Barbecue genesis is often so. Backyard boasts become challenges. Backyard pride becomes competitiveness. Backyard brews become confidence . . .

Or maybe it's just the fun.

Or maybe it's something deeper.

"Men get together and do things: Fish, play cards, hunt," says Terry Black of the Super Smokers team. "But to me nothing is better than a bunch of guys getting together and doing the male bonding thing and barbecuing. Putting a fire under meat happened after the hunt or after the cave man caught a fish. It is the pinnacle of those activities. A celebration sometimes of our 'manlyhood.'"

Claud Mann (Chef Claud on TBS's *Dinner and a Movie*) says: "It's that sense that everything will be OK. You've got the fire, you've got meat in the fire, and for our ancestors that was a big deal." Fire and meat is ingrained, primal. "I like the simplicity of meat and smoke. I also play drums. Drum is one of those things that man has been doing since the very beginning.... That's what I like about barbecue."

Says Steven Raichlen, author of several bestselling barbeque cookbooks: "People who get involved with food very generally are people who like the act of cooking for somebody, making food for somebody. It lies at the generosity of our species.... On top of that, you layer the idea of competition, which is an old way to fuel excellence; you layer a love of gear, because everybody sort of tinkers with their pits and designs for pits and it's just fun; you add the primal joy of just setting stuff on fire."

Peyton Turner's Grills Gone Wild team started in what he describes as a "*Survivor*" moment." He and friends from college and law school form the core of the team. After graduation, "we got together and took one last trip down to a place that we had in Beacon Hill, Florida. One night, we had about ten people sitting out on the beach, with torches and a bonfire. There may have been one or two...coolers full of beer involved. The bonfire got us talking about grilling and then the once-a-year reunion talk came up and the two just went together."

The barbecue pit is something of the original black hole, sucking unsuspecting light particles and normal people into its inescapable depths. Al Roker did a TV special on the Memphis in May World Championship, and the next year had formed a competition team, he enjoyed it so much. Two cookbooks later...

Claud Mann and Ed Richardson's introduction to competition barbecue came when working together on a Southern Living Presents profile of Memphis in May for Turner South, Claud as on-camera host and Ed as producer. They, too, formed a competition team. No barbecue cookbooks yet, but their Barefoot in the Pork still competes after several years in the Memphis in May backyard division, taking a third in 2005.

Cooks stumble into barbecue, they're drawn to it, they're raised on it. Sometimes they're simply invited to it. Natural Born Grillers began when John David Wheeler was recruited by his sister, then employed by the Tunica Mississippi Chamber of Commerce, to cook at the Tunica contest. A tall man who, if he were to take on a few more pounds, might be described as burly, John David can grind out an order sufficiently well, but usually his voice is relaxed and smooth, his laugh deep and friendly. Some of his barbecue colleagues call him Big John (Birm calls him Baby Huey just to be cantankerous, and Ken Nottingham says, "Finger-pointer is what I call him"). John David wears his hair at near crew cut length; his mustache and goatee, the same.

To take up his sister's invitation, John David, owner of a construction company and a real estate firm, traded some plumbing work and some cash with a friend to acquire the Big Show. "It was not the Big Show as it is today," he says. "It had a different trailer, it had fish cookers on it, it had a turkey deep fryer, it wasn't nearly set up for barbecue as it is right now." (Read: the love of gear, the love of tinkering.) "We didn't expect to do good and did worse than that. Didn't get the rib done, burned the shoulders up, but had a good time." (Read: the primal joy of just setting stuff on fire.) He turned to a family friend, John Maki of Custom Cookers, for tips. "He helped me out a lot at the very beginning—helped me with some dry rub, helped me out with blind boxes and different things.

Rusty Voigt fires up the Twatney hog cooker with a neat flame-throwing toy

"Our next contest was Southaven." Hometown Southaven Mississippi. "We finaled in shoulder. Second contest. Sixty-five teams. Didn't have a damn clue what we were doing. I had on a pair of those big rubber black gloves. I tried to put plastic gloves—the regular gloves we wear now—on over right there before the judges and they just popped. And I said the hell with it and just reached in with those black gloves. They were nasty. Third-place shoulder—Natural Born Grillers!" But they'd gotten their taste. Fallen into the original black hole.

Jerry Dyer got his taste of barbecue competitions back in '80s when a colleague saw an ad for a local competition. They applied. Got in. Things were different then; the competition that Pit Connection applied to was one of the first Memphis in May championships. Pure and Sinful's barbecue roots stretch back to that time, too, when Dan Puryear lived in Memphis. He cooked in some early Memphis in Mays. "When I moved to Richmond in '93 or whatever, there was nothing like that around," he says. Dan is unbarbecue slim, with a playful smile. "I was looking looking looking, and there was nothing advertised as a barbecue competition on the East Coast. And all of a sudden you started finding these competitions edging closer and closer to us. So I decided...*me*...I don't think Lisa had a clue what I was doing...so I started building our smoker out here. We built it from scratch. And I said we are going to start doing competitions, and I'd done competitions before, and we're going to see how we do."

Pure and Sinful's growth was typical of new teams. "The first year was kind of rough. Everybody was getting frustrated because we didn't do anything. But the second year we started getting a little nibble here, a little nibble there. Last year we really started taking off. And that's when we started winning checks and trophies. And I think the community knows that we're here."

Though there's the occasional tale of teams who take a grand championship the first time out, the pay-your-dues trail is as common in barbecue as it is in life (well, why wouldn't that be true, since barbecue is life?). Rib Ticklers is a team out of Batesville, Arkansas, that has risen quickly to the top ten, but they started out with typical stumbles. "There's a local competition," says Chris Beller while cooking in Caruthersville. "We attended it a couple of years ago." He turns to teammate John Harris. "How would you measure our success?"

John says, "Umm, we weren't last."

Says Chris: "Once."

For Pure and Sinful, the difference between year-one frustration and year-two nibbles: "Knowing who's responsible for what," Dan says. "What happens when."

"Year one we had too many people," Lisa Puryear says.

"They just wanted to come in the area and sit around and

drink beer all day," Dan says. "In year two, it came down to, We're just taking the people who are really into it. Now we got down to a core group." (At the other end of the team-size spectrum, when asked how many people his team has, John David says, "Seven or eight hundred." In Galax his team numbers fourteen, though some will be devoted to operating the vending operation.) "We've come a long way," Dan says. "And every team goes through this: After you do it for two or three years, people start fading out, going away, losing interest, and you have to reorganize pretty much after two or three years. I've seen it with many teams."

In fact, when Richard Lackie of Sweet Swine o' Mine describes the quick collapse of one of the first teams he was on, he refers to it as "In typical barbecue fashion..." He says, "There's a lot of intermingling of teams. When you join a team, you're automatically a vegetable chopper. Once people get their time, they either become an important part of the team or they go somewhere where they can be.... Egos get in the way, or if you have four great cooks on a team, you're kind of wasting a good cook because you have three categories." In another conversation, Tango of Natural Born has said, "We're so competitive, that we get on each other's nerves." Tango and company have a long way to go, though, before matching the ultimate in competition and nerve-wracking. One team was banned from not only the Tennessee Funfest competition but also from the Memphis in May circuit entirely for fighting. With themselves.

Clara Scarritt of Porky's Pride followed a variation of the vegetable chopper route. Clara is easygoing, proud of what she does and enjoying it, too, based on her rising, hoarse-husky laugh when she tells a story. "I had always been on the other side at our local cook, International City Fest, going to some friends' tent that were in competition and hanging with them all weekend, being fed and beered." When she found out that one of her friends she and her husband met up with every Friday night had a team, "I had a fit. I told him I would love to be on a barbecue team and would work my butt off washing dishes or doing anything they needed if I could join." From "lots and lots of pans and dishes—in cold water, mind you," Clara progressed to rib cook and rib presenter and to the official team title of Rib Boss. "No, you don't see too many women in the front line presenting, although they *might* have a lot to do with the prep and cooking behind the scenes but are never mentioned.... I still think there are judges that don't quite believe that I cook the ribs and just present as a novelty to possibly gain points." (In her transition from "being beered" to cooking, she echoes Dan's assessment of team roles. "Being on the cooking side has shown me how that friends' team should have kicked us out and let them get on with their prep work.")

For many teams, family provides much if not all of the core group. At Smoked Encounters of the Third Swine in Galax, it's father Chris and nine-year-old son Sean, and the gentleman who introduces himself with "I'm just the father-in-law," Sean's grandpa Charlie Bubel. On competition day, Sean keeps the time as his father packs the blind box, and he stands at parade rest during his father's presentation to the on-site judges. Kids on-site are relatively common at barbecue competitions. Youngsters guarding the front gate. Youngsters greeting judges. Youngsters delivering hot, wet towels on plates to judges like flowergirls and ring-bearers. Even youngsters with their own teams. Several competitions sponsor kids' divisions, and there are some serious cooks in those divisions. A kids" 'cue winner in Mt. Carmel went on to compete in the WCBCC backyard division—and made the finals.

At Bowling Green, Kentucky's, Balloons, Tunes and BBQ competition, Cameron Ellison races around the Hickory Pit

Stop cooksite with the archetypal four-year-old's fervor that has archetypal parents and onlooking gray-hairs the world over saying "I wish I had all that energy."

One day before the competition, Cameron's mother, Tammy, was talking about the sauce that her husband Jeff and the Hickory Pit Stop cooking team were going to continue using during their cooks.

"Mom!" Cameron chided. "It's not a sauce. It's a *glaze*."

At Hickory Pit Stop, Cameron is more than just the son of head cook Jeff and team presenter Tammy. Because when four-yearold Cameron corrects Mom about the *glaze, Mom!*, he should know. He created it. And a black-mango-based glaze, at that.

But Cameron has an up-and-coming challenger for the honor of the youngest one on the circuit. Sandra Aylor, an impending mom when she took the MBA judging seminar in July 2005, is a team ambassador for the Memphis in May world championship. "This year we had one team—Papa Pig and the Posse—cater to our unborn child during the contest," she says. "They all called her by name and made sure I always had water when I passed by their booth, and they even let her—me—sample their prize-winning "Anything But" Seafood dish before it was turned in for judging. She is being spoiled by MIM and she is not even here yet." So, will the child's first baby food be tomato-based, mustard-based or vinegar-based? "Since I prefer tomato-based and [husband] Kyle prefers vinegar-based, our newborn will probably like mustard-based everything!"

Several of the Galax teams are pure family affairs. The Pit Connection is composed of husband, wife, daughter, son-in-law. Hawg Wild is husband and wife and kids. The Nervous Wreck Cook'n Crew is husband, wife, two sons (and one son's girlfriend). So-Co is husband and wife (their baby is along, but probably didn't help much). Pig Pounda is pure family except for

Ricky Miller, who's known the Kerces long enough that he might as well be family. And of course, father, son and "just the father-in-law." What does Chris's wife think about the competitions?

"She doesn't mind it," Chris says. "She knows I enjoy it."

Judge Gregg interjects, "Better than a strip club."

Young Sean says, "She wouldn't go to those."

Sometimes it's family, sometimes friends, sometimes organization members, sometimes groups of employees…and often those groups of employees work together at restaurants. Super Smokers out of St. Louis participates in the circuit in part to promote its Super Smokers chain of barbecue restaurants. The year that Smokers took first-place hog at Memphis in May, owner Terry Black was on the phone to St. Louis media within minutes. Cooking-savvy, marketing-savvy and media-savvy, Terry could almost dictate the stories for the media word-for-word on the spot. Among the Galax teams, Jack's Old South came out of commercial sauce roots. John Bennett's So-Co is John's attempt to peer out from the restaurant kitchen door into the competition world for the first time. John has chef's training in his background (as well as a pursuit that might eventually serve him on the barbecue circuit—political science); he has completed a portion of the Culinary Institute of America (CIA) coursework. He's trying out another side of cooking, temporarily defecting from the CIA to the KGB (Kooking Good Barbecue—if you spell *cooking* the way the Chick-Fil-A cows spell "Eat More Chiken").

When Ron Passmore and Gary Kerce stand in the Smokehouse on Pig Pounda's first arrival in Galax back in June, they represent an intersection of dreams. Ron Passmore dreams of getting his Smokehouse into competition; Gary dreams of parlaying his competition experience into a restaurant. Each are a ways away from pursuing the ship-in-the-night goals. "I get closer," Gary tells Ron, "and then I back off. I get closer, and then I back off."

Also heading in Gary Kerce's direction of competition to commercial are John David Wheeler and Chris Birmingham of Natural Born Grillers. Their vending at the Galax competition is a hint of their next commercial endeavor. They're investigating Memphis-area locations to sell carryout—smoked shoulder, smoked turkey and the like.

The circuit has launched any number of such careers. The Ricky Rover Rooter Roasters team of Campbell Hill, Illinois, gave Leroy Rieckenberg something to do in retirement and then dragged him back out of retirement when the Roasters started getting catering requests. Pork Improvements formed their team as friends who worked at the same joint. Almost literally so. Most of the team members were prison guards. They competed successfully for a while, got the bug, and bought a different kind of joint—a restaurant (adding to the menu, of course, barbecue).

Mike Mills translated his Apple City Barbecue Team success into a barbecue restaurant in his hometown of Murphysboro, Illinois. Then to his not-hometown of Las Vegas, Nevada. Then to another of his not-hometowns, New York City, and the Blue Smoke restaurant. And even those restaurants likely began with a few friends...and a beer.

Back where this story began, Chris Carter is saying, "I have a friend of mine who makes all the steelwork for me; he also has a company that manufactures commercial gas grills and stainless steel cookers and tow trailers. He's the guy that really got me into this. Him and I were the ones having the beer. He kind of challenged me to go cook with one."

It's the challenge, stated or unstated. To Guido of Porkosaurus, there's competition even when there's no competition. "Every backyard cook is practicing in his or her way," he says. "They're working to be the best, even if they don't have their sights on competition.

"It all goes back to your backyard, firing up your barbecue, inviting your friends over. That's what really everything revolves around. What better hobby can you have than where you cook to practice it, and have a couple beers? I mean, what better hobby? You're firing the grill up, you're infecting the neighborhood with amazing smells of smoke and hickory and apple and whatever you use, and everybody's coming over and going, 'Man, what are you cooking this weekend?'

"'Aw, I'm practicing.'

"'You're practicing?'

"And we do practice. We're actually having a backyard cookout," Guido says, "but we're really practicing."

12 ACOLYTES OF THE CHURCH OF BARBECUE

"Murphysboro? That's a damn barbecue church up there."
– John David Wheeler commenting on Murphysboro, Illinois–the city, its annual contest, the teams that have come from there

Friday evening, July 15, Galax. A barbecue veteran is chatting with Cody Cline, earnest newcomer. "How many shoulders do you have?" the vet asks.

"Four," Cody says.

An almost-acceptable answer. One pork shoulder for each of the on-site judges, and one for pulling meat for the blind.

"It's good to have more." More to choose from, and, critically important, something to serve to the finals judges should you be so fortunate as to entertain them. "But you'll be OK," the vet says. "If you make finals and don't have a shoulder, one will appear from somewhere."

Like magic.

Nothing that this particular veteran would recommend, of course—it's against the MBA rules to enter meat you didn't cook yourself. But it has happened that the Pork Fairy has left under a team's pillow a shoulder that the team can cook in mere instants, or that the team actually had enough shoulders but forgot where the last one was until another team helpfully discovered it for them, or that "Hey, can I take back that shoulder I cooked but stored on your grill next door?"

Other items appear for teams in need in storied barbecue magic, the way that extra chairs appear if you're a new team and you don't have enough seating for the finals judges, the way extra ice and napkins and advice and encouragement and, dammit, energy appears from other teams.

Saturday, June 18, Germantown/Memphis area. At the Tennessee Funfest, Natural Born Grillers has made the finals in two categories: whole hog and shoulder. After the scores for each categories have been tallied, two contest officials take a computer printout listing the finalists, their preliminary scores, and the time their finals judges will arrive out to the teams. The officials drive up to the teams in a golf cart, and teams are watching for them.

At the Funfest, the officials drive up to Natural Born during shoulder judging. The hog finalists have been named, and Natural Born is on the list. During ribs judging, the official team begins visiting the shoulder finalists. Cheers from around the park as the first two shoulder teams get the good word. Birmingham has already worked his grapevine; he knows that Natural Born has made it to finals even before the golf cart turns onto the row where the Grillers' area is positioned.

"Let's see the paper," he says when the officials approach.

One of the officials shakes her head. "We're going over there," she says, waving her hand in a motion that could include any of a number of teams.

Birmingham knows otherwise, and he and the official give each other crap for another minute or two until Birm gets the paper he knows he's going to get.

Later, after the rib scores are tallied, the cart comes down Natural Born's row a third time. And stops. One booth short.

At Pit Panthers. The first-time team stationed next door to Grillers. Natural Born has not made rib finals.

Yet, when the finals judges arrive at the Pit Panthers cooksite to evaluate their ribs, they are seated at Natural Born's table, on Natural Born chairs, and drink from Natural Born water glasses while being cooled by Natural Born's industrial-sized fan. All things lent quickly to help out an understocked and underprepared new team. The judges had sat at that very table, on those very chairs, cooled by that very fan, twice before when visiting Grillers earlier in the finals. The ribs are served from a platter donated by the Basty Boys team, and placed on Basty Boys plates. The presentation made by Pit Panther Doug Slater has been well-coached by members of the Parrothead Porkers. "We owe that trophy to friendship," Doug says. "If it weren't for the friendship of everybody on the circuit that we have, we would never have got that trophy. Our ribs were good. They were damn good. But being able to present like we did, was only because we have friends on the circuit."

When the finals judges leave, members of the aiding teams and others converge on the Pit Panthers. "The honeymoon is over," declares Tango (cooking with Basty Boys that day). "Your greenhorn status is gone. As G.T. said, your cherry has been busted."

Says Doug, "All three of those teams that helped us, they said, you got your help, don't ask again."

Doug and others who have succeeded with help can very likely ask again. The stories of teams helping one another are rife. Gwatney won grand champion at Memphis in May with a hog that had been slathered with Sweet Swine o' Mine mustard. In Galax, Gwatney team members help Pig Pounda muscle its hog cooler into position, Sweet Swine helps So-Co get a fire going, John David observes David Hair of Jack's lighting an unopened bag of charcoal in the firebox of a cold grill and advises, "Make sure that paper don't burn off before you put that hog in there, OK?—put a little of that flavor on there" (with Alice Cooper's "No More Mister Nice Guy" from someone's sound system—maybe Natural Born's—playing in the background). Small stories, but commonly everyday. Cooking tips are shared with the new teams—and that's how teams grow in general. That's how most of the teams in Galax grew.

Not cooking in Galax is Pat Burke, head cook with the Tower Rock team and formerly with the old Apple City team, out of Murphysboro.

Yet, cooking in Galax is the very same Pat Burke...or at least the spirit and the cooking techniques of Murphy's Pat Burke. Pat doesn't conduct cooking classes per se; it's almost as if he is a walking cooking class. And several of his students are working to follow that walk in Galax.

"I'm a good student," says Rick Dalton of Gwatney. "You just ask Pat Burke. He told me, 'I think I taught you too much.'"

Early in his barbecue career, Natural Born's Chris Birmingham made a point of traveling to competitions where Pat was cooking, just to watch. He'd done the same with George Holder of Pyropigmaniacs. "The only way you're going to do that is watch somebody do it or help somebody do it, who understands what they're doing," Birm says. So when he was advised, "You go to Marion, Arkansas, find a guy named Pat Burke—Tower Rock," he took the advice. "I sat there watching him and I'm amazed, you know, how he carried himself. He says, 'You wanna learn what I do, feel free to come to any cook.' About six straight cooks, I get in my car or truck and I drive wherever he was. And get there about 2, 3 in the morning. I had a job, had to be there every day." And he watched, learning from Pat Burke and George Holder and champion cook John Willingham "how they carried themselves. You learn that you cook barbecue in steps, and you'll notice with us, everything's got a method behind it." Ron Passmore and his 3 Pigs and a Lady partners did much the same thing when preparing for the restaurant business. They traveled the country in an RV, volunteering time at various barbecue restaurants to learn secrets and best business practices of the trade.

John Akins, head cook of the Huish barbecue team, cooked with Pat Burke as part of his apprenticeship; John is in Galax, though not cooking this weekend. John has attended judging school and is now doing actual judging to learn to improve his own presentation and cooking. He has a goodly amount of skill as it stands—entering the weekend of July 16, the Huish team has scored 10 MBA circuit points, putting Huish in a three-way tie for fourteenth. (Ironically, the head cook for one of the other teams Huish is tied with—Sweetness of Hog—is also in Galax and not cooking. Gene Johnson of Sweetness is helping Natural Born Grillers run their vending booth.) One of the things John learns in Galax: "I was really surprised at how much smoke flavor was on those meats there." After Smoke on the Mountain, John set to work on ways to get more smoke into his product. As John says, "Actually, Pat Burke had told us to do this awhile back."

Chad Allen is head cook of the eventually appropriately named Old School Cookers. His is a relatively new team. On his third cook in Caruthersville, his area was next door to Tower Rock. Chad said simply, "Mr. Pat's been real good to me." *Real good* means the three hours Pat spent with Chad Friday night giving him tips and instruction, and *real good* means something as simple as lending rags to Chad on Saturday to wipe down his grill with.

Mr. Pat teaches cooking and he teaches attitude. "Pat Burke set me straight about bellyaching," says Richard Lackie on Friday night in Galax. "He said, 'Look at your scores. If across the board you have seven scores on flavor and four of them are nines, don't blame the judges.' He said you have to look for trends. If you see a trend in your scores, then you know you've done something wrong. He said if you don't see a trend, if it's mixed up, then maybe there's something going on. But he said if you look down and there are four or five scores that are the same, you can't complain.

"It was after Tunica once, I was mad as hell. I said, 'What do we do? What are we doing wrong? Our on-site judges are giving us perfect scores.'

"I looked down, and saw every blind flavor score was 9. Blind killed us. I went from cocky to humble in about two seconds. Tenderness or flavor, you're dead. Dead. Especially if you have a trend."

The good teams learn this lesson. The almost-good teams wallow in self-pity and have another beer. They wouldn't—as Master Burke and grasshopper Lackie do—evaluate why the scores might have differed from on-site to blind. The almost-goods declare the on-site judges as right and the blind judges as stupid for disagreeing with the on-site judges. But that's why there are two styles of judging.

Mr. Pat teaches how to show off. Where Birmingham and others learned cooking, and Richard and others learned attitude, John David was among those that learned presentation. At his first visit to the Memphis WCBCC, John David says, "I went and listened to Pat Burke, went to listen to Jack's Old South and Bad Bob's, listened to Custom Cookers. I picked out about six teams and all I wanted to do was listen to presentations. I got a little bit from each one. That really helps out a lot to do that."

And Mr. Pat provides motivation. He gave a goal to Myron Mixon. "You know who I hunted down?" Myron says. "Pat Burke. He was the man. You can't run from the best."

The teachers are out there. "We're a spoiled young team,"

says Ryan Guthman of Goin' Hoggin', "because Mike Mills sat us down for *hours* before the first time we ever did it, he sat us down and broke it down for us." Mike Mills, known as The Legend in barbecue after his Apple City team took three straight WCBCC championships.

"As a team, we don't want you to give us your secrets," John Akins says. "We would like for you to give us the *short-cuts*. Put us on the same playing field that you're on. And I'll use *my* secrets against *your* secrets. We've had a lot of people that's helped us get us on that same playing field. Curly Tail Smokers have done that. Pat Burke has done that."

And the students teach, as well. In Caruthersville, Chad Allen of Old School says, "Natural Born Grillers took us under their wing," and at that competition, Rick Dalton helps Chad with sauce tips. In Butler, Alabama, Rick invites new team Killer Hogs over to watch him prep his hog. Killer Hogs took what they learned to their next competition, where they placed third—the very first hog they'd cooked on the circuit. Ed Richardson of Barefoot in the Pork cheers the concept of apprenticeship: "Go to an event and spend a few days with a real competition team," he advises. "There is no shortage of work to be done, and the teams are always very positive when it comes to helping teach the process to someone who is truly passionate about learning. Barefoot in the Pork would never have accomplished what we have without folks like Pig Pounda Kappa, Tom & Jerry's Global Porkers and our northern cousins the Bastey Boys."

In Columbus, Mississippi, Doug Slater of Pit Panthers points to a team across the way. "This is a first-year team over here. We've been over there helping them, passing it down more or less. It's not that we're some great team, but we've learnt what the judges are looking for. Little small things, such as putting your baste on the underside of the meat, so when you put it on your tongue…And just a little thing like that goes a long way."

"If they get the knowledge, 50 percent will share it," Pat Burke says of other teams. Of the growing teams, he says, "If they want to learn, they'll take the knowledge away from you."

The knowledge, the help, appears from somewhere, from everywhere.

Walt and Larry O have benefitted from outside team compassion themselves. At a non-MBA some years back, the two were teamed with Jim Johnson. "This being our first competition," says Walt, "we didn't have a good brisket. Jim Johnson and I cooked a brisket—we had some recipe with Jack Daniel's in it and stuff like that. Larry had a brisket recipe that he had done fairly well with as Two Fat Larrys. The problem was that in the shuffling of the meat on the grill, his brisket had gotten shoved over a hot spot. So when it comes time to pull the brisket for competition, we pull it out and his brisket looks like a meteor—black, smoking meteor. We looked at our brisket, and our brisket didn't look bad, but it tasted like liquorice. It was *awful*. We're going, 'Oh crud, we don't have anything to turn in.'

"Willingham was next to us, and he said, 'Well, you know, I've got some scraps from my entry, leftovers and stuff like that. You guys can use that.'" Larry cut the brisket donated by Willingham—John Willingham, multi-championed John Willingham, cookbook author John Willingham—who even helped glaze the entry as Larry and company packed it into their blind box.

"We ended up getting fourth in brisket," Walt says. "And Willingham got eighth." The fourth place slot gave Walt and Jim and Larry enough additional points to elevate them to grand champion…using borrowed brisket.

"So," Walt says graciously, "we asked Willingham to be in our team picture."

A couple of years later, it was Larry handing over the gift of winning. Larry bakes a pretty good cake on the grill, as evidenced by his dessert-category victories. Two years later, at the same competition as the brisket-sharing, "A girl across the way had a birthday," Walt says, "so Friday night Larry gave the team a chocolate cake. They went and turned that in on the dessert contest against his chocolate cake the next day, and they beat him."

Larry considers this again. "They beat me with my own cake. They didn't eat it. I gave it to her for her birthday."

"That was sort of payback," Walt concludes.

Walt is still looking for the secret for his own brisket. At one point in the Galax weekend, he tells Pig Pounda's Gary Kerce, "Some night I'm gonna have to get you drunk again so you'll tell me how to cook a brisket."

Perhaps Walt and Larry and Jim should have turned their meteor in anyway. Chris Carter of Smoked Encounters tells the story of a neighbor at a contest the year before: "They were cooking a brisket. It was about 2 or 3 in the morning, the cooker caught on fire. Of course, he's trying to pull it off there. He takes the brisket and throws it on the ground. He didn't have a fire extinguisher. We had one. We ran over and sprayed the fire, and of course the spray got on the brisket and everything. He turned it in. He took third place."

13
STARRING HOG-EYE PIERCE

"Men will cook if there's danger involved."
−Comedian Rita Rudner

Saturday, August 6, Caruthersville, Missouri. "It's all part of barbecue," says Brad Cheatham, of the Carbondale Eagles, as he returns to his hog prep at the Meat on the Mississippi competition in Caruthersville, Missouri. "Clean your hog. Sew up your neighbor."

Next door, Sweet Swine o' Mine's Pat Rooney is walking it off. Sweet Swine in the interval between Galax and Caruthersville has purchased a new box smoker, which moments ago was laying across Pat's leg. As he and teammate Mark Lambert maneuvered the grill to a spot at the back of their site, Pat backed into an packed-up tent, tripped backwards. The cooker toppled with him, onto him. Mark reached him first, but Brad Cheatham was there only a few moments later, himself. Though Pat's knee was hurting, after a minute or two, he was able to get up and start walking it off.

"Didn't that cooker do that to you one time before?" Brad says.

Pat explains that this is a new unit.

Ron Passmore and Dr. Noah talk with vendor coordinator Jim Davis

"It's broke in now," Brad says.

When it's clear that Pat hasn't been seriously injured, Brad regards the cooker, shakes his finger at it. "Bad cooker! Bad cooker!" Someone later jokes that it's good that the smoker landed on Pat's knee instead of his head. Would've been a shame to dent the smoker.

Later, as Pat works in front of the hog cooker, someone asks him, "How you feeling?"

"I'm not feeling today," Pat says. "I got a job to do. I got plenty of time to whine later."

Wednesday, July 13, Galax. Jim Davis is sitting in his golf cart directing his wife and son in laying down yellow duct tape on the curbs, designating spaces for both teams and the vendors on the cross of Main and Grayson. He shouldn't be there at all.

Jim had—no pun intended—first crack at one of the competition carts, because he broke his leg prepping for the competition. Returning to the street after inspecting the First

National Bank building, Jim hit a slippery spot. "The next thing I knew, I was looking up."

Broke his leg. Left his toes purple. His doctor recommended surgery. Watching his family work, he pats the paperwork in his hand—team lists, vendor lists, hand-drawn street maps and site layouts. "I got this to do." He then gestures toward the cast over his right leg. "I don't have time for that. I've spent the time pretending that my leg isn't broken."

He's not even supposed to be driving the golf cart. He and his walker are supposed to be passengers. Even so, after his son works his way down Grayson with tape measure and duct tape, Jim puts his good foot, his left foot, on the gas and carts down to supervise.

Plenty of time to whine later.

At a later whine time, on Thursday at the Galax Smokehouse, Jim has been asked to deliver a copy of his site map to Ron. Before being joined by Walt, Larry and Jim sit at a table and talk about Jim's strategies for getting good vendors, and about arranging team and vendor spaces on the two streets that will be closed off for the event.

Larry comes to the table prepared. "I have something for you."

Jim says, "What's that?"

Larry bequeaths the pink suspenders.

"Oh," Jim says, examining the dancing piggies. "I thought it might be a fifth of Jack Daniel's."

Larry teases, "I heard you have trouble walking sober."

A few minutes later, two tables down, a Smokehouse customer moves the wrong way, sends ice and Pepsi splashing onto the Smokehouse floor.

"You wanna walk over there real quick," Larry kids Jim. "You still got one more good leg."

At a yet-later whine time, on Friday, John David Wheeler

of Natural Born Grillers sits in another commandeered golf cart, watching Myron Mixon and Jack's Old South set up, and exchanging friendly smart talk with Myron and fellow Jack's Old Southerner David Hair. John David, like Jim, is using the cart as a motorized gurney replacing the surgical gurneys the both of them should by all rights be on. John David was scheduled to have surgery the week of Galax—for a herniated disk in his back—but he, like Jim, postponed the knife to complete his barbecue obligation.

David Hair is fetching a tool for the hog prep—a hacksaw that teammate Nick "Flash" Cochran will use in a few moments to cut off the hog's feet. "I'll fix you right up," David says to John David as he brandishes the hacksaw (blade length, about two feet). "Cut that right out." *Clean your hog. Sew up your neighbor.*

"If I thought it'd feel better," John David says. "I'd do it, brother, I swear."

John David's injury isn't barbecue-related but it *is* barbecue-aggravated. Heavy items, awkward items, and, in the case of John David as presenter to on-site judges, a lot of time standing up and sitting down and standing up again during the presentations. Nine presentations during preliminaries. Potentially as many as three more if you make it into finals.

Though not a dangerous sport, barbecuing does involve occasional appearances of fire, knives, heavy objects, and the law of the famous Mr. Murphy. "It ain't a cook," says Pigs in Paradise's Craig Fager, "unless I get something pinched, poked or cut."

September 2003, Murphysboro, Illinois. The Annual Murphysboro Barbecue Cookoff was winding down. The Da-Nite Outback cooking team was presenting its ribs to the finals judges, and the Carbondale Eagles were prepping to receive the finals judges when they finished at Da-Nite. Next door to the

Eagles' cooksite, M&M Cookers' Mark Arnold and his son Josh were hooking up their cooker trailer to their pickup. They had not made finals, though they were confident they were "in the money"—that is, a fourth or a fifth in rib.

The team had gotten the pickup positioned in front of the trailer, but they'd misaligned the ball of the hitch and the trailer tongue. A half-inch. Mark leaned over to try to bring hitch and tongue into alignment while Josh pulled the pickup back the half-inch by the tailgate. "When he did," Mark says, "the tailgate come down, cracked me in the head, knocked me out. Josh fell backwards into the grill. We were both basically in trouble."

Doug Boyd was helping Da-Nite with the ribs presentation when he heard the commotion. Mark relates the tale as it was told to him, "When he heard somebody was hurt, he just jumped up—you know, a volunteer firefighter, that's what he was—he ran down there and took care of us until the ambulances got there.

"He really thought my neck was broken. When I dropped, they told me I just went limp, and was in an awkward position anyway. My face hit first on the ground. When I came to, he was there. I had no clue who he was. He got some rags and slipped them around my neck to hold me steady. Everybody was wanting to help me up and get me up, and I was saying 'I'm all right.'"

Doug said then, "No you're not, Mark. Trust me, I know what I'm doing, you're not all right. You're bleeding, and you need to just lay here."

Clean your hog. Sew up your neighbor. "When it happened," Mark says, "Brad and them guys from Carbondale Eagles seen us, they were right beside us and they jumped over there, as quick as Doug got there. And they stood there and kept everybody away, the crowd and whatever, and were trying to calm Joshua down" until Doug was able to attend to him. "He took care of Josh, and made him lay still. Josh ended up with three cracked ribs, and beat up big time on his back. He had bruises from his hip to his head."

After Mark and Josh were taken away to the emergency room, the cookoff participants didn't receive any status reports. "No one knew how bad we were hurt, they just knew that we were hurt." As the awards ceremony was about to start, the status report came in the best way possible: in the form of Mark and Josh walking up the middle of blocked-off Pine Street toward the stage. The assembled crowd broke into applause.

"I ended up with some stitches on the top of my head, and a real good knot." And a fifth-place rib that day.

"And the tailgate had a big dent in it. Big dent."

Clean your hog. Sew up your neighbor.

July, 2005, Galax. Smoke on the Mountain, once underway, remains accident-free. Though the Tango-encroached bench in the Farmer's Market might give slight argument to that observation. And down on Grayson Street, the vending contingent of Natural Born Grillers on Thursday evening got something of a jump-start to their hearts when they jacked up one side of their vending trailer, the side along the curb, trying to level the unit, and it slipped off the jack with a creak and a bump. No one hurt. Just a little unexpected movement.

A good thing, since Brad and Doug were a few hundred miles away.

14

JUMPIN' JACK'S FLASH CAN'T COOK WITH GAS GAS GAS

"Let that hog a little suntan. Rules don't say anything about cooking with sun."

— Boyce Winters just before his teammates move a tent to put their hog in the shade during Friday prep in Columbus, Mississippi

Friday, July 15. "Get some ice on that," Larry O instructs.

He's not offering medical advice. He's doing his job as a meat inspector.

Hawg Wild's hog is on the edge of being a little too wild. It floats in the water that fills the Hawg Wild cooler, not doing the backstroke, but warming up to it. Literally. Larry checks and sees that the hog is still under the required temp of forty degrees, but threatening warmer now that the ice bags that floated along with the hog no longer contain ice.

The Friday of the competition, Larry visits each team, making sure that the meat that they will cook meets contest standards. "Barbecue," say the rules spelled out specifically on the contest brochure, "is defined by the Smoke on the Mountain Barbecue Cooking Contest as pork meat (FRESH OR FROZEN AND UNCURED) prepared only on a wood and/or charcoal fire, basted or not, as the cook sees fit, with any consumable substances and sauces the cook believes necessary.

Ken Nottingham and Chris Birmingham of Natural Born Trillers prep shoulders.

MEAT FOR THE CONTEST MAY NOT BE PRECOOKED, SAUCED, SPICED, INJECTED, MARINATED, OR CURED IN ANY WAY, OR OTHERWISE PRE-TREATED PRIOR TO OFFICIAL MEAT INSPECTION." (The "consumable substances" part tickles rep Chuck Doan when he covers that point in the judges' training; the actual phrasing in his course outline is "nonpoisonous substances," which, Chuck points out, "I don't think we have to worry about today." He looks at the other reps. "I think we're all still alive.")

Meat inspection is rarely the rep's job, but Galax is a new competition and no one has the necessary experience. Larry checks hogs and ribs and shoulders and chickens, too—for the Anything But competition.

After Jack's Old South passes meat inspection, Myron Mixon and Nick "Flash" Cochran wrestle their hog out of the cooler built into the front of their rig. (Another team on the circuit, Goin' Hoggin' out of Murphysboro, has the right idea.

They have named and labeled the cooler they use to transport their hog to competitions…the Hog Coffin.) Myron's hog is big, and even dead, puts up a good fight. Flash is wiry and not much heftier than the hog, but he's determined to win the battle.

Myron and Flash manage to get the hog partially out of the cooler. The two of them rest, and the hog rests with his head peering over the side, looking like a lolling porcine rendition of Kilroy Was Here. George Nicely of Grillers is watching. When he sees the hog propped against the side of the cooler, staring macabrely off into a void, he chirps in, "Honey! I'm home!"

Myron and Flash struggle with the hog, carrying it to the prep table where they plop it down, gutted-belly-side up. There's a quick moment when the scene looks like a WWF professional wrestling promo, with the feared Man in Black about to flip the evil HOGG over his back and bodyslam him to the ground. The evil HOGG even seems to be taunting the feared Man in Black, as a good trash-talking professional wrestler should. The evil HOGG is sticking his tongue out. His dead purple tongue. "That's something you don't see on the Food Network," someone says.

What you don't see on the Food Network: the open-eyed hog, spine and ribs exposed in the open body cavity, skin slick and bland after having been scalded to remove its hair, blood trickling from its mouth down the upside-down snout, like the fake blood on an action movie star after a fight scene and before he wipes it off bravely with the back of his hand. What you don't see on the Food Network: the pinpoint hole, tiny tricklet of blood, in the center of the forehead, where the deed was done. What you don't see on the Food Network: the glassy dead stare.

The judges usually don't see that stare, either, even though the hog is cooked with its head still on (and occasionally the cliché apple stuck in its mouth just before judging begins). Many teams cover the hog's eyes to avoid injecting extra squeam into squeamish judges. One of the persistent surprises of people new to the circuit—whole hog means whole hog.

Days before, Galax-Carroll-Grayson Chamber of Commerce President Leesa Morris and Executive Director Judy Brannock were discussing this very surprise. "I understand that some have the head on with the eyes and you see it on the grill," Leesa had said about the upcoming competition.

Judy commiserated: "I can't look at a fish on the table without covering its eyeballs up." Judy would appreciate the eyeball-masking efforts employed by inventive cooks when presenting their hogs to judges. Some teams get lucky; the pig's eyes are already closed on delivery. When that luck doesn't play out, sunglasses have been utilized, so have simple foil wrapping, and strategically placed garnishments and decorations. And in one case, the eyeball-masking was literal: a Freddy Krueger hockey mask. That hog was being cooked by the Carbondale Eagles, who were hiding the hog more from themselves than from the judges. "We normally do good when we got a damn ugly pig," head cook Brad Cheatham says. But figuring the Krueger mask was tacky, they took it off before judging began. That particular damn ugly pig got them a second place. It's the cookin', not the lookin'.

Gary Kerce of Pig Pounda Kappa solves the squeamish judge problem by removing the hog's head before cooking it. Other teams actually perform the shiver-inducing surgery of removing the eyes themselves.

The hog now wrestled to the table, Myron and Flash flank it, pulling the gutted chest cavity open further and then pushing down hard on each side to manually do the work that a rib-splitter normally does. In pushing, they end up rocking the hog back and forth a bit, unintentionally see-sawing until the chest cavity is open sufficiently. If his hog hasn't been butterflied by his butcher, Gary Kerce will do the job himself. Aligning the blade of a cleaver along the hog's spine, he'll take a hammer to the top of the cleaver, splitting the spine until the hog opens properly.

Next, the feet have to come off. Flash brandishes the hacksaw that David Hair had offered as a surgical tool to Natural Born's John David, and begins hacking and sawing. An onlooker says, "They cut the feet off so he don't run away."

This one don't run away.

Birmingham over at Natural Born Grillers uses a cordless power hacksaw to cut his hog's feet off. While performing that operation at the Tennessee Funfest some weeks previous, a kid—the son of a member of another team—watched Birm with the look of gaping-at-the-car-wreck. "You're torturing God's creatures!" he said.

His mother said, "It's just a pig."

Several booths down, Richard Lackie of Sweet Swine o' Mine wishes his just-a-pig were a little smaller—perhaps so that it was *literally* just a pig. In the livestock world, a pork creature 125 pounds and over is technically described as a hog. Under 125 pounds, and it's technically a pig. At the other end of the spectrum, at a different competition, "We had a team whose hog fit in one of those blue coolers," Larry O says. "The rules say the hog has to be at least 85 pounds. We're not the barbecue police, but it looked like someone's poodle." (Over 125 pounds, hog. Under 125, pig. Under 85, poodle.)

A hundred and forty-three-pounds this one is. Lackie notes that every twenty pounds of pig means three to four inches on the grill, and this one has a few too many pounds translating into a few too many inches to fit his grill the way he'd like it. An onlooker notices the length, too. He points to the cooker. "Will he go in that thang? Looks like he's longer than that to me."

"He is," Richard says. "We're gonna have to do pig yoga.... He'll be in the lotus tonight.... He might be sitting on his haunches tomorrow." (Pig yoga mantra: *Mmmmmmmmmm.*)

Pig Pounda's beheaded hog has automatically solved Richard's problem of pig length. Gary likes his hogs bigger than most, around 190, 200 pounds. Removing the head allows such a big hog to fit on the grill without resorting to meditation.

With hogs, get much over 150, and you usually extend more than the need for grill size; you extend cooking time. As it is, Richard will cook his 143-pounder 24 hours; most hogs are on the cooker for around that length of time. On the other hand, Gary Kerce cooks his beheaded 200-pounder for just 22 hours.

The Sweet Swine o' Mine hog is lying on its back, just like the conquered Evil HOGG and Gary Kerce's Headless Hogman of Sleepy Hollow. He'll stay that way, pig yoga or not, when placed on the grill. Most hogs on the MBA circuit are cooked belly-up these days. A few years back, most were cooked belly-down, in what is known as "racing style" or "running" or "saddle down." At Galax, the Kings Cooking team is racing their hog on its tum.

The belly-down cooks believe that racing style allows fat on the back of the pig to render down through the meat, flavoring it. They also believe that racing style is more traditional...and more attractive on the grill. "We can cook ours so where it looks right," Winfred Geer of Porky's Pride says.

The belly-up cooks believe that the open cavity retains juices and moisture with less danger of retaining fat, and a greasy feel. Gary Kerce likens the open cavity of the hog to a soup bowl; it retains juices, and the cavity supplies its own naturally flavoring soup bones. "A lot of people go to the store to buy bones to make soup with, and the reason they do it is the wonderful flavor."

Belly-up also gives them easier access to the interior of the hog should they want to baste or inject during cooking. To handle such access, Kings is prepping their bellydowner with a "suitcase" cut; the skin of the hog is sliced along the spine and then down on each side, so that it can be lowered, like a large flap, to reveal the meat for bastes and such. "The secret to cutting a hog," says Winfred Geer as he takes a box-cutter to his hog, "is not making it look like it's been in a knife fight." When done, to protect the meat and to preserve the look of the hog for the judges, the skin is raised again, closing the hog like a suitcase. Don't forget to pack your floss.

The cavities of racing style hogs are generally filled with something to support the meat and/or supply moisture during the cook. Teams have employed pork butts, oranges, wrapped hickory wood, crumpled aluminum steam tray pans, and bricks wrapped in foil.

For Richard and Pat Rooney, just as with most of the other hog cooks, the injections begin now, before the cooking, as he preps the Sweet Swine hog for surgery.

Sweet Swine uses multiple needles when doing injections, plunging several in at a time and leaving them there. They go into the hog's hams first. Trace a line from the pig's tail to its first back leg joint. That's the ham. With a hamful of needles sticking out, the pig looks like the cartoon cowboy returning from a raid in Injun country with a turkeytail of arrows imbedded in his politically incorrect cartoon behind. A more modern analogy comes to mind looking at this arsenal of imbedded injection needles—acupuncture needles. Richard Lackie offers some credibility to the analogy: Dr. Lackie, cook by calling and dentist by trade.

As Dr. Richard preps, an onlooker says, "Better make sure those teeth are numb before you pull them."

"He won't mind," Dr. Richard replies.

Townsfolk observe hog prep at Sweet Swine o' Mine.

Lackie moves the position of the needles up along the hog, injecting as he goes along. The needles go into the tenderloin after ham injection is finished, and eventually on to the shoulder.

Over at Gwatney, Rick Dalton has two sets of injection needles. Large veterinary needles for the ham, smaller cooking needles for the other parts. The ham is bigger and denser than the rest of the pig, and requires more injection of moisture. Therein lies part of the art and challenge of cooking whole hog: three different cuts of meat—shoulder, loin and ham— that must be cooked intact on the hog, all at the same time. Three different textures, thicknesses, densities. And your goal is to have them be equally tender when served to the judge.

Back at Sweet Swine o' Mine, a local woman watches the hog prep. "Is it like top secret what's in the injection?" she says.

"Absolutely," says Pat Rooney.

This seems to miff the woman. "Excuse me for asking."

Pat and Richard say in unison, "You didn't ask."

"We didn't say no," Pat says. "You just asked if it's top secret."

"Actually, it's pretty simple," Richard says later. "Brine, some sweetening, to keep it moist. And the loin, you cook it on its back like this, you can't really get a whole lot of flavor into the meat. You can't really put a rub on the loin or do a whole lot with the loin. It will still taste good."

Richard's hog is 143 pounds. Pre-injection. "He weighs about 153 now," he says after he's done juicing the hog.

Next, surgery. Jim Davis and John David Wheeler can decline it, but the hog can't. Using an electric hacksaw, Rick Dalton at Gwatney cuts the back ribs away from the spine and then makes parallel cuts about four inches from the first ones, forming two still-attached slabs of baby back ribs. Gary Kerce at Pig Pounda is using a drill-like Dremel tool to accomplish the same thing. The loin backs, near the spine, are situated high along the arc of ribs, near the spine—and in fact, the phrase "living high on the hog" refers to a lifestyle that allows you to indulge in such a prized cut of meat.

Rick and Gary's surgery allows them to access the loin section of the hog easily, and to work their rubs deeper into the hog. A second advantage is appearance on the grill. Gary notes that the rib bones will curl slightly during the cook, and precutting them stops them from popping up through the meat. At Jack's Old South, Myron accesses the loin by punching the injection needle between the ribs.

At Gwatney, Rick and Hal Berry are ripping off paper towels, wadding them, stuffing the wads into crevices of the hog to soak up blood and condensation. They want the meat relatively dry before the mustard flies. Birmingham, Dalton, Lackie—they and others slather the open meat in the cavity with mustard, more as binding agent than flavorizer. They lay down

Jackson Pollock lines of mustard, then spread it out over the meat with gloved hands.

Then the rub. Mixtures of salt and paprika and cumin and Kool-Aid (yes, Kool-Aid) and worcestershire powders and sugars and instant coffee (eek, not often, but, yes, instant coffee) and favored commercial seasonings and what have you, according to the cook's taste and successful experimentation. In fact, judges and new teams alike would likely be surprised how often the ingredients of great-grandpa's secret recipe for rub, sauce or baste are readily available because of FDA regulations requiring their listing on the labels of the commercial products that are the real source. Why waste time and money on failed experimentation, and on preparing successful results for competition, when you can buy damn tasty stuff by the bucketful? The commercial stuff is usually doctored, or combined with other commercial stuff. More than one team prepares its table sauce a mere *half-hour* before the judges first arrive—a few glugs from that restaurant-sized plastic bottle of commercial marinade, a few more from this one over here, a couple of scoops from that jar of sweet stuff, and a little brown sugar, heat it up…and great-grandpa's secret recipe emerges into the land of presentational tall tales.

Once the rub has been liberally applied, the cooks let their hogs rest (usually while they themselves rest and self-inject some beer). The resting allows the dry rub—in essence, a dry marinade—to work its way into the meat. At this stage, Birm at Natural Born covers the hog with a black plastic. The image of body bag is inescapable.

Next, hogs are transferred from the table to the grill. Many teams prep their hogs on large aluminum trays with shallow sides to catch juices, then bring the grill's grate out to the hog. Gwatney's hog grate has held dozens of occupants, and their stays have left their traces. The outer edges of the stainless steel rack are blackened by smoke, gradating toward the center into a more brownish loop where hogs of varying sizes have occasionally covered the grate, and leading to a relatively clean area in the center in the rough outline of pig body, pig head, pig legs. The smoke outlines make the grate look like the Grill of Turin.

All three competition cuts of meat (whole hog, shoulder, ribs) are generally prepared this way (with, of course, the unavoidable cook-to-cook variations). Inject, if it is the cook's preference, the hog and shoulder (the thinness of rib meat precludes any value of injection). On all three cuts, slather with mustard or Italian dressing or whatever the cook's preference might be. Coat in dry rub. The coat of rub may be applied all at once, or there may be successive coats at this stage, as done by Natural Born Grillers. Let rest for two to four hours. Place on the grill. Cook. Baste during cooking (sometimes with a concoction that looks and tastes awful, but cooks down just fine). Wrap in foil two to four hours into the cooking process to help retain moisture and protect the outside of the meat from getting too dark; in other words, "Be (um, where's the aluminum foil) prepared," because the line is commonly mentioned on the circuit: "If you ain't wrappin', you're lyin' or losin'." Glaze a half-hour or so before the judges arrive.

The goal with all three categories is to enhance flavor, and match the flavors of the injections and the bastes and the dipping sauce and the meat itself to each other. And to make it look good.

Prepping the shoulder has many similarities to cooking the hog. The shoulder itself has several muscle groups, several consistencies of meat within it. Down along the leg bone—the shank portion, also known as the picnic arm—there's less fat than up near the shoulder itself—the Boston butt portion of the shoulder. "Picnic's a lot leaner meat than any other portion of the shoulder—it's almost hamlike," Myron says. Because the shank is less fatty, it dries out faster. A sheath of skin and fat covers the shoulder when it comes from the processing plant. Most cooks leave about three inches of the fat layer on the shank in order to protect it during cooking. Down at Natural Born shortly after 11:00, Birm, wearing a translucent plastic apron and a bill-turned backward ball cap, is trimming and evaluating. "These three are good shoulders," he says with quick sweeps of his hand. "The others…" He has choice words for the non-choice cuts of meat. Too fatty; not enough meat. In trimming, eighteen to twenty pounds in original weight will be whittled down to sixteen to seventeen pounds, primarily by removing skin and fat.

Not all the trimmings are discarded. Some will be placed on the hog, insulating certain parts of it to keep heat down in areas that cook hotter than the rest of it.

Over at Pig Pounda, Gary has the outside of the shoulder, the skin side, facing up as he works it on his prep table. He pulls the skin back, removes the layer of fat underneath, and replaces the skin. He then flips the shoulder over and sets it on the skin. He explains, "That makes a real good nice bark"— meaning outer layer—with no fatty, oily taste.

Like the hog, the shoulder will cook for a long time, upwards of an hour a pound for most teams. When Birm's done trimming, slathering and letting the hog rest in dry rub, he aims to have the shoulders on the grill at 3:00 for serving to the first judge at 11:15 Saturday morning.

Ribs are a different story entirely. Some cooks are beginning their rib prep early in the day Friday; Sweet Swine is done trimming and applying dry rub by noon. Others, like Gwatney and Pig Pounda, prep them later; Roger Kerce at Pig Pounda won't start until after midnight. Ribs will hit the grill early morning, starting around 5:00 AM, depending on team preference. The first rib judges will arrive at the teams at half past noon.

The prep process takes time because of the number of pieces of meat that will be readied. At the Kennett competition, a judge asked Brad Cheatham of the Carbondale Eagles how many ribs he's cooking.

"Seventeen," he said. "One case." Cases are sold by weight, so the number of racks in a case can vary. The more active teams cook a case each time out.

"How many shoulders?"

"Eight."

"How many hogs?" The question was a joke.

Brad snorted laughter in response. He pointed to his hog grill. "There are thirty-two hogs in that cooker, if you can believe it."

"Yeah, and only two going in," said teammate Daryl Ukropin. "So they've been busy."

There was only one hog on the Eagles' cooker—most hog teams cook only a single hog. Occasionally, a team will cook two. In Galax, Gwatney's Rick Dalton is smoking two hogs.

As a final step for hog prep when he competes, Winfred Geer restores the flaps of his racing-style hog and begins to sew them together at the top with loose, Frankensteinish sutures. "Lacing it up like a football," teammate Henry Geer says.

Winfred says, "It's a pigskin, ain't it?"

15 SING A SONG OF PIG PUNS, POCKET FULL OF WRY

"What's the name of the team that don't have a name?"

– Judge John Rox in a judges' briefing after reps announce that one of the teams has no outward display of its name

Friday afternoon, July 15. The curious public is gathered as Pat Rooney and Richard Lackie prepares the Sweet Swine hog. They're curious about the injection needles, about slathering the hog in mustard, about barbecue in general.

"You use a sweet sauce?" one asks Richard.

Richard explains his sauce. Has some sweet to it. And why do you ask?

The onlooker points at the team banner. "*Sweet* Swine o' Mine."

The explanation comes again, the play on words that continues to be less and less connective as Guns n Roses continues to sink into the Frankie Valli/Creedence Clearwater/Boston land of sometimes-remembered oldies.

No matter how many times Richard has to explain the name, no matter if it ever gets tiresome, no matter that, as Richard admits, "it can escape you sometimes," it's unlikely that he'll change it. Sweet Swine o' Mine is branded upon him.

Literally.

Whereas Airpork Crew ultimately declined the opportunity for tattoos the weekend they swept the Mt. Carmel Ribberfest cook, Richard and four teammates succumbed a few weeks after they took first place in the shoulder division at the World Championship Barbecue Cooking Competition. They adorned ankles with a drawing of the WCBCC cleaver and the initials "SSOM." No changing it now. The Puns n Roses moniker is theirs forever. (And by the way, here's a tip from Pat Rooney: "I tell you one thing you don't want to do. Put insect repellent on a new tattoo.")

Aging pop references is one of the reasons the New Pigs on the Block (punning the boy band "New Kids") changed its name to Pigs in Paradise when it returned to the circuit (their interim name "New Pigs II" lasted just a contest or II). That's why teams are at this writing resorting to rap and hip-hop puns (for example, Notorious P.I.G.) that five years from now will likely have people scratching their heads.

At least Porkosaurus won't suffer the effects of passing time.

At Galax, Pit Connection is another name that has not been affected by aging. The name has been around since the early '80s when head cook Jerry Dyer hooked up with four other active-duty marines who were teaching at the Millington Navy Electronics School. They held a contest for a team name; the winning entry was a student's suggestion—an electronics student, mind you, thus the connection to "connection" in Pit Connection.

Other team names at Galax need "connections" as well—they need varying degrees of explanation. Self-explanatory are Nervous Wreck Cook'n Crew and Hawg Wild. Kings Cookers needs only a bit of explanation (the King in the origin of the name is a certain beer brand no longer associated with the team and not a Memphis-based hip-swinger and not, oh, Henry the VIII).

Natural Born Grillers will survive its pop-culture roots in the movie, *Natural Born Killers.* (Team leader and founder John David Wheeler originally wanted to name the team after the Quentin Tarentino hit, *Pulp Fiction.* But Pork Fiction was already taken. Had he considered it, so was Reservoir Hogs. Would he now consider naming the team Grill Bill? or Kill Grill? And would the source of the name be the first or the second *Kill Bill* movie?)

And Smoked Encounters of the Third Swine? If you're gonna do a pun on a pop-culture title, do it with something that will stick in people's memories, like a Stephen Spielberg movie. *Close Encounters of the Third Kind.* (Spielberg's other movies lend themselves to varying degrees of pigs-ploitation. Saving Private Porcine? That one has not been used. Jowls has been used though recently discarded. Jurassic Pork has been used, as well.) The problem with the otherwise memorable Smoked Encounters of the Third Swine is its lack of *precision* in the memory. Galax participants have referred to it as "Porked Encounters of the Third Time," "Swine Encounters of the Third Kind," "Something Like Close Encounters of the Third Kind," and "Third Encounters of the…umm . . ."

Jack's Old South? People call head cook Myron Mixon "Jack" almost as often as they use his real name, especially if they haven't yet met him. The Jack in Jack's Old South is Myron's father, who developed the team's sauce. The full name of the team, by the by, is Jack's Old South BBQ Sauce Cooking Team.

So-Co Smokehouse is short for "southern comfort," the hospitality, not the alcohol. On the other hand, consider another team on the circuit, J&J Cookers, so named for Jim and Jack (hint: no one on the team is named Jim or Jack).

Gwatney? The team used to be called Super Clean Smokers, after a sponsoring automotive product and not pride in their culinary hygiene. The team's current name is another automotive reference (though it sounds like a pretty good name for an English stout)—officially, the team is named after car-dealership Gwatney Chevrolet, which took over team sponsorship.

Pure and Sinful—ah, stealing is a sin, a pure sin, and the members of Pure and Sinful have stolen the name. Well, not really. Team leader Dan Puryear is a fan of a Richmond, Virginia, rock band named, yes, Pure and Sinful. Good name for a barbecue team, Dan thought—and he approached the blues rockers to ask if he could share the name (not to mention a little cross promotion). Pure and Sinful, audio edition, said yes to Pure and Sinful, edible edition. (Considered but discarded: Dan and the Divas.)

And Pig Pounda Kappa? Alas, exploring that name might take you as long as landing a summa cum laude. But let's do: Gary Kerce was looking for a team name that was "something different, something unique." A fellow Gary worked with, a university student and, likely, a frat rat, came up with a suggestion. Go Greek. "Pig" had to be in there. "Pounda" was from the poundage of the pig. "Kappa," the Greek word for the letter K for Kerce.

Team names across the circuit range from the straightforward (e.g., Memphis Barbecue Society) to the outlandish (e.g., Church of Swinetology) to the think-about-'em-for-a-second (e.g., Shigs in Pit).

And the puns, oh the puns. How many puns could a pigpen pen if a pigpen could pen puns?

Well, a whole bunch. Barefoot in the Pork, The Hogfather, Porkcrastinators, and Magically Piglicious! (perhaps thinking the pun is a lucky charm). The Grill Sergeants. The Boarddello. The Spice Is Right. The Best Little Boarhouse in Memphis. Hog Rock Café. Dr. Frank-N-Swine. Pig Newton. These are indeed grills gone wild, especially the team named, um, Grills Gone Wild. (Logo: debutantish piggy lifting her shirt to flash her piggy teats, three rows of them, though tastefully covered in a trio of bikini tops.)

And the just plain playful. Rib Ticklers. Grand Masters of Cooking Disasters. Ribs for Her Pleasure (overheard from an unrelated team as they pulled the membrane off the backs of St. Louis spareribs: "You want a natural condom?"). Flying Pigs. We Don't Cook Sheep. Squeals on Wheels. Smoke 'em If You Got 'em. Oink, Cackle and Moo (from the KCBS circuit, obviously). 4 Wieners and a Weber. Pork 4 Skins (The name came from a bit of slang with a commercial bent. It was Pork for Money—"Skins" being slang for dollar bills, as in a golf skins game; however, that explanation didn't prevent one awards emcee from refusing to say the name when announcing awards at a competition some years back). And you gotta love that cooking team from England: The Mad Cows (they cook pretty good, too—the Brits won the 2004 Jack Daniel's Invitational).

And the smartass. Literally. The Central Texas Smartass Cookers, out of Rogers, Texas. In that buttish realm is the Breasts and Butts—the caption of a picture of that team appearing on the Florida Barbecue Association website noted, "Yes, there's another name for this team, but it's a family event."

And the just plain honest: Old Farts. Or the Ugly Brothers barbecue team (slogan: Proving yet again that men, even Ugly ones, rule the grill"), with male team members Les Ugly, Big Ugly and Bud Ugly, and female members Farphrom Ugly and Nadevenclosto Ugly.

And when in doubt, use this formula: "Smokin' Fill-in-the-Blank". Smokin' Guns, Smokin' Elvises, Smokin' Joes. And Misfits and T's and Pig Express and Hoosiers and Badgers and Dads and Roos and Moos and Moose and Poobahs and Triggers and Butts and Clones—and Irish and Spiders (and bears, oh my).

But there's only so much punning, wordplay and plain ol' fun that can go around. There have been at least two teams called "Pork Que," one pronouncing it with the profane reference it results from, and one pronouncing the "Que" as "kay" (as the Spanish do), so that his team is pronounced "Por-kay Pigs. And that's n-n-not all, folks: Holy Smokers II adopted the II when they found themselves at a previous competition right next to another team named Holy Smokers. A Bubbacue from Evansville, Indiana, and a Bubba Q from Houston. Two sets of Bastey Boys, one with the "e", one without. (Noted on the back of a tank top worn by a female Bastey Person: "Full Contact Co-Ed Naked Barbecue Team: The Bastey Babes.")

For the intelligent porker: iQue.

In fact, it's surprising that there isn't a Pete Townsend-inspired "Who Are Que?" (with CSI investigators doing an autopsy on a whole hog). or "Que Are You? or…the mind boggles about the possible *who/you/que* puns. Including "Mad About Que," after the hit Helen Hunt/Paul Reiser sitcom from the nineties. At least the phrase "mad about you" predates Hunt and Reiser, so the name ends up being quite timeless. The Mad About Que team originally called itself "Sauced Swine," but the phrase's "she-sells-seashells" pronounceability sent Scott and Teresa Cutler on a helenhunt for a new name. (When it comes to some other team names, the hell with selling sauced swine by the seashore, try running Ricky Rover Rooter Roasters over that tongue of yours three times fast. Or the Peter-Piper-pickled-pepper-peck-picker-reminiscent Pigs, Peppers and Blues.) Scott and Teresa's next choice was Parrothead Porkers, and although not registered with the non-existent Federal Bureau of Barbecue Eponymy, that name was already featured on another team's shirts. One of Scott's next suggestions was "The Smelly Pits."

"I'm not wearing a T-shirt with 'Smelly Pits' on it," Teresa protested, apparently blinded by good taste.

Nonplussed, Scott said, "You could put on the back, 'Come

smell my pits.'"

For some reason, "Mad About Que" won out.

By the by, Scott Cutler takes heart when learning that there's already a team out there named The Pit Sniffers. And another is using the slogan, "People Love to Smell My Pit!" He says, "I told you all it was a good idea!"

16 PIGS PROVE AGAIN (SEE "NOAH'S ARK") THAT THEY CAN MAKE IT THROUGH THE RAIN

"Look Ma, no mud!"

– subtitle of the WCBCC recap in the Memphis Barbecue Association Newsletter, Summer 2005

Friday noon, July 15, Galax. The WXII TV 12 noon weather-cast is being broadcast live from Galax. "What's left of Dennis," says meteorologist Austin Caviness, straddling Grayson and Carroll Counties in the middle of Main Street and talking about the former Hurricane Dennis, "is an area of low pressure, still camped out over Kentucky, and therefore the moisture's still wrapping in from the southwest. Showers and storms will be scattered around again this afternoon."

Later, about quarter of 3, Al Norton looks up from his work on the main Gwatney rig, points north. "It's not looking good," he says to his teammates. The sky is almost black.

By 3:00, thunder is rolling. "I heard that!" Chris Carter of Smoked Encounters exclaims.

"Nah!" next-door-neighbor Dan Puryear calls out from inside his tent. "Think positive!"

Close to quarter of 4, it begins to rain gently in Galax, Virginia.

At about the same time, as Austin Caviness has pointed out, the high pressure system squatting over Kentucky yanks moisture out of the southwest and curls it toward the northeast. Southwest of the Kentucky system, in the path of the moisture curling northeasterly, is Southaven, Mississippi, just over the border from Memphis. Southaven, where Natural Born Grillers calls home.

In Southaven on Friday, a more vicious rain falls. Four inches. Four inches in the space of, in differing estimates, thirty minutes to an hour. An older subdivision sometimes called Autumn Woods 2.9 miles away from the home of Natural Born Grillers' John David Wheeler as the Yahoo Maps fly and less than half that distance as the crow flies begins to flood. Water and mud sweeps into Autumn Woods, flowing down the streets, flowing into homes. Forty-eight houses eventually become near houseboats.

On the news that night, a TV cameraperson follows one of the residents back into his home after the floodwaters recede. "Y'all wipe your feet before coming in," the resident grimly jokes as he slops onto mud-soaked carpeting in his living room. "Man, I tell you," John David says later, "you haven't seen anything, though. I mean, people say 'I saw it on the news'—water was just about waist-deep, and everything from the waist down was just ruined. Mud was ankle-deep in the houses. I never seen anything like it. I've never seen a flood before. You see it on television and stuff, but until you witness it…." For a moment, he's lost for words. "It's weird."

The Autumn Woods residents discover that the floodwaters have brought valet parking to Southaven: a car parked on the street has been moved to the neighbor's driveway. "The water came right through the middle of his house and the next-door house," says John David, "and his girlfriend's car was in the driveway and [the flood] moved it back to the road, and his was on the street and [the flood] floated it over to the neighbor's. That's where the rush of water was. That's one of the houses I adopted." His company, Wheeler Construction, adopted two houses "to finish them, to get people back in." The others were eventually adopted by other construction companies, local merchants and area churches. And where else could he lend his expertise? "We cooked for the volunteers and the victims themselves"—Birm, primarily, along with Wayne Booth of Red Hot Smokers, cooked ribs and pulled meat and chicken and burgers the weekend after the flooding.

In Galax on Friday, the rain falls with summer-shower lackadaisicalness and not with waning-hurricane ferocity. Tango, unaware of weather patterns anywhere else but Galax, says "C'mon rain!" as he looks at the stormclouds. Weather might give his team an edge—it won't affect his cookers; it might hinder others' efforts. Down the row at Pit Connection, the rain indeed forces the team to get a later start on cooking than they'd planned.

Asked if the rain affects his cooker as he stands on his primary trailer rig, Rick Dalton gestures up with both hands to simultaneously signal "doesn't matter" and "I got a big-ass roof above me." He says, "Other than us getting wet?"

Four weeks later, the Big Pig in the Sky will punish Dalton and other innocents for his cavalierly confident gesture.

Friday night, August 13, 2005. At the Butler Fest cook in Butler, Alabama, Rick is on his way to the grandstand. In a minute or two, at 7:30, Butler Fest officials are to announce the winners of the Little Porkers ancillary contest. Five kids cooked up chickens earlier that day, and Rick was among the "celebrity judges" that rated the entries, being the head of the reigning world champion barbecue team and all. Among the other judges was another reigning champion—Alexa Jones, Miss Alabama 2005. Miss Alabama is much easier on the eyes than

Rick Dalton, which is probably why she and not he got to wear that little crown throughout the competition.

But at almost precisely 7:30, sprinkles fall. "I'm not going," Rick says, turning back toward his cooksite. "It's raining." And there are things to be done at a cook site during the rain.

Looking up as he arrives at the cooksite, he sees evidence of the wisdom of his decision. Earlier that day, a local had shrugged off some ominous clouds. "The weather doesn't come in from over there," he told Rick as he nodded at the darkened horizon then. "Comes in from there." He pointed to where, now at 7:30, a mass of black clouds like a thick smothering tarp thrown over the horizon are moving in. A few minutes later, the deluge slams down, and the wind rushes in with it.

First, the scramble for odds and ends. Paper towels blow off prep tables and unroll themselves across the cooksite. The team covers stereo speakers with black garbage bags just as they'd done in Galax. Supports holding team signs are blown down, picked up, blown down again. Then, a more serious scramble. Rick grabs the bracing of one of his two pop-up tents covering the food-prep area. Another teammate grabs the other prep tent in the same way. The wind swoops in, threatens to lift both tents and their human anchors off the ground. Rain pours. Next door, the wind knocks down the primary tent of Ain't Your Daddy's Barbecue. A rough introduction to barbecue competitions—this was Ain't Your Daddy's Barbecue's first competitive cook. As the Ain't Your tent goes down, Rick says, "There goes that one." But he's not referring to the next-door rookies' tent; the one he'd been holding has almost simultaneously collapsed under the wind and rainwater.

Down at the other end of the competition-site, Natural Born Grillers are working equally as hard, with equal levels of unsuccess, to save their prep tent. Birmingham and Ken Nottingham push up against the tent top with a broom to push out the water that's collecting there, spilling it out over the sides. At the Gwatney site and all along the midway, cooks and cook helpers are doing the same. Grillers can't keep up with the rain; the tent collapses. Knowing that there's probably little risk to their primary tent, anchored as well as it is, and knowing even more that if there is risk to the tent, no human intervention will save something of that size, the Grillers duck into their RV to wait the storm out. Signage on the Grillers' plastic picket fence acts like schooner sails—the wind pushes one sign-festooned wing of the fencing in toward the site several feet, despite the heavy metal feet anchoring the fence.

Rick and very quickly two other Gwatney teammates join in grabbing the second prep tent. The wind is a bit wicked now—it blows the hog cooler on the back of one of the pickup trucks open—the hog cooler is a chest model deep freeze, with insulation seals, and a heavy top door, and the top door doesn't open easily.

The mud that normally plagues the often-called "Memphis in Mud" championship comes calling in Butler, Alabama, as water washes across the grass site. "A river runs through it," Lance Freemon says as he slops through it, holding the tent.

Silence settles in, briefly. Lighting snaps. Lance, Rick, and Al pop away from the tent faster than the lightning itself as a slight electric jolt pulses through them. Lance drops to the ground, and for a moment there's fear that he's been seriously injured. But he's OK. Just getting the hell out of the way. Lightning had struck a nearby water tower; one of the cooks said he could see it surging along the ground, from the base of the water tower and along team row.

The next day, on-site judges will be advised to judge teams "from the waist up." When making their area and personal appearance evaluations, judges will pay no attention to mud— they are not to consider anything the cook cannot control.

"Sometimes it rains," MBA rep Randy McGee tells the judges-in-training in Memphis the week after Galax. "Lots of times it rains. Lots of times there's mud. Sometimes there's mud this high" and he holds his hand palm down at the level of his waist. He's referring to a contest in Oakland, Tennessee, earlier that year. Rain and, yes, mud that had to be plowed away like snow with a snowplow…and leaving snow-drift-sized mud "curbing" in front of the teams' tents. Gwatney laid down forty-five twenty-pound bags of mulch to give themselves non-sloppy flooring in their tent.

Barbecue competitions are rain or shine, and mud or shine, and flood or shine. Rudy Lindenberg of the Rub 'n' Cue team recalls several years ago at Caruthersville, Missouri. The competition-site is right on the Mississippi, which flooded the day before the competition. Teams were ankle deep before the water receded; the competition now known as Meat on the Mississippi might just as well been known at that time as Mississippi on the Meat. (By the by, Caruthersville is in Pemiscot County, Missouri—"Pemiscot" being the Native-American word for "liquid mud.")

The competitions are held despite any manner of acts of God.

There are the insects. Winfred Geer of Porky's Pride talks of a competition where "a mosquito went by—had three ticks on it."

There are, well, the insects. While giving the cooks' briefing in the grass before the bleacher-seated cooks at Vienna Georgia's Big Pig Jig, MBA rep Randy McGee suddenly danced a bit. Not of his own volition. Randy said to the assembled cooks, "I'll be telling the judges tomorrow not to count down for fire ants."

There are the tornadoes.

Well, tornado.

At the 2004 Memphis in May, the contest site was evacuated when a tornado bore down on Memphis—with the contest site in its path. Most people cleared out; some stuck it out. A champion of sticking it out is Myron Mixon of Jack's Old South. He found a way to stay in the park, even though it was being cleared by the police. From his vantage point, he could see the winds pluck up tents with fickle tornadic selectivity. "You'd see one tent blown away, and the one right next to it would be untouched," Myron told *Maxim* magazine. "It was like God was picking and choosing which barbecue He liked."

And speaking of Myron and acts of God, there's the nothing-in-particular-but-bad-luck:

Friday night, September 23, 2005. At the Charlotte 2005 competition, people around the contest site begin looking to the sky when they hear the popping of fireworks. But there are no fireworks. The pop-crackling sound was not fireworks but firewood—a huge branch breaking free in a breezeless evening from a drought-afflicted pecan tree. A power line partially cushions the branch's fall, and suspends it. Some of the branch reaches the ground; some of it lies atop the truckcap of Myron Mixon's pickup. It misses Gary Kerce's pickup, just a few feet away; someone spots the keys still in the pickup, and backs it away from the branch and the electrical line.

The jokes start falling as hard as the tree limb but without near as much snap. "They're trying to eliminate the competition," a police officer says when she arrives on the scene.

A nearby cook says, "I've been injecting that tree for a year now…"

"There are easier ways to get wood," someone calls out. "Bring a bag of charcoal."

"Myron's switching from peachwood to pecan."

"You know there are rules against cooking with electricity."

A yellow caution tape goes up. A real one. Not a "Danger:

Men Cooking" novelty tape like some teams use. The police won't let Myron move his truck until they can make sure that they can get it out without the branch sagging further and snapping the electric line (it would eventually be safely extricated). Gary Kerce, who'd gone back to his hotel room, returns to the site after being alerted to what's happened. "Gary," Myron says, "you know you can't disturb the scene of the crime. Get your truck back in there. We need another cushion."

And there is the heat that gripped the States during the summer of 2005. As the jokes go, *It was so hot....* It was so hot in Butler, Alabama, in mid-August, the organizers decided to move the competition to November 2006 almost immediately after the end of the 2005 competition. It was so hot that there were jokes that cooks were putting their products in their cookers to cool them off. At one point during that weekend, Gwatney's Lance Freemon stood in the cook area, a cold, wet washcloth draped over his head and face, smoking a cigarette. He resembled some sort of smoke-breathing alien. But he was a bit cooler.

Fortunately, in July 2005, Galax does not suffer from such extremes, even in this unusual weather year. The Friday rain is intermittent and brief, and the cooksite—on pavement—will accommodate the weather. "Any time we're on concrete, we're happy," Richard Lackie says. The mountain air is warmer than normal this year in Galax ("To the locals, this is hot," Ron says Thursday afternoon, with the temperature surging to a wicked seventy-two degrees), yet cool compared to what other competitions have faced and will face. ("You guys are from Memphis, Tennessee—that's a plenty hot place," Austin Caviness had meteorologized to Pat and Richard during the noon weathercast.)

July in the mountains is part of the design of the timing of Smoke on the Mountain. No other competitions on the MBA circuit brave the heat this time of year, which explains the two weeks between the Kennett-D.C. weekend and Galax's event, and the three that ensue before the circuit picks up again after Galax, in Caruthersville, Missouri. July in the mountains is one of the reasons for Sweet Swine o' Mine's participation. That and a "wild hair." Says Richard Lackey, "We saw the brochure, and we said we weren't driving eleven hours to compete. But we got to talking, and saw there were no cooks in July." Smoke on the Mountain had originally considered a February timing, but the weather argued against it. Contests are also snow or shine—as evidenced by the precipitation at a 2004 competition in Memphis called the Polar Fest—but Galax decided not to risk it.

Shortly after 8:00 on Friday, the rains come again. When they start, Cody Cline is under his tent talking with Larry O, who is offering Cody instruction, and encouragement. When he hears thunder, Larry says, "There's someone else who's wishing you luck."

"And this weekend," Austin Caviness had said noontime, "we'll actually build in some heat, as if we needed it, because we're already plenty humid. As high pressure builds off the coast, we'll still have a chance for afternoon showers and storms, but I think our coverage this weekend will be more like 30 percent."

Whoever was wishing Cody Cline luck with the thunder would on Saturday determine just how accurate Austin was.

17

'CUE MEETS JOHN 'CUE PUBLIC

"I wish the Elvis impersonator were here. Then we'd have it all!"
– An onlooker at the corner of Grayson and Main yelling to no one in particular while vendors and teams set up

Wednesday morning, July 13, 2005. "Now I want to ask you something," Maurice Vaughan says to Ron Passmore on WBRF radio. "I can tell you folks, this is big big big and for goodness' sakes if you have something on your agenda other than a trip to Galax this weekend, consider changing that because you do not want to miss Smoke on the Mountain....And we are honored to have the one, the only Ron Passmore, who with his partners owns and manages and runs the Galax Smokehouse. Good morning, Mr. Ron Passmore. Welcome, sir."

"Hey, good morning Maurice."

"I'm telling you folks, this Smoke on the Mountain event, this competition, this barbecue deal that we're talking about, this starts at 10 AM on Friday morning, is that right, Ron? It starts at 10 AM and it lasts all day long until Saturday morning about 2 AM right?"

"Absolutely. The entertainment's scheduled the whole time."

"Wow. What sort of entertainment are we talking about?"

"A lot of local folks during the day. Friday night at 7:00, free to the public, is the Embers."

"The Embers? The original Embers?"

"Yessir. They start at 7 at night until 11 at night. Then on Saturday night after the awards ceremony at 6, we have a band called the GTs who do classic rock and oldies."

"Now are they gonna be performing on the Grayson stage downtown on Grayson?"

"Yessir."

"OK, and speakers everywhere," Maurice says, "everybody's welcome, there's room for everybody."

In addition to the headline dance bands (and to the barbecue itself), visitors are expected to be drawn to Galax on competition weekend by a flow of local mountain music throughout each day, by a classic car "cruise-in" held in a parking lot across the street from the police station, and by food and handmade crafts from the vendors that Jim Davis has gathered. On the section of Grayson east of the gazebo, a crafter will demonstrate old-time blacksmith skills on an antique anvil. Over on the south part of Main, a booth will be filled with detailed wooden models, stained and varnished to a beautiful sheen, of biplanes and jet planes, trains and tractors, space shuttles and helicopters, and, of course, guitars and fiddles. On Grayson, the culinarily inclined will be able to buy fine handmade cutting boards. And Jim Davis and family will be vending themselves—handmade Celtic and Native American jewelry, and theme-worthy hand-carved jade pigs.

Saturday, September 10, Bowling Green, Kentucky. Walt and Larry are repping the Balloons, Tunes and BBQ competition. Among their judges for that competition is Terry Rider, a member of Walt and Larry's Mile High barbecue team. Terry and seven others are finishing up judging blind shoulder; Larry is watching over them, along with the contest chairperson and other volunteers. Larry says, in part to add a bit of conversation to the proceedings, "Don't you think the organizers have done a fine job? They have music, balloons, a carnival . . ."

"A clown," Terry adds cheerfully.

Larry pauses. "Terry used to be on our team," he says to the others.

"Until about fifteen seconds ago," Terry says.

Music, balloons, a carnival…typical of the for-the-public events that accompany most barbecue competitions. In the case of Bowling Green, two nights of music, some showing off of Corvettes made at the local GM plant, vendors and raffles and even free notarized living wills, and a balloon launch. As final scores are being tallied, dozens of hot-air balloons are being inflated with dragon-snort bursts of flame. The balloons rise from their sides toward the sky slowly, jostling each other, like vast primordial amoebas waking up and flowing away.

Caruthersville staged a pageant for young beauty queens. Overheard during the announcing of the two- to four-year-old division: "We got some future Miss Americas here. Just remember to say 'World peace' when they ask you."

Friday, September 23, Charlotte, North Carolina. Two hours away from Galax, and two months after, the Charlotte North Carolina Blues, Brews & BBQ teams up with cookbook author signings and culinary cooking demonstrations by chefs from the adjacent Johnson and Wales culinary school as part of the "Charlotte Shout," a monthlong celebration in September. And while the clean-clean chefs are working to demonstrate culinary preparation, the Hogway Speedway is running pig races on a closed-off intersection next to the barbecue cook site. The piglets race around an oval not much longer than thirty yards total to get to a prize plate of cheese puffs, while Dennis Cook calls the race Pimlico style. "We need hog callers to get these hogs to the finish line," he tells the assembled crowd over the PA, "because they sure don't want to go through that fence down yonder where those cookers are!"

Local involvement with a competition can be a bit more

direct than the public simply attending related events:

Wednesday, July 13, Galax. "Tell us something about some of the local people you were mentioning,"Maurice Vaughan is saying on-air.

"There's two ways to enter," Ron says. "You can run with the big dogs and enter the professional competition, or if you want to start out slower and just see how your product compares, you can enter the Patio Porker division."

"Patio Porker division."

"They're the amateur division."

Maurice is laughing, enjoying it. "Patio Porkers!"

"And you can only smoke ribs, but your ribs will be judged by a certified Memphis in May judge, so you can get a true idea of where you stand alongside the big dogs. If you win this competition, if you place first in the Patio Porkers, there's a cash award, and we pay your entry into the Smoke on the Mountain professional competition in 2006."

"My goodness. Now when you barbecue, do you just barbecue beef or pigs or chicken or what all can you barbecue? That's a question, isn't it?"

"In the Memphis in May, the only thing you can do is pork."

"Pork, pigs."

"It's just about pork."

As opposed to competitions run by other sanctioning bodies, primarily Kansas City Barbecue Society (KCBS) and International Barbecue Cookers Association (IBCA). All circuits talk the same language of barbecue but in distinctly different and heavily accented dialects. "Kansas City has got their thing and we got ours," says Memphis Barbecue Association rep Chuck Doan, "and different contests and different groups bring different things to the table."

Figuratively *and* literally.

As Ron has pointed out to Maurice, the MBA circuit brings

to the judges' table pig, pig and pig—whole hog, pork shoulders, ribs. The Kansas City Barbecue Society circuit cooks…well, as Society co-founder Carolyn Wells has been quoted, "If it moves, we cook it." (Does that limit the entries in the KCBS's usual Dessert category to Jell-O?) KCBS teams cook pigs and pigs (ribs and butts), beef brisket, and chicken (Cornish hens accepted) as their primary categories. And dessert. Even when the two circuits agree, they disagree. They agree on pork ribs. However, using pork *spareribs* is relatively common in KCBS competition, only occasional in MBA cooks, and usually by new teams. Loin backs are the MBA ribs of choice. (And, more specifically, the MBA ribs of choice are usually baby backs, which are the loin backs from pigs weighing 100 pounds or less.) The IBCA competitions cook pig-specific (spareribs), pig-general (anything not a sparerib), beef brisket, chicken ("one half fully jointed domestic chicken that includes a breast, wing, thigh, and drumstick"), "open" (anything that's not beef, pork or chicken—including but not limited to "goat, mutton, fish, crustacean, wild game, or wild fowl"), beans (some meaty beans in Texas, apparently). And dessert (made at home or on-site).

Ron explains to Maurice on-air, "Now, there *is* a competition called Anything But, which is an ancillary contest on Friday, which means that you can cook anything butt—B-U-T-T—pork. That's where you want to enter a beef product or a seafood product, you can do that on a Friday night. That is not a part of the professionally sanctioned competition. It's a local competition. If you want to barbecue possum, as long as it's not pork."

Somewhere along the line, Ron has come under the impression that the commonly held *"Anything But"* competition is spelled the same way that you spell "pork butt." Butt such a small spelling faux pas can be forgiven given the vague universe of barbecue orthography, where any word can be mangled to end up with a piggish pun in team names and in barbecue literature.

(Quoted from the Memphis Barbecue Association Newsletter: "of course, membership in the Memphis Barbecue Association has more than its fair share of porks—errr—perks!" And the name of the monthly publication of KCBS is *The Kansas City BullSheet*.)

The word *barbecue* itself is an orthographic challenge. On the back of the Gwatney Championship Barbecue team rig are painted the words "Bar-be-cue Made Simple." The food may be made simple, but the spelling isn't. There's no way to misspell the word *barbecue* unless maybe you throw a Z or an ampersand into it. So many ways to spell the word that started out as *barbacoa*. There's barbecue, barbeque, bar-b-q, bar-b-cue, bubbacue (actually a team name), BBQ, B-B-Q, barbicu (in pre-Revolutionary War writings), barbacue (same). Oftentimes today, the cooking is called Que for short, and Q for shorter. And the shortest version of the word, the letter Q, is visually appropriate. In your mind, rotate it 90 degrees to the left and see the fat little piggy and its tail.

So, Anything But can be Anything Butt in Galax, and "Barbecue With Altitude" can be "Barbecue With Attitude," as it is misprinted on the final version of the competition poster—the version with all the sponsors' names on it. Ron shrugs off the misprint. Not critical. Nothing that can be done about it. Besides, "Barbecue With Altitude" is new to Ron, but it is not new to barbecue. Similarly, "Smoke on the Mountain" is a competition name new to Galax but not to barbecue—other competitions have been so named. Nothing wrong with that. There are only so many names to go around, and some are obvious. Smoke on the Water (no mention of fire in the sky) in Evansville, Indiana (MBA), where the titular water is the Ohio River, and Smoke on the Water (still no mention of fire in the sky) in Pine Bluff, Arkansas (KCBS), where the water is a lake, and Smoke on the Water (nope, not yet) in Winter Haven, Florida (also KCBS).

Then there's the Big Pig Jig (in Vienna, Georgia) as opposed to just the Pig Jig (in Columbus, Georgia). There are the Ham Jams (one in Philadelphia, Mississippi, and one in Oakland, Tennessee).

Balloons were big in 2005: Balloons and BBQ (Greenville, Mississippi); Balloons, Tunes and BBQ (Bowling Green, Kentucky); Barbeque, Blues & Balloons (Madison, Indiana).

The Fests are various: Hog, Pig, Barbecue, Fun, Ribber and Ribber (Madison, Indiana, and Mt. Carmel, Illinois, respectively—or was it the other way around?).

And were we talking about puns? Like Bellevue, Nebraska's, Red, White & Que, or Asbury Park, New Jersey's, certainly-Springsteen-inspired GuitarbeQue.

Unlikely to be duplicated is a straight-between-the-eyes competition name: The Texas Dead Cow Cookin' & Bean Fixin' Extravaganza, in Wichita Falls, Texas.

And in the realm of competition-name puns that coulda/shoulda been: St. Louis Barbecue Fest might have learned from Caruthersville's Meat on the Mississippi...for, of course, Meat Me in St. Louis. Another coulda/shoulda actually appeared, as a typo, on a website listing upcoming competitions, as "The 1st Annual World's Oldest Barbecue Competition," until the typo was subsequently corrected to read "The *31st* Annual ..." Maybe next year at Galax Ron can conduct the 1st Annual World's Oldest "Anything Butt" competition. It could be the beginning of big things...)

"Big big things happening this week in Galax, Virginia," Maurice is saying just before signoff, "and folks, our observation is please, put us on your schedule—we'll see you there. Here we go, it's Kenny Chesney, number seven this week, it's "Keg in the Closet." Boy, we're rolling out a keg at the barbecue this weekend. Ha hah!"

"Actually, we are," Ron says off the air as Chesney begins singing. "This is the first time beer has ever been sold in public in Galax. Keep your fingers crossed it goes well."

"I'm sure it will, yeah," Maurice says. "I'm sure it'll be fine."

18

THE SUSPICIOUSLY COINCIDENTAL RHYME OF *BOOZE* AND *BARBECUES*

"I think it's beerthirty."
– Overheard around 11:30 AM during team setup in Caruthersville, Missouri

Thursday, July 14, 2005. When on Thursday the beer-vending truck pulls up to the corner of Grayson and Jefferson—what will be the westernmost end of the Smoke on the Mountain beer garden—Judy Brannock approaches the driver. "Where do you want to put this truck?" she asks.

"Wherever you think will sell some beer," the driver says.

The conversation marks an oddly historic moment. For Galax. Not for barbecue.

A picture on the website of Grills Gone Wild depicts the team building their pre-gone-wild grill. One of the workers stands beside the partially completed cooker holding a beer. His companion sits *inside* the open cooker like it's the cockpit of a Maserati, holding, yes, a beverage. Caption: "Grills don't work without beer."

Few cooks do, either.

And for that matter, even fewer barbecue competitions. Accounts of eighteenth-century barbecues have regular references to whisky and beer and toddies and revelry. And in an article called "Barbecue and Beer," Darryl Beeson writes, "A former finals judge, who prefers anonymity, says 'One year I created my own judge's category: What Does It Taste Like With Beer?'"

The organizers of Smoke on the Mountain and the city of Galax itself knew of this affiliation long before the competition began. And they changed a couple of things because of it.

Alcohol sales, police chief Rick Clark tells the cooks at their Friday evening briefing, will be allowed on the street during the competition weekend. "This is the first time in the history of the city"...he pauses..."legally." In its century of existence, Galax had allowed no outdoor sales. For that matter, indoor sales...legally...are fairly recent to Galax. "The Chamber of Commerce, who is the licensee for this event, would ask that if you come into the licensing section, which is from Main Street," he gestures east to indicate where Main meets Grayson, a sliver of which teams can see through the bank's glass back door, "back to Jefferson," and he gestures west, "that you drink the beer that you buy there [and not anywhere else]. The Virginia Alcohol Beverage Control board will be here and enforce the law. The law is, you can't leave with an alcoholic beverage you bought in that area....And they're really serious about what they do. It's not that I'm not serious, but they're real serious. And they'll come back on Miss Brannock." He pauses and gives that expression of pre-smile. "We don't care about Ronald."

Not that Galax up and discarded its century-year-old ban on public sales without some consternation. In its July 4 edition, *The Galax Gazette* had mentioned "a carefully monitored beer garden" in its preview of the competition. Says Fire Chief Hankley, "We've got the Fiddler's Convention which is notorious for wonderful music, but it used to be notorious for hell-raising and drinking. They went through several years there—this is fifteen, twenty years ago—where it was rough, so people were kinda cautious. It's still a pretty good step for the city to go, OK, we're going to try this. What I'm proud of is the fact that they said, 'Hey, we're going to go ahead and take that next step.'"

There are also rules for drinking along the main strip of the competition, the streets where the teams are housed. In the Commonwealth of Virginia, chief Clark explains to the assembled cooks, "the law prohibits the public consumption of alcoholic beverages. I have instructed my officers that you're here to have a good time. We're not going to run around and sit on your containers. If you're like staggering and throwing up in the middle of the street, it's another story."

"Just be respectful," someone summarizes.

"Thank you. 'Be respectful' is a great way to put it....Be nice, be discreet, have a good time, enjoy yourselves. On behalf of the city, our goal is for you to leave here and go home and tell people what a great place this is."

Earlier in the week, Judy Brannock—chief Clark's Miss Brannock—summarized the alcohol policy more swiftly than chief Clark did. "If they drink responsibly, and have a good time, that's OK," she said. "If they show their hind-end, they're gone."

In her way, Judy has pointed out that this weekend, the only sauced butt allowed on the menu this weekend is pork butt.

Only Mel can get away with holding his beer in an uncovered container on the streets of Galax (and showing his bare hind-end, to boot). Mel, the Natural Born Grillers silver metal pig mascot. By the end of one competition, Mel was tipped back so he sat on his behind, his legs pointing out. Someone had lodged a beer can between his front legs.

The delicate acknowledgment of alcohol in Galax has in part led organizers to not provide beer or other drinks in the judges' hospitality area. There will be drinks upstairs for VIPs, but leav-

ing a tapped keg untended might lead to problems of self-polic-
ing since the hospitality room opens out on Main, and not into
the "carefully monitored beer garden." Drinks in the hospitality
room run toward the safer water, soda, and sweet tea.

Saturday afternoon, July 16. After completing his judging,
Skip Sawyer stepped out of the hospitality room with a plastic
cup of sweet tea in his hand. Chatting with another judge about
judging a non-MBA contest, he is saying, "…you're sitting at a
table, one of the category's chicken, so…"

"Iced tea here?" someone interjects.

Skip ignores the interruption. "…You're sitting there with
a sample…"

"That is tea, ain't it?"

Skip looks over at the interrupter, a gentleman wearing a
volunteer T-shirt, pointing at Skip's tea. "Yeah."

"Good."

Skip says, "Are you one of the undercover guys?"

"Yeah, I'm one of the undercover guys." It's hard to tell if
he's serious, or simply a volunteer policing for alcohol and jokingly going along with Skip's question.

Skip says, "You're welcome to sniff it." He'd heard that the
ABC—Alcohol, Beverage Control board—was going to employ
undercover enforcement.

"I won't sniff it. Just the fact, beyond there"—he points to
the banner hung between two sawhorses at the end of Grayson,
with "Absolutely NO Alcohol Beyond This Point" hand-print-
ed on it—"I thought, 'How'd he get by me?'"

So, with no alcohol in the hospitality room, Larry O had
covered one obligatory Saturday-morning judges' briefing
point quickly. "Alcohol," he said that morning. "Again, just wait
until after the judging." Rep Randy McGee in one of his briefings at another contest reflected the sentiment. "When you go
outside today, I ask that you be friendly, careful, helpful, atten-

tive, to these teams. I want you to enjoy yourself. Don't go out there and be quote sober as a judge." He meant figuratively quote sober as a judge. Be open. Have fun. But be *literally* quote sober as a judge. Despite the informal category created by Mr. Beeson's anonymous friend, MBA *guidelines* strongly discourage alcohol consumption before or during the judging process. (KCBS *rules* prohibit alcohol consumption before or during judging, and a judge caught drinking before or during judging will be dismissed and replaced.) Alcohol changes taste buds, shortens attention span, slows thought processes, slows *the contest* if enhanced judges begin to lose track of time. Both contests and teams have adjusted old ways to help prevent such problems. Used to be, some contests would open full bars at 9 in the morning in the hospitality room. Used to be, teams would offer a selection of drinks to judges, from wine to beer to mixed drinks, *during* judging. Now they serve water. (Interestingly, MBA literature still suggests that Saturday morning is a good time for the ancillary bloody Mary contest.)

At the cooks' meeting the day before, on the other hand, Larry had this note for the teams: "Beverages. I always say, avoid alcohol. That's not you. You can drink all you want. But don't feed the judges alcohol. And if you have a drunk judge, let us know and we'll replace him with another drunk judge."

And drink-all-you-want has happened in barbecue on, oh, more than a couple of occasions. Beverage consumption leads to such tales as the head cook who was so schnockered that he began mixing and *drinking* his own special cocktail—vodka and the team's barbecue sauce. Or the cook who would drink so much he'd pass out in his chair. His helpful teammates would then duct-tape him to the chair. This happened so often, Larry O says, that "he had his own roll of duct tape."

Those tales have comical elements, but there are of course the sobering tales: the team that lost its rig in transit and didn't realize it; the inebriated cook who stumbled away from his site and into a pile of rocks, cutting up his face; the cook who couldn't compete the next day because of his Friday night DUI arrest. Chief Clark touches on this on Friday to the cooks: "I will tell you that Virginia has the strictest driving under the influence laws in the United States. We strictly enforce that."

And it's not that drinking is required at barbecue competitions. David Hair likes his sweet tea. Flash likes his Mountain Dew. Larry O likes his Vanilla Coke, though Larry jokes about the dangers of soda pop: "You can put something in it. Take the poison out of it. Put some medicine in it."

And sometimes medicine of a different sort is needed:

May, Memphis in. Doug Slater, head cook of Pit Panthers, was toting a beer keg on his shoulder back to his team's area. He was bumped while walking, and through a Rube Goldbergian sequence of events, ended up on the ground with a gash above his eye. His first reaction: "Is the keg all right?" His next reaction: head off to the ER to get stitches (ten of them, eventually).

As he left for the ER, a member of another team "saw me walking back like this with my hand over my eye, all blood. He got up and went down to my team, and said, 'Who's the S.O.B. that Doug got in a fight with?' Just another guy from another team. Comin' to find out to see if I was all right, one, and to see if I was in a fight, to see if he could take care of the sonofagun that hit me. Needless to say, all my team members took care of the sonofagun that hit me, because it was a keg of beer. They all whooped his ass pretty well."

19

A BIT OF BROADWAY MUSICAL COMEDY COMES TO MAIN STREET GALAX

"Sometimes presentations are funny. Some are serious. Both are OK."

– Larry O, instructing judge trainees

Friday evening, July 15, Galax. "Do this." Larry Ohrberg holds his arms up and pirouettes. It is a Bolshoi audition he is destined to fail.

It's shortly after the cooks' meeting, and Larry is giving Cody Cline of Nervous Wreck Cook'n Crew a personal seminar in on-site presentation. Cody has already turned in his Anything But entry—deer ham. And "Deer Ham" could be the name of the little improvisational theatre now being staged in his booth. The Deer, as played by the titular Nervous Wreck who has just now opened his deerish eyes and noticed the headlights. The Ham, played by on-stage Larry Ohrberg.

Cody watches Larry's spin move. "You do that for the judge?" he asks.

"No," Larry says. "You don't want the judge there for that." Larry explains that the spin, done in front of other team members *before* the judges arrive, allows for quick inspection to make sure the cook isn't marked with grease or grime that

184

judge might spot and deduct points for. He has already advised Cody to move anything unrelated to judging behind the tent to reduce clutter, and to make sure the area is swept and clean-looking.

Now Larry begins a mock presentation so that Cody can view what's involved, and learn some of the strategies he'll employ with judges the next morning.

"Get you some gloves," Larry says. "Surgical gloves. Where are you cooking the shoulder?"

Cody points out the shoulder cooker, the bigger of his two units.

"Here's what I'm going to do," Larry says, and begins playing the part of Cody Cline. "They're going to come up to you and hand you a judges card. You're going to look at it, make sure it says Nervous Wreck on it. It will say order number—make sure they're in the right order. Now, 'Welcome to Nervous Wreck,'" he says to the imagined judge. Larry holds up his left hand. "I've got a glove on this hand already." Larry O as Michael Jackson. "And you've got your other glove. You shake their hand"—gloveless. "I'd like to introduce you to my team. This is my wife, Mary Ann, this is my brother, my cousin, my son, my daughter. We're a family team, and this is our first competition." Larry moves comfortably into his improvision, weaving what he knows of Cody's background with presentation conventions and with his own experience as half of Two Fat Larrys. "Mary Ann" is a wife thusly woven. Cody's wife's name is actually Sharon, and Larry's wife's name is Mary Jo.

"Then as you're talking to them, you put that other glove on. You're looking at them in the eye. That way they know you've got gloves on. Then you come over here. 'Now this is our cooker.' Tell them a little about your cooker. Remember, you've got fifteen minutes from the time you greet him." He advises Cody to appoint a team member who will give period-

ic timing warnings from behind the judge. "Fifteen minutes."
Part of what Larry knows about Cody is that he likes to talk
about his cookers and how he came to be a cook, so he's stress-
ing the time limit. Others have fallen into the trap of devoting
too much time to talking cooking units and too little time talking food and eating it, too. One cook—during finals—once
spent his entire fifteen minutes at the cooker and the judges
were forced to leave before eating a thing. "Fifteen minutes.
You have to welcome them, you have to do a presentation, they
have to look at the meat on the grill, they have to look at it on
the plates, they have to check it for tenderness. They eat it, test
it for flavor. Fifteen minutes. You might practice with a dry run
tonight after I leave. 'This is my cooker. I build all my cookers,
I work at such and such.'"

Larry goes on to cover the opening of the grill to display meat
and garnish, the mechanics of gracefully seating a judge while
meat is being taken off the grill, the presentation of the meat at
the table. And the show goes on, Cody drinking it in, until…

"I'm starved, bring it on!"

Larry and Cody look up. Neither knows the woman who
has just come into the tent. She is part of the theater, too—the
real part. "Y'all gonna give out samples?" she says.

"These are the professional teams," Larry explains, then
directs the woman and her companion to the vendors down on
Grayson Street.

"This will happen, too," Larry says to Cody when the
woman is gone. "You need someone to run interference." He
advises Cody to appoint someone as gatekeeper, someone to
keep such intrusions away. "While you're doing the presentation, they'll be standing out here, like this." (He affects his
straight-faced Buckingham Palace guard pose, hands folded
defensively in front of him.) "They'll be polite."

No polite gatekeeper is needed for the other interruption

of the evening, when two judges stop by to say hello. Larry introduces Cody and the team to Roy and Jane Barber—judges, contest organizers, former reps, former judge trainers (including student Larry O). "Roy invented barbecue," Larry says. "Back when they first invented fire." Cody, on the other hand, is a new hand on the circuit. "This is his first competition ever."

"Oh my goodness," Jane says.

"I met Cody when I was up here in March, " Larry says. "I kind of suckered him into this. But this is where it starts."

"That's right," Jane says.

They chat for a time, then exchange best wishes and wishes of luck. When Roy and Jane leave Larry's impromptu theater, no one knows that Jane will return the next morning, scorecard in hand, to evaluate just how closely Cody has followed Larry's advice—which, in a couple of cases, is not at all...

SONGS THAT CHOIRBOYS
DO NOT SING

"Barbecue is a weird combination of immaturity and intensity in a twenty-four-hour period."
– Richard Lackie, Sweet Swine o' Mine

Late Friday and into early Saturday, July 15 and 16. Pig Pounda's Ricky chats with a Galax local night owl. Ricky's real name is Carl Richard Miller, but his childhood friends the Kerces knew him by his middle name, and have called him Ricky ever since. A while back, Gary Kerce hosted a *How to Barbecue* instructional videotape; he called his friend Carl at the beginning of the tape, being all formal and all, and slipped and called him Ricky at the end of it.

The Galax night owl obviously has not seen this informative videotape, and has been quizzing Ricky and his teammates about barbecue all evening. And all evening Pig Pounda has been forthcoming with information.

Ricky stands on the Pig Pounda rig, which looks a bit like a traveling theater displaying the set of Ribberdance. From his stage, Ricky tells his audience of one the secret to barbecue. You could almost set it to music:

You party a little bit.

You take a break.

You party a little bit.
You take a break.
You party a little bit.
You take a break.
You party a lot.
You take a break.
You party a little bit.
Then the judges come and you're serious.

There's some partying going on this Friday night at Galax, though relatively little. The night before, a couple of teams had hit almost all of the local bar scene (two bars, no waiting). But now most folks are simply drinking beer or not drinking at all while cooking or preparing to go to sleep to get ready the next day. Right now, the Pig Pounda "party" is a party of two, in marked contrast to Friday night activities at some competitions.

Friday night on the barbecue circuit is party night, but not as often as broadcasters with big microphones and TV ratings to worry about would lead you to believe. TV loves to play up the *par-tay* when they cover Memphis in May or any other event that attracts revelers, like the Big Pig Jig. The costumes, the music so dense you could cut it with a chef's knife, the liquor sluices sculpted out of ice blocks that drain alcohol into the mouths of prone young citizens who would other-wise be pondering cancer cures and writing poetry while lying prone before an ice-block sluice of alcohol at a frat house. And there's that rare sniff of a team smoking some-thing other than pig.

At Memphis in May, the parties are loud and well-attend-ed. This past May, Chris Mills surveyed the crowd drinking beer and pina coladas and various other libations in the booth of the Flying Pigs barbecue team. "I don't know a single person here," he said as people pushed past him to get to the grazing table, where chips and beans and wings and pulled pork sat over steam trays. Chris has acquaintance with members of the Flying Pigs team, and he supposed he might know a few of the team members' friends at this party. Especially since he runs Flying Pigs. But the partiers had taken over.

The revelry at the smaller, less media-visible competitions is lower-key, and more social than what hits the small screen. Take the Late Night Porkers out of Murphysboro. The team knew how to party, with music played so that people conversing could actually hear each other. And they served, on cold competition Fridays late in the season, a party-worthy kettle of "liquid apple pie" heated over an open fire. Liquid apple pie: Apple cider, cinnamon schnapps. Warm and warming.

The Pork 4 Skins booth was once *the* place to stop first at Murphysboro, the fore-described damn barbecue church. Come one, come all, sip martinis, renew friendships. Down the way, Super Smokers treats their special guests to a Cajun buffet. Charlie Hagene of Porky's IV shares his armadillo eggs (jalapenos stuffed with cream cheese and coated with bratwurst meat). The Carbondale Eagles team stirs its witches' cauldron of chili, though the chili doesn't tingle with Eagle Jimmy G.'s home-grown double-double-toil-and-trouble hot sauce that he sets off to the side for folks he knows can handle adding it to their bowlfuls. Other teams set up roasters of pulled pork, baked beans, chicken wings, ribs—with sides of chips and slaw and steamed garlic potatoes.

Unlike poor Chris Mills at Memphis, the Friday night partiers are usually entertaining close ones. Family, sponsors, friends, judges. At Bowling Green, Gwatney entertained reps from the nearby Corvette plant (because Gwatney sells a few of them thar cars at the sponsor's lots). In Galax, Gwatney invited just one person to join them for their team Friday dinner; this time, steaks.

Competition locale affects Friday party size. The more

local teams in a competition, the larger the pool of partygoers to draw from. Cody Cline and Nervous Wreck is the only local team at Galax, and he's concentrating too much on cooking to worry about entertaining. In fact, he prefers to cook alone in general—even when cooking for a family event or a party.

Walt notes, "Like John David says, the people attracted to barbecue aren't necessarily choirboys, and I'm not sure I'd get myself involved if they were."

In fact, choirboys have maintained their distance from barbecue from the very start of this style of cooking originating in the Americas. In the Caribbean, speakers of the Tupi language called the framework they cooked meats on a *mukem*, which French explorers adopted into French as *boucan*. And the woodsman-type fellows who cooked this way were called *boucaniers*. Apparently the woodsmanish boucaniers were less than law-abiding citizens. We know them by our word describing the rogues' ventures into piracy: *buccaneers*. No choirboys they.

The not-necessarily choirboys at Natural Born Grillers are not playing calypso, nor are they chanting "sixteen men on a dead man's chest" (and in fact the "yo-ho-ho and a bottle of rum" chorus might be better sung by Gwatney, as Rick Dalton offers swigs of high-quality single-barrel rum to nearby teams).

Despite the tastes of rum, despite the music (particularly when his music-loving sponsor joins the team), Rick notes, "I seldom have anything going on Friday night. Pat Burke rarely has anything going, Myron never has anything going." In fact, stroll down the rows of teams at Memphis in May on Friday night, and you know the serious teams, the teams that have a good shot of walking the stage Saturday evening. They're the ones with just one or two people sitting chatting, weathering the decibels that sometimes is recognized as music that blares around them. Especially on rib row, where there's no need to be on-site Friday night (teams in the WCBCC can cook only one category), the booths of the serious boys are shut down, tent walls pulled down, dark. The teams are back in their rooms, sleeping. Or having a steak dinner before they set to sleeping. "I'm there to cook and do my best job," Rick says. "If I have a huge-ass party going on, I can't pay attention to what I'm doing. And I got derailed up at Galax quite a bit. I get derailed a lot everywhere, people coming by to see me and I should be very thankful for that and I am, because of people wishing me well, wishing the team well, because of success that we've had."

The Friday party at Galax is down on Grayson Street where the Embers are playing. Along Main Street, the teams are mostly in Ricky's "take a break" mode.

10:00

Tracey and Andy Royer of Pit Connection sit in chaise longues before their grill, reading. To themselves. They are putting the shoulders to bed, but they don't need to put them to sleep.

In one of the tents, two kids play solitaire. On a laptop. Twenty-first century and all.

Over at Natural Born Grillers, Birm is basting his shoulders on the Big Show.

10:30

At Natural Born Grillers, a table is piled high with Boston butts, and red meat rub is flying. Butts aren't on the menu for MBA competition—they never are, though butts are a perfectly acceptable KCBS entry. These butts are on the menu for vending the next day.

Street lights bathe the teams to a point; teams are illuminated from inside with their own portable lighting. Fluorescents are built into some of the bigger rigs.

11:00

Miss Pat at Pig Pounda is prepping greenery for display the next day. Inside the Pig Pounda trailer, in the air-conditioned kitchen that as yet lacks an ironing board, she splits the stems of green onions and places them on ice, so they'll curl and "flower" for, as Miss Pat phrases it, "a little extra flair" on the judges' table setting.

During presentation, the flowered onion will be nestled alongside a cherry tomato and a small American flag into a bit of kale on a glass plate etched with the Pig Pounda logo. Black and white napkins in napkin rings will flank a full place-setting of place mat, silverware, and water goblet (slice of lime) on a glass coaster—and in the center of the table, a metal pig with damp towels for hand cleanup on its back.

11:30

Nick "Flash" Cochran has armed himself with a twelve-pack of Mountain "Caffeine" Dew. Sitting in his lawn chair, he is gearing up for the long haul as Jack's Old South's night man. He's babysitting the cookers, and has even tucked one of them in with a big, smoke-discolored blanket to provide a little extra insulation against heat loss.

Activity—even work activity—along the row of teams has quieted down. Flash's teammates have gone off to sleep in their motel rooms. Like many travelers, team members often stay in local motels—the number of rooms depending on their budget. Sometimes the entire team will take a single room. It's usually only a place to catch a shower and some sleep, so more lavish accommodations often aren't necessary. The folks at Pit Connection and Smoked Encounters and So-Co and others sleep on-site, respectively, in their tent and in lawn chairs, in on-site cots, and in their truck. At the Caruthersville competition, Lynn Moss of the Firehouse Smokers combined truck with on-site by clearing out tables under the team booth canopy and driving the truck under it. Motel room on wheels. At the same competition, Pigs in Paradise next door used a hammock as part of its booth display; one of the team members put it to practical use for Friday-night snoozing.

"It's toughest when everything's asleep," Flash says. "That's when it's hardest." He's on guard to keep the fires going, to keep the cooker temperature constant, to keep the water pan full, to keep himself awake. Generally, Flash will hold some site prep work back to work on through the night—finish tent setup, put tables in place, clean the rib grill, "something to keep you moving."

At competitions, he says, you can tell when other night men have fallen asleep. You can see failure to stay awake when smoke stops issuing from stacks. You can smell failure to stay awake when water pans go dry and start to burn. The water pans that lie below the meat grates on many cookers are filled with water and other liquids like apple juice; gently steaming, never boiling, they catch juices from the meat while helping to maintain constant heat and a good bit of moisture. At a recent competition, Flash saw that a neighbor's fire had gone out and no one was around to restart it. His first reaction was to be neighborly and stoke the fire, but decided to stay away from the grill for fear of being accused of "messing with it."

This is your nightmare: Your night man falls asleep. The grill goes untended. This is almost always a disaster.

Your dream: You make finals.

Your restless sleep: Your night man falls asleep *and* you make finals.

Your bizarre restless dream-sleep: Your night man falls asleep during the World Championship Barbecue Cooking Contest vs. eighty other shoulder entries *and* you still make finals.

It's happened. You succeed and you have no idea how or why.

Just as the early makers of Ivory soap goofed in mixing a batch only to find the damn stuff floated, fortunate mistakes grace and curse the barbecue circuit. There's the story of the team that unknowingly switched a rub for their Friday-night quick-cook for their guests with their carefully concocted rib rub...and made finals. There's the story of Da-Nite Outback cooks running short on sauce, so combined two of their differing sauces at the last minute...and getting raves from the judges. (The good news was they had a good sauce. The bad news was that to duplicate it, they had to make batches of two completely different sauces and combine them late in the process.)

At Natural Born Grillers, Ken Nottingham is the night man. Ken is as low-key as the quiet hours he haunts. His voice is soft and rich with drawl when he evaluates the job. "It's fun, I guess." He takes another swig of his beer before making the rounds—hog cooker, the Big Show, back to the hog cooker. There's another name for the night man: "sacrificial lamb."

Rick Dalton of Gwatney is his own night man, along with Lance. Rick bastes his shoulders for the first time (in the parlance, he "mops" them), at the sevenhour mark for cooking.

Midnight

At Smoked Encounters of the Third Swine, Chris Carter has brought out the cots. He's somewhat awake, and will catch spots of sleep between checking the cooker and the fire. A few feet away, young Sean is buried somewhere in a sleeping bag on another cot, sleeping soundly. For Chris, the night is part of the challenge. And the fun. "When you get the rookie people," he says, "after they have to do a night shift, either they come back or they don't come back. You can tell whether they really like it or not."

Half a block away, the beer garden and the music stage have shut down. People are still milling about, socializing, quietly.

Judy Brannock stands at the corner of Grayson and Main, outside the doorway to the A Place in Time antique shop, along with Chief Clark and a couple of Galax police officers. The evening breeze is cool, and Judy and the officers are chatting casually.

"How many people tonight?" she says to the chief.

"I'd say three to four thousand."

"Is that good?"

The chief says, "Oh, hell yes."

Good indeed. In its July 27 edition, *The Galax Gazette* would report police estimates of attendance at 8,000 people each day, Friday and Saturday.

Bit by bit, Judy's fears are being allayed. Earlier in the week she'd been worried about ordering too many T-shirts. Sales at the gazebo directly behind where Judy and Chief Clark chat were good enough that by Friday evening, only twenty T-shirts remain. Larry O gets his wish in leaving the public wanting. Judy is also pleased to hear praise for the competition when Tango stops by—including appreciation of the mountain setting. A few weeks before, at a Missouri competition, Tango tells them, he heard a sound familiar to him from his military days. "I thought a squadron of planes had taken off—it was a squadron of mosquitoes. They had numbers on their wings." (In St. Louis 2003, they *were* squadrons of planes—U.S. fighter jets roaring overhead for an Independence Day air show during the judging. The fighters had numbers on their wings, too. The fighters were slightly bigger than Tango's mosquitoes.)

Back at the site, Birm's working the shoulders. Each shoulder comes off the grill. He removes the cloth that's been covering the shank, dips the cloth in oil, replaces it, and wraps the shoulder in foil. Some of the shoulders are repositioned to account for heat variations on the grill. "That's old-school cooking right there," he says.

12:30

Sweet Swine's Pat Rooney, Richard Lackie and Amy Milam are killing some time chatting with a couple of guests, including Kell Phelps, publisher of *The National Barbecue News*. On the table where they prepped their hog that afternoon, where they will entertain judges the next morning, they've set up a portable DVD player. They watch, in bits and pieces between conversations, *Napoleon Dynamite*.

Chip Davis of Kings Cookers zips by on his transportation of choice—a razor scooter.

1:00 a.m.

On a table stage right of the opening in the Pig Pounda rig, Roger Kerce is prepping ribs. This is much later than most; Richard Lackie had completed his rib prep before chatting with Austin Caviness on the WXII Friday nooncast, even though those ribs weren't scheduled to go onto the grill until 6 am Saturday morning. Roger works just short of a case of ribs—fourteen slabs, stretching away from him along his work table. (It would be truer to barbecue parlance to say "fourteen ribs." "Rib," "slab," "rack" and "side" are synonymous, and in conversation the quicker way to refer to "slabs of ribs" is to just call them "ribs." As in "How many ribs are you cooking today?") Roger has set aside four racks that will go uncooked. Each will become a "demonstration rib"; each of the three preliminary judges will be shown how Pig Pounda goes about its rib prep. They hope that such demonstration helps lead to a fourth demonstration—to the finals judges.

Roger, like most other rib cooks, begins by stripping a thin whitish-to-translucent membrane from the concave side of each slab. Most rib cooks concur that this membrane makes the ribs tough to pull apart, and blocks the smoke penetration. A few leave the membrane on during cooking, on the theory that the membrane slows fat rendering and helps retain moisture. But for these cooks, the membrane will likely come off before the judges arrive. The occasional team will cook ribs hanging from a hook, perpendicular to the ground. For such ribs, the membrane must stay on to keep the slab from falling apart when the meat tenderizes during cooking.

Membrane removal is discussed by some as if it were a magical art—primarily newbie cooks who hadn't had to fret over such rib prep on home grills. They're new to the membrane removal game, and at first it seems a chore difficult to grasp. Literally. That membrane is slippery. At its core, membrane removal is a matter of lifting a bit of the membrane off one of the bones, securing it, then pulling it away like removing a Band-Aid from your son's tricycle-fall scrape. To get a purchase point, a tool of various preferences is slipped between the membrane and a bone, often in the middle of the slab, sometimes at the end. Tools of preference include standard knives, fish filet knives, shrimp deveiners, those metal rod thingies tooled to form a bottle opener on one end and crimped up at the other to get a purchase on pop-tops, and, in the case of Crash Dummy Walt, a Phillips-head screwdriver.

Once the leverage point is established, the cook further lifts the membrane either with the tool of choice or with a finger (try your pinkie—you can slip it underneath more easily). From there, use one of four established styles of membrane ecdysis.

1. If beginning from the center of the rib, simply continue lifting up while the membrane "tents," pulling away from both sides simultaneously. Or,

2. Grab the membrane with something that will counteract the slipperiness. A paper towel works just fine. If starting from the west end of the rib, lift and tear eastward. From the east end, lift and tear westward. (Don't you love detailed instructions?) Or,

3. Twirl the finger that you've inserted between bone and membrane so that you wrap a portion of the membrane around

it, allowing you enough purchase to pull the membrane away (see directional instructions in point #2, above). Or,

4. Find a butcher or meat supplier that delivers the ribs with the membranes already removed, as the occasional team does. Or,

5. Get another member of your team to do it. You're the head cook, after all.

For Roger Kerce, this is the beginning of an hour to an hour and a half of rib prep. The Carbondale Eagles devote three team members and a considerable amount of time notching out small bone fragments that can remain on the meat between the bones after they are cut. The now-retired Orange Blossom Cooking Team sent their ribs through a bandsaw to give them perfect uniformity of bone length. Perfect rectangles were their slabs. Some teams remove the meat "strap" from across the top of the rib, to give the rib uniform depth for look and for cooking consistency, and to eliminate a piece of meat whose grain runs perpendicular to the grain of the meat between the ribs. "Now why would you want to do that?" Richard Lackie says to one of his preliminary judges on Saturday when he explains to her why his ribs retain the strap. It's a great cut of meat, including parts of the bacon, he explains as he serves her another couple of bones.

Teams examine the ribs carefully, scraping off whatever fat they can find, and looking to avoid "shiners"—places where the bone is exposed through the meat. It's not unusual to see a team member holding up a rack of ribs by one end and examining it as carefully as reading a contract for the fine print. (Overheard at Gwatney during rib prep: "Slide that knife toward you. Shave that sucker.")

Roger spreads dry rub over the back of each slab. Then Roger allows the ribs to sit awhile (perhaps allowing him to follow Ricky's recipe by engaging in the "non-take-a-break" portion of barbecue success) until the rub gets tacky.

Next Roger turns the ribs over to rub the other side. Upon achieving the proper state of tackiness, the ribs are stacked in a cooler to marinate for six hours. Most will go on the grill at 8:30 AM. Five racks will be set aside to go on the grill later—they will be "staggered" so that they will reach the desired doneness at about the cross-your-fingers time the finals judges arrive.

Emptied of the ribs, the top of the rib-prep table looks like it's been stenciled with a long row of ghost I's using dry rub.

1:30

Gwatney is at the nine-hour mark on the shoulders, and Rick mops them again.

Next door, Ken Nottingham of Grillers sprays baste on the cloth that covers the shoulder shanks, then begins unrolling the foil around the shoulders so that he can lift it over the shoulders and wrap them.

Nearby, Galax police officers are chatting with team members and a couple of locals that are hanging out late when Birmingham pops out of the RV. "Hey, brother, where's the moonshine?"

One of the officers begins chanting, "LaLaLaLaLa," the kid's "I'm not listening" song. He says a bit sternly, "You don't have no moonshine. You left it in the city."

Down at Jack's, the night men are conferencing. Richard Lackie chats with Jack's Flash, now *non* jumpin' Jack's Flash, as he sits quietly, a bit wearily, in his lawn chair.

Roger at Pig Pounda stokes the fire, begins to prep the rib grill.

Others sleep beside their cookers—Cody Cline, the Pit Connection crew. The entire Pure and Sinful team is likely sleeping in their motel rooms. Their site is closed, abandoned. So is the So-Co site. Both teams are cooking only ribs, and will start up later in the morning.

2:00

Chip Davis of Kings Cooking turns his shoulders over, which the Kings cooks do every hour. Such turning of meat is relatively rare on the circuit. Cooks generally don't like to disturb their product, and they take as few opportunities to open the grill and throw off the temperatures as possible. "Trust your thermometers," reads a cooking tip on the Natural Born Grillers website, then repeats an old saw heard occasionally: "If you're lookin', you ain't cookin'." Not turning the meat also means less chance of accident. There have been any number of dropped shoulders in contests. Dropped hogs, too. There's not much more three-stoogish than—as displayed at a contest in Evansville, Indiana—sleepy grown men with perhaps a beer or two in them trying to flip a whole hog, with two twisting in one direction and two in the opposite direction. Especially a hog that—in the case of the double twist that nearly tore that particular hog in half—had been basted in butter. Real people reenacting "slippery as a greased pig" cliches.

Richard Lackie checks the hog fire. From his location somewhat near the middle of the row of teams, he can hear music coming from both ends of the contest. Country music from the south end's Kings Cookers, and "Is-that-Natural-Born-or-Gwatney?" from the north end. The answer to Richard's question: both.

The music flows down the street. Hank Williams, Jr., has put a pig in the ground, and he's put some beer on ice. And all the rowdy friends aren't coming over; they're already here tonight.

2:15

The Ingham brothers—Birm*ingham* and Ken Nott*ingham*—work together to inject their hog. Birm catches an eyeful of smoke, has to back off and wipe his eyes. When they get done injecting, the two of them unroll the foil they have prepped underneath the hog, and set to wrapping the pig itself.

2:30

Bathed in the fluorescents built into his main rig, Rick Dalton injects his on-site hog. "I'm hitting the places where I know I'm going to pull from." Then he sets about wrapping the hog in foil.

He swings over to the back of the site and the blind hog cooker, lit by a floodlight mounted on the cooker. The hog inside, in contrast to the on-site hog, looks dry, dark. The head is practically detached from the body. Cooking "blew the head off," in the parlance. There's a hole in the meat along the ribs. "Blew out the side."

"We call this 'the ol' Spare Parts hog,'" Rick says. "This one's real ugly, but I only have to pull some meat off it." The judges will never see the hog itself; just the meat in the blind box.

Rick refills the water pan on the blind hog cooker, injects Spare Parts, notices that juices are pooling in the body cavity near the neck and head. With a knife, he makes two quick stabs through the point where neck meets head; the juices drain into the water pan. He then covers the hog in foil.

"Spare Parts," he says, "see you tomorrow," and claps the cooker door shut.

2:45

Tango brings out ribs cooked for vending and shares them with the four police officers talking at the north end of the contest, near the crunch-enhanced wood bench in the Farmer's Market.

3:00

There's a bit more activity at Pit Connection. Reading is somewhat more active than sleeping, anyway, and in their lawn chairs, Tracey and Andy are again reading.

Next door to Pit Connection, Ken and Birm have joined Flash to chat a bit. Tango scoots by in a golf cart, stopping only to call out, "Flash, you giving Birm some barbecue lessons?"

3:30

Shift change for King's Cooking and Sweet Swine, at about

the same time. Paul Goforth and Pat Rooney arrive (separately and on foot and not on scooter); Chip and Richard knock off to catch some sleep. On this trip, Sweet Swine is running short-handed, and has no dedicated night man. The only baton they exchange in their relay is wakefulness. The Kings cooking baton isn't much more substantial as sleepy nightman Paul Goforth arrives on-site. He's left with the cookers going and a quick update from teammate Chip: "Rib sauce is on one side, barbecue sauce on the other. It's all ready to go." For other teams, the changing of the guard is a bit more formal. Michael Brown of Grand Masters of Cooking Disasters uses the white board mounted on his rig to log time and temp and what wood is added to the fire when. This allows the cook that follows him to know exactly what was done in preparation.

Rick Dalton prepares to wrap his shoulders with Lance's help. With a series of metallic rips, Rick creates a multilayered crisscross of aluminum foil. One by one, the shoulders come off the grill, placed in the center of the crisscross. Rick injects each one—and each one swells slightly like a meat balloon—then wraps the each shoulder, using one length of foil from one direction of the cross, then a second length of foil. He places the wrapped shoulder aside; Lance places the next shoulder in the center of the aluminum cross, returns the wrapped shoulder to the cooker, working to keep the door closed as much as possible.

4:00

The work done, Rick relaxes a little bit before heading off to bed. He pours himself a whisky and waits for teammates Hal Berry and Rusty Voigt to relieve him. When they arrive, he'll catch a quick nap at the motel and arrive back at the site at 7:30.

4:30

The ruckus begins.

21

MORNING HAS BROKEN, AND WE KNOW WHO BROKE IT

"Another good memory is standing on the hill by the motel, looking down on that lovely little town and watching all that smoke drift up from the barbecue cookers."

— Sheila Daniel, recalling the morning of Saturday's judging

Saturday, July 16, Sunrise–6:17. Dawnlight the morning of the competition. "It's starting out to be a great day," Al Norton of Gwatney says to a passerby. Birdsong. The occasional scraping sound as charcoal is refreshed. Cooker doors creak open, creak shut. Smoke billows silently from stack after stack after stack. Billows quieter than morning birdsong…

Birdsong. Man shouting, "Let's go, Grillers! Let's have a little music. Crank it up, Big Daddy!" Jeff Holmes of Hawg Wild is still irked by the music from Gwatney and Griller speakers that played long into the night, long into the early morning. "That was the most ridiculous thing I ever heard of as far as a little respect for some neighbors here," Jeff says later that day. He says he put in a protest to officials, but the music continued to play. "So," round about 4:30, in protest of the music, "I set off the alarm in the truck. Let the horn go off."

Hawg Wild's protest seemed to have affected his immediate

neighbors more than anyone else. Pit Connection roused from sleep. "I don't know if they were sleeping in there but they came out and stuff like this and I think they're a new team, and I felt bad, but maybe they were tired of the music, too." And a member of another team expressed more concern over the dawnlight shouting—and a few words that were in it—than the music.

With or without the help of ruckus, the Galax cooksite begins to wake up. Some parts of it more slowly than others.

When Richard Lackie put his ribs into the cooker at quarter after six, it was fifteen minutes too late, for his liking. "I had the old AM/PM problem this morning," he says—an alarm clock mistakenly set to give him an early *evening* wake-up call. "But it's not a bad thing," he says. "The trend is more pull these days"—that is, a little less tenderness—so something short of his preferred doneness might actually work in his favor.

Next door, John Bennett is a bit behind on his ribs, too. He had trouble with the fire in his cooker. Pat Rooney came over and next-door-neighborly helped the competition fire up the grill. John normally cooks only with apple wood. But he has deemed that his supply is too old, so he's building his fire with a mix of charcoal and wood chunks. It is, he says, the first time he's cooked that way, and he's having trouble getting enough heat. John fans the fire now…electrically, with a table electric fan, perhaps something of an inventive first on this circuit.

"This your first competition?" Richard Lackie says.

"Yeah," John says.

"Awesome. Nervous?"

"Not really," John says. "I just came for the experience."

"Good. Ya gotta do it."

"I wanna get some feedback doing this."

"Hope you get good judges," Richard says. "The first time I cooked, I was presenting. I was a little bit nervous, but not with that product or anything. So I'm sitting there talking to my judge, and after I get done with my spiel, I'm like, 'So, how long have you been judging? You know, this long, and I noticed his name was George, and maybe looked a little familiar, and he starts talking, 'Well, I've got a barbecue team,' and 'I go, oh, really!, what's your barbecue team's name?' And he goes, 'Pyropigmaniacs'—who had just won grand champion at Memphis in May in rib. Mid-to-late nineties, you went up against them in rib and you're dead. So I just turned white. He was the one judge who came back for feedback, because you're not always lucky enough to get it, unless you beg 'em to come back. He come back and says, 'Your flavor's better than mine. Get your tenderness down, you got me beat.' We finaled in shoulder, got drunk and ordered a Backwoods at 11 at night. Called down to Louisiana....My second cook, I got second place. I went from thirtieth in that cook to second place. And I got grand champion the next cook."

And when Larry O stops by to say hello, he asks John, "You ready?"

"Not really," John replies.

Down at Natural Born Grillers, Ken Sacrificial Nottinglamb says, "I'm stressed as usual," as he checks the temps on the Big Show. "Oh baby, talk to me," he beckons, perhaps to the temperature gauge, perhaps to the wrapped shoulders themselves. This is "magic time," John David says later. The shoulders better be ready by now. When John David arrives on-site at Natural Born Grillers with sausage-and-egg biscuits and coffee, he is impressed with what he finds his night man doing. "Ken learned how to cook," he says later in half-joking amazement. "Ken used to watch the damn thermometers. Now he's pacing around, saying 'Ain't there ain't there ain't there.' I said, 'What's wrong with Nottingham?'"

"I was showing 'em how to cook," Ken says.

"See how they treat you?," Birm says to Ken.

"He was pacing around," John David says. "And he's checking things, touching the meat, saying 'No it's not,' and

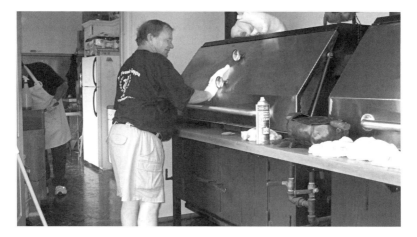

Ricky Miller of Pig Pounda Kappa tending to his grills.

I'm like *damn*."

Ken gives the crap straight back. "Put this on the record: the only reason he seen that actually happen was that was the first contest that he was here at 7. He's learning what really goes on here, is what it is. He thinks he just shows up and its all done, it just happens."

It is indeed an earlier arrival for John David. His back pain sent him to bed earlier than normal. He'd not been up into the night, and had not heard of the problems with the music/truck horn exchange, and indeed won't hear about it until later that day.

Cody Cline gets his ribs on at 7:00—ten racks. By quarter after 7, Cody and wife Sharon work a broom. Al Norton works a leaf-blower. Had the competition been on grass, rakes would have been deployed to clean up team areas. Dan Puryear works a folding chair. His ribs are on the cooker, and he's catching a quick nap, hat down over his eyes. Jumping Jack's Flash works a hose, as does Jeff Holmes, clearing debris with a hard spray. The teams are working to remove anything that would distract the judge (overheard at one site at the Tennessee Funfest: "Hide that yellow hose—it catches the eye"—or perhaps it was clashing with the building behind it) or would work against a perfect "Area and Personal Appearance" score. Cigarette butts and beer-bottle caps emit sounds that only judges can hear, and judges will zero in on them in a second. Grease spots, smudges, smoke residue around a cooker vent…

Birmingham at Grillers hoses down the grills and weathers a joke about using water sprays to maintain temperatures. Lance Freemon of Gwatney polishes the sides of the rig and the grills. They *all* polish the sides of the rig and the grills, as well as backs and fenders and countertops. Just before judging at the WCBCC at 2005 Memphis in May, a Super Smokers team member was spotted applying Armor-All to one of the cooker's trailer tires. Keith Roberts of Pigs in Paradise cringes when he tells the story of the judge who told him that he'd wanted to give Keith a 9.8 or 9.9 in overall impression but dropped him to fairly damning 9.0 when he noticed a spot of barbecue sauce on the grill. The cringing people listening to the story agree that that's awfully harsh.

Most important, the teams are making sure that there's "no drunk uncle" lying about, as rep Randy McGee phrases it. "They should at least put a table over him, and a tablecloth." (Larry notes, "He was the one who was supposed to hold down the fire.")

Because of the on-site presentations, MBA competitions entail more work, more expense, more equipment than competitions on the KCBS and similar circuits. More judges means more meat (and cooking a whole hog virtually defines "more meat"). And on-site presentation leads to larger areas, seating for the judges, booth decorations, tent walls masking food-prep areas, team uniforms and bright smiles on Saturday. In contrast, KCBS teams have only to turn in their food on Saturday. KCBS cooks don't have to worry about the legendary drunk uncle; KCBS cooks can *be* the drunk uncle.

Volunteers uniformed in gray T-shirts are scrambling within

the bank building to have it ready for the continental breakfast scheduled to begin at 7:30, for judges' check-in beginning at 8, and for the first blind check-in at 10. The blue volunteer T-shirts are reserved for Chamber members; this is one of the few times Ron and Judy will be color-coordinated.

At 8:00, Walt and Larry begin their rounds of the teams. Their official goal is to hand out blind boxes—one foam-plastic container for each category the team is in, and up to two plastic cups and lids if the team is going to submit sauces with its entry. The boxes are labeled with a removable sticker listing team name, category, and turn-in time. At each team, Walt and Larry state the official time; synchronizing watches is easier in the days of cell phones pulling the time from satellites. But that isn't quite as easy in Galax, with several people out of cell coverage. Walt and Larry also confirm the blind box delivery deadline that's printed on the box label; that deadline is also the time the first on-site judge for that category will arrive.

Then, for each team, "Good luck today."

Teams are solidifying their presentation areas. Remaining tent walls go up. The presentation table is set up—chairs for presenter and judge arranged, tablecloth laid down, napkin and plate and other dinnerware. Sometimes silverware. "Some of the teams might have silverware sitting on the table," Randy McGee tells judge trainees. "It's a trick. They do it because they think it looks good. They don't want you to pick up a fork and a knife and eat barbecue." Reps advise teams that the best way to keep judges from using silverware is to not give them silverware. Brad Cheatham of Carbondale Eagles tells of a judge who couldn't decide if he liked Eagles or another team better. The judge used knife and fork as the deciding factor. "We had some silverware on the table," Brad says. "He saw a couple water spots on it. Got knocked out of finals because of a couple water spots. Go figure. To say the least, though, we threw the silverware away."

This move would go unnoticed by most judges (well, so would water spots), but other teams tell tales of silverware *demanded* by the judges. Once when the Magnolia Smokers refused to supply silverware to a visiting judge, the judge took the spoon from the sauce bowl, stuck it in his mouth to clear the sauce, and proceeded to spoon-feed barbecue to himself.

As Larry O told Cody Cline in his Friday-night coaching, the night before, "If they use a fork, they got no business judging barbecue....The correct way to judge barbecue is when you're done, you should have sauce from this ear to this ear. And it's permissible to have it on your scorecard."

Mack Walker was the hog cook with the old Airpork Crew team. "You already got a fork," he once said as he spread the fingers of one hand, "and it has five prongs."

Decorations are put into place. At Natural Born, little pig figurines, tuxedos and sunglasses and all, overhang the lip of black plates. Tango—gruff-looking Tango who looks like he should be a boxer or a boxer's manager and not a garnisher—cuts peel and pulp from oranges, leaving delicate orange-peel baskets, handle and all, that he'll fill with grapes. Birds made of squash, palm trees made of carrots and trimmed green pepper "fronds"—these are the heights of Tango's table garnish artistry.

Around 9:30, Tango wraps the Natural Born ribs. They'd tried something different with these ribs—starting with a cold smoke. As opposed to a hot grill, a cold smoke means starting the cooking at a lower temperature. Some say this keeps the pores on the meat open longer, allowing more smoke presentation. Ken begins to take shoulders off the grill and place them in coolers. They will rest there awhile before being returned to the grill for judging at 11:15.

First judges show up at 10:00 for whole hog.

Thirty minutes away.

KICKOFF OF THE ASS-KICKING CONTEST

"Anyone who's not here, raise your hand."
—MBA rep Randy McGee as a judges' meeting is about to begin

Saturday, June 16, 8:30 am. The contest begins, the contest that Crash Dummy Walt has described to Ron and Carlene as Ron's SUV climbed the mountain from Winston-Salem back to Galax on Wednesday night.

Between beginning of Saturday-morning judges check-in and distributing the judging assignments, during the time that judges would be drinking coffee, greeting old friends, swapping horror stories, catching each other up on their real-world lives for better or for worse, Walt and Carlene would be scrambling to make sure each team had three on-site judges for each category entered, and that each blind table would have its four judges. No gaps. No unassigned judges. He would be, as he said then, "busier than a one-legged man in an ass-kicking contest."

In Kennett a few weeks before, the one-legged man managed to kick one judge into whole hog on-site and whole hog blind at the same time. "I hope you're hungry," rep Randy McGee said with a smile before working to rearrange the assignments.

The kicking contest is officially underway as Walt visits the

Walt Brown speaks to gathered judges Saturday morning before judging begins.

check-in table. As each judge came in, his or her name was checked off a list, and the judge was given a name tag. It's a matter of identification to one degree, a kind of a little "Hi! I'm Freddy!" chest display—though most judges will already be sporting their official name-included judges badges. The name tags serve as identification of another sort—ID'ing the guilty.

At 8:53, Walt bends over the table.

Two name tags remain. Two unclaimed name tags mean two no-shows. At least two other judges who must take on additional categories to fill in the holes (more than two in the real world, as the no-shows would likely have been themselves assigned multiple categories). As Judy might say, two more hind-ends for the one-legged man to kick. (Surprisingly, Larry doesn't nominate Jim Davis for the job of one-leggery.)

And their hind-ends might indeed be kicked. Kicked from participating in the contest next year, if the organizers so choose. Walt has advised Carlene to "record the no-shows."

Granted, no-shows might result from extenuating circumstances. Car trouble. Family crisis. Other unanticipations. But accepting a judging invitation is regarded as making a serious commitment.

Two other judges, a few days ago, had called to explain that they couldn't come to the competition because of an emergency gall bladder operation. Those judges will certainly be invited back next year—they followed protocol, gave the organizers fair warning, and even had an excuse that didn't have to involve a note from Mom. (Elaine Lyons was the judge who thought she was suffering a heart attack when she asked friends to take her to the emergency room—the problem was not with her heart, but with her gall bladder. The operation went well, "but I never did get my doctor's note" to give to Walt, Elaine later jokes. At another competition, a finals judge showed up late to the briefing—a pretty severe no-no in itself—with an acceptable excuse. He was also in emergency surgery. Except he was the one performing it.)

Walt was ready for the warned absences. He was also ready—mentally, anyway—for the additional two absences; they happen every contest.

Walt crosses out the no-shows from his assignment sheet. Then, before Larry O begins the judges' briefing, he retires to the back to work with Carlene on reassignments. The ideal is to assign the newly empty slots to judges who have only one category. But almost all the judges already have two categories— they are "doubling" in the parlance. Another ideal Walt won't be able to achieve is to assign the doubles to the hog and ribs categories—that gives them a little spacing between their duties. Several of the judges end up "tripling" in Galax—they will judge all three categories. They'll be eating *more* than the finals judges do. On-site, they'll eat about the same that finals judges do—visiting three teams and tasting three samples within a category.

But likely a tripling judge will also serve in the blind, meaning at least *four* samples and possibly as many as *six*.

It's a rare judge that dislikes doubling—hell, it's simply more good eating. One year in Memphis, a *Southern Living Presents* camera crew was interviewing judges for a half-hour special on the World Championship Barbecue Cooking Contest. "If you can sum up barbecue in three words," the producer asked judge Annie Sisson, "what would they be?"

No hesitation: "More! More! More!"

Tripling, however, is something more of a challenge, and in fact official MBA judging guidelines discourage it strongly.

Just after Walt and Carlene finalize the details of the judges assignments, Ron and Larry are welcoming the judges out in the bank lobby. It's 9:00, and the mandatory briefing begins.

Alex Brown is one of the twenty-five assembled judges who listen attentively to briefing words he's heard dozens of times before in his ten years as a judge. Alex has come in from Reston, Virginia. A friend and fellow D.C.-area judge had alerted him to the Galax competition, and he later saw advertising for the competition. "I'm like, 'Where is Galax?'" he says. "'It's in Virginia. I'll try to support all the Virginia barbecues.' I had no idea where Galax really was."

Alex's road to judging and eventually to the unknown Galax began simply, and typically. "I like to eat." Seems obvious enough, yet there are a couple of judges that don't like to eat…meat, anyway. You hear the story from so many teams that it begins to sound like an urban legend. Pet alligators flushed down the toilet that are now rampaging through the sewer system. The adopted chihuahua that turns out to be a huge rat. The vegetarian judge politely chewing, discreetly spitting meat into a napkin, boldly turning in scorecards. That last one is *not* urban legend, however. Turns out that a couple of certified judges are acknowledged vegetarians.

Alex Brown is not one of them. "My dad used to barbecue for the Masons when I was a kid, and so I'm used to seeing folks in the backyard cooking all night long," he says. "It was something enjoyable, you know, the little kid running around." Years later the big kid was running around, and he caught wind of some smoke in the air near where he lived. "They had the D.C. Barbecue Battle in Georgetown, and I went over there as a spectator. Sure enough, I saw all these people walking around getting this preferential treatment."

At that competition, Alex asked someone, "Who are they and how are they getting to eat all that stuff?"

"They're judges."

"How can I be one?"

That was in June of that year, Alex says, "and by October I had taken the class and I was *hooked*."

Probably everyone in the abandoned First National Bank building has taken "the class"—the judges' training seminar that is usually held in Memphis but is occasionally given in such far-flung places as D.C. and Mt. Carmel Illinois.

"Used to be," rep Randy McGee has said, "judges were just handed scorecards and told 'hurry back.'" The used-to-be is no more.

Used to be, judges were locals and friends and contacts invited to sit down with teams and scribble scores and continue the drinking that they may have (probably have) already started. But such loose and inconsistent recruiting led to problems, from team complaints to last-minute scrambling for warm judging bodies to small political wars about who was and who was not invited and how could you snub the richest guy in town? So Memphis in May began a judge-certification program. Potential judges now take a daylong class, and must judge two contests as "trained" judges before receiving certification. Most MBA competitions now strive for 100 percent certified or trained judges, knowing that teams prefer being evaluated by the qualified.

And the briefing Larry gives this Saturday morning, as much a part of the blah-blah-blah as the cooks' meeting the evening before, is both standard and mandatory before the judges are given the final instruction to "hurry back."

A couple of tables back in the Galax judging area, Roy and Jane Barber listen attentively to words they've heard dozens upon dozens of times before and they themselves have spoken dozens of times before. They are among the ones who have *given* "the class." As former Memphis in May reps, they have done what Walt and Larry are doing today many many times. They taught the judging seminar for a time—they taught *Larry* and maybe another thousand judges—and now they judge when not working as organizers of the Tennessee Funfest competition.

Roy and Jane heard of the contest from an invitation in the mail. They are on a list of certified judges maintained by the Memphis Barbecue Association, a list that was provided to Ron Passmore. Roy and Jane, from the Memphis area, first came to judging in 1991, before classes started, though a class of a different sort got them involved. Jane was teaching decorative painting, and one of her students was the judging chair of a competition in Clarksdale, Mississippi. The student knew Jane liked barbecue, and invited her and husband Roy to participate. "We both became instantly interested in this sport," Jane says, "and we also noticed we might like to get in on the administrative part." They took the judging seminar in September 1991, began rep training in '92, were fullfledged reps in '93.

At Alex's table, Terrie D'Amato listens attentively to words she's heard dozens of times before in her seven years of judging. Al Roker brought her to Galax in something of the same way Roker brought Smoke on the Mountain to Galax. "One day I was sitting in Battle Creek Michigan, bored to tears," she says, thinking of perhaps using her baking skills to volunteer for a state fair pie-baking competition or something. "Well, I'm flipping through the channels and I come across the Food Network and there's Al Roker at Memphis in May. It's like 'Well, now that is the coolest thing—I gotta do this.' Get online, find the Memphis in May website. In like a month they were having a judging seminar down in Memphis. So I called and signed up and went down for the course. Went down to Memphis from Battle Creek, fourteen and a half hours, and took the class. Been doing it ever since."

Terrie was also on that list of certified judges provided by the MBA.

Toward the back, John Akins, head cook of the Huish barbeque team listens attentively to words that are rather new to him. John came to Galax, as well, in response to a mailed invitation. But his name was not on the list that Terrie and the Barbers are on; his was on a separate list, one that would be soon be integrated into the master list of judges. John took "the class"—the MBA judging seminar—the previous April; students from that seminar also received a mailing from Ron Passmore.

John's motivation for taking the class, recall, was to learn barbecue from the *judge's* perspective. John says that the class, in learning what judges are taught to look for, affected his presentation more than his style of cooking. A ten-hour trip into Galax for John, so he turned it into a mini-vacation, bringing along his wife and daughter, and mother-, father-and daughter-in-law.

In John's class was Terry Jo Litchfield, who'd been waiting since last year to attend the judging school. With the class under her belt, she says, "It's not exaggerating to say I was ready to test the pork!" So ready, was she, that she decided to accept the invitation to Galax, despite the fact that she's from

Manhattan, Kansas, about a thousand miles away. "I decided this road trip would be spontaneous over and back so we could stop and see whatever along the way. I figured we could go out one way, through Kentucky, and back another which was through Tennessee by way of North Carolina. Of course this meant driving was the mode of transportation." Mini-vacation for Terry Jo meant family travel, as well. "Along with me came my mother, an aunt, and an uncle."

By the time the meeting begins at 9:00, Walt and Carlene have settled all the judges assignments, and are watching as Larry addresses the assembled judges.

There are the usual pleasantries and the unusual pleasantries: "This is a first-year event for this," Larry says, "and these people have just been amazing. They never even went to the organizers seminar. What do you think of what they've done so far?" The response is a round of applause. "Today we have twelve teams. That's not very many." (And in fact the MBA generally requires that a competition draws fifteen teams to avoid going into sanctioning probation the succeeding year.) "But we have the top five in the world cooking right here. We also have a couple of new teams out here, too, who have never cooked in competition. We're really proud of them because they've stepped up to the plate."

Larry shapes many of his comments and his requests around newness. The contest and its volunteers are new; spend some time talking about what you're doing with the judges' assistant—known as a contest "ambassador"—who will be assigned to you when you visit teams on-site. Go back to the new teams and give them feedback. Don't ask teams to feed the judges' assistants as they might at other contests, because the newbies might not have enough meat to feed others. Teams that don't feed the ambassadors may feel like they're at a disadvantage compared to those that do. The volunteers will have plenty of chance to eat later. Besides, Walt points out, not bringing in the ambassador can avoid any manner of faux pas. "I had one ambassador who said, 'Wow, that's the best rib I've ever had!'" right in the middle of the presentation.

Ron adds, "I would like to say all your ambassadors have never seen barbecue like this in their lives. God bless them, they're doing the best they can to help you. Feel free to coach them about exactly what you want them to do. They'll do whatever you want."

"Don't tell them that," Larry jumps in. "They'll believe you. You don't know these guys."

"Please don't assume that they know what you want," Ron says.

Larry says, "I'm going to go get my car." Needs a good wash.

And Larry shapes many of his comments around the old standards, the words that Alex and Terrie and Roy and Jane have heard so many times before:

When you get your cards, check for conflicts. "A conflict doesn't mean that someone you partied with last night. It means that the cook was your spouse's divorce attorney, and you're looking for an apartment now. It might be the guy who sold you a car that blew up and didn't qualify for the lemon law. That might be a conflict. A conflict means that you don't feel that you can judge that team fairly."

Treat all teams equally, to the point that if you ask a question of one team, ask the same question of the others. When Linda Booth of Red Hot Smokers addressed judges-in-training, she talked of courtesy to the teams. "I don't like to see a judge walk up with a cigarette in his mouth" —she pantomimed a last drag of a cigarette, a flick to the ground, a grind of cigarette butt with the toe of her shoe, then she extended her hand theatrically to the imaginary head cook about to greet her—"'Hi. I'm here to meet you.' I have a real problem with that." When a new judge at the Mt. Carmel Ribberfest did just that before greeting his third shoulder team, he explained jokingly to the team greeter, "Someone just told me that you guys hate when a judge does that, but I'd already done it to the first two teams, so I had to do it to you to be fair."

Pay attention to timing. "The judging times are: hog, 10:00; shoulder 11:15; ribs at 12:30; finals at 1:45. We want you to be here for your judges assignments at least fifteen minutes ahead of time." We don't have enough judges to replace you, so we're at your mercy right now." At the cooks' briefing, Larry noted that the contest was short of judges, and that the teams would know that they were really in trouble if Walt showed up with a scorecard. Ten minutes minimum at each team, fifteen minutes maximum.

Finally, "Remember, honesty and integrity of the judges is the most important thing....That's why," Larry says as so many other reps have said at so many other briefings, "that's why you get paid the big bucks."

There is indeed no pay to judges, other than the food itself. And the goodie bag.

Ron Passmore has interpreted the judges' supply list provided by the MBA as gospel, and the suggestion for a goodie bag as one of the commandments. Unlike the commandments, and more in line with the pirate's code in *Pirates of the Caribbean*, the call for goodie bags is a "guideline." Not all contests give them away. In fact, there's just so much goodie-ing that one can have in one's life. A barbecue judge is either crazy or simply not on the circuit enough if he or she actually pays money for a pen, a pencil, or a notepad. Note-jotting goodies are second in giveaway frequency only to the obligatory apron. It's rare for a judge to walk away from a competition without an apron, and sometimes more than one.

Of course, these aprons are rarely used. They hang in

closets, aging and drying out, like tobacco from the rafters of a Kentucky barn. One enterprising judge put her aprons to excellent use, however: She cut them up and sewed them into a commemorative barbecue quilt.

The apron in the Galax Smoke on the Mountain goodie bag is of good material, with a big reproduction of the competition logo boldly presented on the front, no sponsor names. Several competition aprons display sponsor names as part of the sponsorship deal.

Also included in **Galax Goodie Bag #1**, the plain brown paper bag (and yes, two goodie bags at Galax):

- United Way pin attached to specially printed "Thank You for participating in the 2005 Smoke on the Mountain Barbecue championship" card (great logo of a pig on a spit, too)
- blue U.S. Cellular paper clamp
- one golf tee, supplier unknown
- Chamber of Commerce refrigerator magnet, depicting a picture of a fiddle superimposed over a picture of galax leaves
- Morton Realty and Auction business card
- greeting card with artwork of galax leaves, with "thank you for being a part of our first 'Smoke on the Mountain'" imprinted in an informal script font on the inside.
- Gazette Press Printing note pad (printed by Acme Printing—um, just kidding)
- coupon for one free month of Wiredog internet service (logo of dog, no pig)
- Bank of America pencil, unsharpened (fill out your deposit slips in pen, please)
- Grayson National Bank keychain, made, according to the sticker on it, in China

- koozie from a local law firm specializing in, among other things listed on the koozie, DUI (good thing they gave judges something to keep their beers cold)

Bag #2 (logoed AXA Advisors plastic bag):
- AXA four-color informational brochure (what a coincidence)
- AXA notepad (did you guys get it printed at Gazette Press?)
- Papermate pen (likely supplied by someone other than Papermate directly)
- 5 Life Savers: 3 peppermint, 1 cherry, 1 grape (unconfirmed if this mix was random or planned)

For all that, the word *goodie* might be a synonym for *miscellaneous*, as anything and everything seems to have wound up in some goodie bag somewhere. Murphysboro gave out easily carried six-pack coolers. Caruthersville, a battery-powered multi-head electric screwdriver. And at various competitions in general: Salsa. Cookie cutters (on one occasion, in a shape you can clearly see is a house after someone points out that it's in the shape of a house). Used casino playing cards. Big-ass plastic paper clips emblazoned with local merchant names. Wood rulers (obsolete things have to end up somewhere, one supposes—why not a goodie bag?). Mini-jars of jelly. Pig-shaped lighters with flame-emitting snouts. Candles. Water bottles. Software on CD. Travel mugs. Car visor CD holders. Combination bottle openers/pop-top poppers. Mini Beanie Babies. Clock/calendar/alarm/calculators. Baskets of apples given by the Murphysboro competition, in the middle of apple country, in its early years. And sturdy rubber beverage huggies, personally purchased by the contest organizers and bearing their names, saying "Thank you for your support." You're welcome, Dave and Lynn McClellan.

The Kennett, Missouri, competition in 2004 sought to include a popular marinade and a barbecue sauce (a pretty tasty one, at that) in its judges' bags, but unfortunately there wasn't enough of each to go around. Marinade and barbecue sauce alternated in the goodie bags, and when the judges discovered this, there was an almost-polite scramble to grab the bag that had their favorite of the two. The marinade won that informal judging process.

Sometimes the best goodie related to the goodie bag is something that, by definition and by laws of both physics and metaphysics, can't be in the goodie bag: The bag itself. Mt. Carmel was known for its sturdy cloth duffel bag. Caruthersville found a sponsor to provide a goodie bucket—a Bud Light beer bucket.

Teams get goodies, too. In Galax, the team bag contains the same items as the judge bag, with the exception of a handsome Smoke on the Mountain logo cap replacing the apron. Caps are nice, but cooks and most other people generally have only one place on which to wear a cap at a time. MBA guidelines discourage promotional items in team goodie bags; they are quickly thrown away unless they're useful. The KCBS Ribberfest contest in Madison, Indiana, had the right idea in 2005. At that contest, Joyce Lindenberg of the Rub 'n' Que team approached teammate Wally Wathen during their setup on Friday night, showing him a roll of duct tape. "I've been looking for that," Wally said (he was worried that they'd forgotten to pack it). "Where'd you find it?

"In the goodie bag," Joyce said. Ribberfest also included a tape measure, a plastic cutting board and disposable plastic gloves (large, a good thing) for the teams, and packets of moist towelettes (from the Iowa Pork Board—slogan: "Pork—Now That's BBQ!") for both teams *and* judges. (Intriguingly, Ribberfest organizers gave toothpaste to the teams and toothbrushes to the judges, hand lotion to the teams and soap and shampoo to the judges. If there is a message in this choice of distribution, it remains inscrutable.) No duct tape for the judges (not even, as one cook quipped, to tape their mouths shut).

The other Ribberfest, the aforementioned Mt. Carmel, Illinois, competition of the cloth-duffel fame, in 2005 once again gave away a goodie bag that was in itself the primary goodie: an insulated pizza-delivery bag. Teams don't have any call to keep pizzas hot. They *do* have call to keep blind boxes and their contents hot as the blind runners dash the distance from cooksite to blind check-in—a distance that can be as long as half a mile, depending on the size of the competition. (Now if they don't deliver that blind box within thirty minutes…)

The Charlotte competition has some truly useful goodies: the meat itself (shoulders and ribs, though not hogs) are provided to teams free from sponsor Smithfield.

For a time, a brand of low-level "payment" in a *very* loose sense of the word was common on the circuit. Says Chuck Doan, "Used to be years ago a lot of teams were big on giving gifts—you know pens, coffee cups, bass boats, things like that."

At the Galax cooks meeting Friday night, Larry O tells the teams, "Gifts. This is an old one. I read this at every meeting." And then he rattles off the policy, bored by its insignificance: "If you have a gift for a judge, we ask that you hold it till the end. Invite him to come back, and give it to him then." He perks up a bit when he knows he can give the policy his own spark. "We don't want to see someone walking out of Gwatney going into the next booth with a Gwatney hat. Now, I saw *you*"—Larry points at John David of Natural Born—"running around with a koozie from Gwatney today."

"He bought me a free car," John deadpans.

"Hey, where's my Natural Born hat?" Al of Gwatney pipes in.

Larry continues, "Some people feel that if you give them a

hat, you're gonna get their top scores. It doesn't work that way. I don't think you're going to influence a judge with a towel or anything like that."

The giving of gifts to judges has now largely died. The jests about bribing have not. Later, during judging, Myron Mixon of Jack's Old South welcomes a judge into his area. "Wait a minute!" exclaims David Hair, who is bending over slightly near the judging table, holding a hundred-dollar bill. "I haven't put it under the table yet!"

A hundred is apparently the going price of joke currency. At the Friday cooks' meeting, Al Norton jokes, "Natural Born puts hundred-dollar bills under the plate."

"We get those in the blind," Larry O says. "No garnish in the box.…The only garnishment you can put in the blind box tomorrow is money. Taped to the top of the lid. We will remove it and Walt and I will dispense with it, that's not a problem. But anything else in there is not allowed and it will be removed."

Once, while repping a contest, Walt and Larry fielded a team-on-team accusation of, well, not bribery but of… something that may not have a word to describe it. When the cook of one team heard that two judges had bought alcohol for a competing team on Friday night (and helped the competitor consume said alcohol), that cook complained to the Crash Test Boys. The accusation probably was grounded in what Pat Burke of Tower Rock frowns on as judges being too "team friendly"—the judges party with particular teams, help them get set up, and in one case even helped a team prepare a blind box just before reporting in to judge that category—in the blind. That's obviously a case of sidestepping both the intent and the purpose of the blind judging. How can you examine a group of "anonymous" blind boxes if you've just packed one of the boxes yourself?

A judge being "team friendly" is a matter of perception. If

a judge singles out one or two teams and is generous with his assistance—or his alcohol—will he also be generous with his scores? Larry O says there should be no such problems. "If you can't judge a team fairly, you shouldn't be judging at all," he says.

And now the *real* payment to the judges is about to be distributed—the passes to the free food. Walt brings out the list of judges and the on-site assignment cards, and the assignments begin.

None of those so offered turn down the challenge of the triple. *More! More! More!*

Here's a true story about handing out assignments, from a competition not in Galax: In the judges' hospitality room on the Saturday morning of the main competition, a single judging table is set up, cordoned off with four decorative plants. On the other side of the plants, about thirty judges await assignments. "I need four judges," says the judging chairperson to the group. Hands shoot up. The chairperson considers, then decides on a process. "OK, the first four people to get to the chairs…" The music that stops in this game of musical chairs is the musical call to the judges. On cue of silence, several judges dash past the decorative plants. Four lucky ones nab slots.

That's how judging assignments are made…*if* you have a judging chairperson with a sense of humor and *if* you have a fun ancillary contest that needs adhere to no rules published anywhere at any time. The detail left out of the telling of this story was that the judging chairperson had announced, "I need four judges for *the bloody Mary competition*," and thus, shooting hands, four open chairs, scrambling judges.

Another way that judges are *not* selected came as a surprise to the organizer of a contest repped by Gary Countz and Sharon Countz some years back. The Countzes flew in for the competition; when the organizer greeted them at the airport, she said, "Didn't you bring the judges?" And wasn't joking.

(The Countzes worked to round up as many locals as they could, conducted a mini judging seminar, and managed to get the contest completed.)

Musical chairs aside, how are judges selected? The reps' computer creates a random matrix, assigning, say, Judge 1, Judge 5 and Judge 7 to Team 1, and Judge 1 and Judge 3 and Judge 4 to Team 2, and so on. Each on-site judge gets three teams; no two judges share more than one team. The program prints out assignment labels for the scorecards, and the cards are grouped, three to a judge. Separately, Walt and Carlene have assigned numbers to each judge of that category, and Walt and Larry now call off names…

Judge 1. "Terrie D'Amato."

"Here."

…and they work through the list, handing out the packets of cards.

For blind, the computer randomly assigns teams to each of the blind tables; judges are assigned table numbers and will judge the entries placed on that table. The dread of every team is to land on the same table as a good competitor; in larger competitions, usually only one team per table has a shot at making finals; they have to survive the table. And if two great entries split the vote, they can knock each other out of finals.

Five minutes of 10:00. The judges, scorecards in hand and volunteers beside them, are ready.

Five minutes of 10:00. Outside the judging chambers, up along Main Street, the teams in the first category are scrambling.

23
BLIND TRUSTS THAT FEW BANKS HAVE SEEN BEFORE

"You can put bacon in the box. It's fine." "As long as you don't spell your name out in it."

— Larry and Walt's instructions in blind-box preparation from Friday's cooks' meeting

Saturday morning, July 16. Nine-year-old Sean Carter with Smoked Encounters of the Third Swine leans over the work table, propping himself on his elbows, cupping a burnished bronze belt watch in his palms. He wears the same white polo shirt and black apron that his dad and his grandfather wear. The cover of the belt watch is flipped open, and Sean stares hard at the time. Time reads fourteen minutes till judging begins.

Fourteen minutes to deliver the blind box, dad Chris Carter prepares for his first category, working next to Sean, to the check-in area. Smoked Encounters is only about a minute's walk from check-in. Even so, time is tight; dad Chris works fast. Wearing yellow rubber gloves with orange palms, Chris has taken meat from the grill and placed it in a disposable aluminum steam-tray pan. At an elevated work table in the back, he works to find the best meat for the judges. The meat that he likes he puts into a blue bowl. It's the meat that, by look and by feel, he believes to be tender and attractive. He shies away from any fat that he discovers. When the bowl is full, he sets about arranging it in the blind box.

Up and down Main Street, teams are involved in similar scrambles. Three cooks work side-by-side at Gwatney. Four flank both sides of a work table, two by two, next door at Grillers. All along cooks' row, with the minute hand climbing toward the pinnacle 12, gloved hands are reaching, testing, placing. The conversation is clipped at almost every tent here in Galax, and all along the competition circuit, in all the categories:

"We're down to twenty."

People are reaching across the tables, getting in each other's way, grumbling, then working like clockwork the next instant.

"How you doin' for bark over there?"

"I don't know about bark."

At Gwatney, Hal Berry slips a gloved hand, palm up, underneath the darkened outer layer of the meat, lifts it gently to give Rick a big section from which to choose a sample. This outer layer is known as the bark. Ideally, it's a little firm, not tough, flavorful, not ashen. Teams make a point to give bark samples to judges because, when the meat is cooked right, the bark shows off the flavors of the rub and the bastes used to cook it. Teams like to include it in their presentations because bark cooked right signals that the whole cut of meat is cooked right. Larry O points out that bark is seen mostly on hog and shoulder. "On ribs, it's usually called 'burnt meat.'"

Cooked wrong, the bark can sink a team. If it looks dark, nasty. If it tastes of too much smoke, or tastes burned. If the rub hasn't settled into the meat and bites back at the judge. Some of these problems can adjusted with a brush of glaze to give the bark a moist, lighter look and a little flavor. Some use a bit of yellow food coloring to adjust the appearance of the meat.

Some use a red tent.

A number of teams—Natural Born Grillers among them—entertain their judges in red tents. Such tents cast warm color on the meat, say the adherents, making it look more appetizing. "When you get into that red tent, you're gonna see smoke ring like you never saw before," Larry O has told judges in training. "Red shirts, red aprons, whatever. It will affect the appearance of the meat." John Akins of Huish serves his judges under an orange awning, though it's a fact of his sponsor's colors instead of a presentation choice. John once encountered a problem with judges wearing transition-lens glasses, though. The combination of lenses darkened by daylight and an orange wash of light made the meat's smoke ring invisible.

"Eleven minutes."

Red tents of course do not help with presentation of the blind box. More often than not, blind boxes are opened not under natural daylight softened by red filtering, but under steely fluorescents that give the meat a little look of freezer blue. That's why vets advise teams to view their meat the way judges view them. Take your meat into a VFW hall and see how it looks under commercial lighting. Let it sit for a while, and *then* taste it. It's gonna sit for a while come competition time. As cook Jimmy Johnson says, "Better cook your meat so it tastes good cold." Teams are also advised to take pictures of their blind boxes just before they close them up and trot them off to check-in. Memory will sweeten the look of the box; the camera will tell the team what the judges looked at when scoring appearance.

Blind-box preparation is a frantic art, done differently from tent to tent. Some dip their meat in a light baste for added flavor before putting it in the box. Others glaze the meat itself with a pastry brush the way they glazed the bark. Some sprinkle a dash of rub over the meat, for flavor and for a special look. Some do none of the above, some all, some a combination.

"Big pieces."

Part of the reason for packing at sprint pace is to keep the meat as warm as possible. It's not unusual to see one team member designated to do nothing but be the lid-keeper—the job David Hair is fulfilling at Jack's Old South. Cook works the meat, lid closed. Cook moves to place the meat in the blind box, lid open—then closed to retain heat. At Pig Pounda, Gary has stationed his whole hog blind box prep right at the grill; other teams usually pull meat into an aluminum steam tray and take it to the "kitchen" to complete the blind box prep. Gary keeps a bucket of ice water nearby. He plunges his gloved hands in to chill them, works the hot meat until it nearly burns him, plunges again.

"How's your time and how's your sauce?"

"I got my sauce."

Rick Dalton is chopping meat, not for eating, but for lining the bottom of the blind box. The chopped meat insulates the box and provides additional heat and, steaming, moisture. If the serving meat drips any fat, the chopped meat will absorb it and disguise it from the judge.

"Good texture to it."

"Down to five."

The teams then carefully arrange the meat so that it looks attractive, appetizing, when the judges open the box. They don't have the presentation tools that restaurants or even other barbecue competition circuits have. No garnish is allowed. Nothing but the meat itself, and the sauce. The cooks can season and sauce the meat right in the box, or send in one or two foam-plastic cups of sauce that judges not only *can* taste along with the meat—they *must* taste meat and sauce together if a sauce is offered. Stories are rampant about great meat killed by bad sauce.

"Too tough."

For the hog entry, teams must place samples of the shoulder, the loin and the ham into the box. Newer teams tend to dump all three in, with no particular segregation. More accomplished teams arrange sections of shoulder, of loin, of ham and of bacon (which is to be savored and not to be judged), highlighted by strips of bark, with as much composition as a Mondrian.

White foam plastic is not part of the color scheme. Larry O cautions new teams to make sure the box is full, that the presentation doesn't allow a lot of container to show, to imply to the judge that you have a lot of meat of good quality, and to help the sample as a whole to retain heat. "We tell the teams," he says, "that they have to feed four hungry judges…and Walt."

"That's overcooked; take it out."

"Behind you."

Teams can compose their presentation Mondrianically, but they are not allowed to "mark" their blind boxes. Nothing that would be considered a trademark that judges would recognize and associate with a specific team. No writing or markings on the box. No punctures—not even a toothpick intended to keep the lid secure. No duct tape. No inclusion of bones (in shoulder and whole hog) or foil, and certainly nothing that could be related to a team, such as topping rib sections with grilled pineapple). In fact, nothing is allowed in the box but meat and any covering sauce. No garnish. And, as rep Randy McGee once had to instruct, no hair. "The hair part's not in the rules," he says. Yet, all warnings in life are based on actual incidents, unfortunately. Randy says simply, "It was gross."

Bones, of course, are allowed in the rib blind box, where cooks pack meat in two- or three-bone sections. Never single bones on the MBA circuit, though single bones are common on other circuits. Sections with at least two bones help retain heat, and give the judge the opportunity to "tear" the meat in testing texture. At one Murphysboro cook, Terry Black of Super Smokers knew his ribs weren't on the money; they were tough, needed another forty-five minutes or so on the grill. Terry's teammate Skip Steele prepped the rib blind box and gave it to Terry to deliver to turn-in. Says Terry, "I get in front of the booth as I'm getting ready to turn it in and I can see Skip, and I'm like, 'You know, I'd better look in here and see what he did.' I lifted the lid up and he's got a bunch of single bones laying in there." The MBA-reviled single bones. "I shut it and looked at him and said, 'You're a very funny man. You are a *very* funny man.' I'm laughing. I'm just laughing the whole way to turn it in."

"I want this thing packed slap-assed full."

Sean is on the watch. Three minutes. Completing the blind box is timed so that the runner has enough time to get it to the blind check-in as close to deadline as possible. The runners know exactly how long it takes to take a brisk walk from cooksite to check-in. They or someone on their team have timed it. Likely more than once. In Galax, the run is no more than a couple of minutes. Three blocks, tops. At larger competitions, it can be a half-mile or longer.

Boxes close. Some teams on longer hikes wrap the boxes in foil, or tuck them into insulated food delivery bags to hold the heat. Thusly secured, they're handed to the runner.

Jack's Old South is not using any insulation today. Myron places the last bit of meat in the box, David closes it, Myron pops a sample into David's mouth and sends him on his way.

When Jimmy G. of Carbondale Eagles darts away from the prep area to deliver the blind box, he regularly announces, "Blind man walking." Here, today, Al Norton shoos runner Lance Freemon away. "Blind, you're outta here. Drive careful."

As David Hair walks his blind box to the judging area, Ricky Miller spots him and calls out, "You need some help carrying that up there?"

David darts his I'm-having-fun smile and a *yeah-right* raise of the eyebrows. "You let me tote yours and I'll let you tote mine."

Moments later, Ricky is transporting a red insulated container the size of a small cooler, holding it by the carrying straps,

24 THE BLIND FEEDING THE BLIND

"They cut me a piece of shoulder. I'm like 'What? You cut me a piece of meat? ...That's like the worst thing you could do.' No, this will never do."

— Judge Alex Brown on the frowned-upon practice of slicing meat in Memphis in May competitions

Saturday morning. While the teams deliver their blind boxes, Larry prepares his blind judges in a short briefing before going to the judging table. In other competitions judges are brought into the blind area and then given their briefing. "We're gonna wait," Larry says. "In another three and a half minutes we're gonna go in there. I like to do the briefing in advance, so that we go in there, we open up the boxes and we eat hot pork. I don't like cold pork and I don't think you do either."

"In there" refers to the blind-judging area. Tables, their tops wrapped in red plastic, are prepped there. Stiff paper plates, plastic knife and fork positioned on paper napkin all neat and tidy, packets of moist towelettes, crackers, pencils (sharpened), toothpicks, bottled water and yellow scorecards.

Runners come through the bank's back door and give their samples to the volunteers waiting there while Walt supervises, pointy finger at the ready. Tango delivers the Natural Born blind box; Nottingham is right behind with two covered cups of sauces. Volunteers Pamela Russell and Brittany Hall check the entry in, removing the team label from the box and placing it on a log sheet. The box and the sauce cups are numbered with grease pencil, and the number jotted on the log sheet. After being inspected for foreign material (foil and the rest), the box goes to one of the tables in the blind room.

Four judges are assigned to each table. "What we're going to do," Larry is instructing those eight judges, "is we're going to open all the boxes at once. We look at them, we judge the appearance score first. We're gonna mark all the appearance scores, then sit down. When everybody's seated at your table, then you know it's OK to get in there and mess them up."

John Akins is one of those judges, and this is part of what he's come to Galax to see—how other teams are prepping their blind boxes. "Our downfall is in the blind, as it is for everybody," he says. "You win or lose in the blind pretty much. To be able to see what actually goes on—I mean, you hear it and people tell you and all this and that, but to be able to sit there at that table, look at everything, taste everything, and go through the cycle of judging that stuff, it's a lot different than what you think."

In the briefing, Larry is saying, "When you get in there, you can talk about anything you want, other than the entries. I want you to have fun today. It's a lot more fun if you get good meat, but I think you're gonna have some good stuff in there."

Don't talk about the entries—independent judging, and all—and don't send other signals, either. When Randy McGee gives his blind briefings, he tells judges, "There's no *mmmmm-mm!s*, and there's no *uccchhhhhhhhh!s*." If you have a spitter, be discreet; don't give it away. "You don't want the judge next to you to miss the rapture of that moment."

Walt tells of a competition he judged where he knew he was in for "rapture" when he reached for a sample the other three judges had already tasted, and found them all watching him to see his reaction.

Larry tells of another competition—ribs category. "I had a sparerib—it looked like a dinosaur bone—it was about this long. I went to pull the bones apart, and the bone broke." Now *that's* overdone. "I did laugh out loud. You're not supposed to do that."

The quick briefing covers other basics:

Meat served with sauce must be judged with sauce.

"Please don't remove any of the food, unless it's already in your stomach." The leftovers are for the volunteers at the grazing table.

"No double-dipping with the sauce." Spoon the sauce onto your plate. Don't dunk meat into the team's sauce container, munch on it, and dunk it again.

At the end of the briefing, one of the judges asks, "What if we have a conflict in blind?"

Larry O replies, "Then I really need to talk to you."

In KCBS blind judging (which is the only judging done at KCBS competitions), six judges are seated per table. A seventh judge is declared the "table captain." The table captain has several similarities to the captain at a restaurant. He or she makes sure everyone is seated and has the proper utensils. (Remember, the only accepted judging utensil is a pencil.) He opens each blind box at the beginning of each category's judging, and displays it to the judges at the table one by one, like a restaurant dessert waitress showing the evening's confections. He doesn't eat. (He's welcome to gobble stuff off the grazing table later, though.) And he examines each judge's scoresheet, looking for incomplete markings, as diligently as a restaurant captain might examine a credit card slip for the proper minimum calculation of the tip.

In MBA/Galax land, the blind judges open their own boxes, and simply gather round the table to evaluate the look of the meat. John Akins is now starting to see what he set out to see—especially in presentation. "You were able to see that some people put a lot of thought into how they put that stuff in that box," he'll say later. Mondrian. "Some of it was kinda funny how people would just throw it in there." Non-Mondrian.

After evaluating the entries' appearance, the judges set to "messing them up." They draw lines on their plates and number the quarters so they can keep track of the entries as they bring them to the plates. Just like the on-site judges will be doing shortly—a bit later in the process because they are at this moment listening to cooks describe their grills and their cooking processes—the blind judges squeeze the meat, tug at it, taste it.

Larry reiterates, "No double-dipping with the sauce" as a double-briefing on the double-dipping.

After tasting each sample, the judges place tick marks near the scores they initially believe the sample deserves. As the judges taste other entries, those marks might be erased and reticked. If a judge has trouble deciding which of the samples is better than another, he or she can return to the sample and re-taste. In KCBS, once your score is down, it is written in barbecue stone.

Unless a judge has difficulty deciding final scores, blind judging moves relatively quickly, and can be done in twenty or twenty-five minutes, while on-site judging takes a full hour. This gives Walt a jump on score entry. He begins inputting the blind scores in the computer as soon as all the scorecards are completed and approved.

Scoring completed, the judges chat about which one samples they preferred. This is part tradition and part Larry's request: "I ask you to stick around the tables afterwards and share with each other what you thought was the best. That's where you really learn—talking to the other judges." A couple swap tables and sample what the other judges had. Larry approaches the first table and asks the judges there, "Which one was the worst?" The judges point. Larry turns away and mock-calls down the hall, "Walt, I got one for you." He smiles as he turns back to the judges at the table. "He falls for it every time."

And the judges fall for the joke none of the time.

MEL AND MS. PIGGIE RESIST THE TEMPTATION TO FOOL AROUND

"Focus."

– Written on a whiteboard inside the Pig Pounda trailer, underlined three times

Saturday morning, 9:55 am. Mel stands guard.

Mel is the silver metal pig figurine, about a foot high, that stands on all fours outside the Natural Born Grillers' gate. He's named after a Memphis-area watering hole that serves beverages to Griller members on occasion, and, despite his silver metallic sheen and the fact that he's wearing a couple of strands of Griller party beads, he looks natural enough that at least one dog has come up to Mel and sniffed his behind.

Mel's waiting for the first judge.

So is Ms. Piggie, next door. Ms. Piggie is a pink rural mailbox on a table immediately inside the Gwatney gate. The mailbox door is cut in the shape of a pig's face; the box itself, comprising Ms. Piggie's body, is supported by four wooden legs.

At gates up and down the Galax contest midway, teams are anticipating. The blind runners have been dispatched. On-site judges will arrive momentarily.

John David knows what to do when they arrive. "I'll run

my trap," he says.

"That's what you're here for," Birm says.

At the gate of Jack's Old South, David stands behind Myron. With one hand, David laboriously traces large circles around Myron's back and makes ratcheting noises. "Time to wind him up again."

Greeters standing outside their booths watch down toward the hospitality room.

"Judges walking."

They're pretty obvious when they hit the street. They'd be obvious even without their badges and name tags and without the escorts wearing T-shirts labeled "Volunteer." They tote clipboards and wear aprons and sometimes hats festooned with pins—the memorabilia distributed by previously attended contests. And maybe sometimes a pair of those pink suspenders Larry so enjoys giving out. The judges are variously power-walking or strolling or shuffling lethargically—whatever it takes to time their arrival at their designated teams shortly before judging is scheduled to begin. Judges hit the first whole hog teams at 10:00 sharp. If they arrive earlier, they are instructed to wait, standing away from the site or facing away from the team so the team doesn't feel rushed. Not that anything is going to prevent a team from feeling rushed. Shoulder judges are scheduled to arrive at 11:15. Sharp. Rib judges, 12:30.

The volunteers that accompany the judges—referred to in Galax, as they often are, as "ambassadors"—are tasked with making certain their judges stick to schedule, and get to the right place. They are not, as Larry instructs at the judges' briefing, "packhorses." They are not to carry cameras or purses or umbrellas, and especially not the judges' scorecards. "It's very important that you never let the ambassador handle the scorecards. We have teams that are still convinced that they influence them."

At that morning's ambassadors' briefing, one of the volunteers asked Larry O, "Do we have a diagram of the different stations?"

"We have a map," Larry said, and joked, "And we're keeping it…. Most of the teams have their names, we have area signs out there. It starts with Kings Cooking—the very first one, number 1—and goes all the way up to the end. The very last one is Natural Born Grillers, and that's number 12. They all have been given an area sign that's out in front of their booth, so you look for that sign."

"When the judges get their scorecards," said Carlene Poole, "they will say area 3, area 9, area 6. The number corresponds to what they are judging."

"If you want to look at this," Larry said, "this is an actual scorecard."

"Don't touch it, Stacie!" Carlene called out. "We'll be dusting for fingerprints!"

Larry said, "The scorecard will tell you the name of the team, and also that little label tells you the area number. So you know number 1's here, number 12's here, so 6 is about in the middle."

Carlene added, "Hopefully."

At 10 sharp, Terrie D'Amato has her untouched-by-human-ambassadors scorecard for Gwatney's whole hog at the top of the stack of three on her clipboard. When Terrie arrives at Gwatney, Al Norton—mustachioed, energetic, theatrical Al Norton—greets her.

The clock is running.

Fifteen minutes.

Al accepts Terrie's judge's evaluation stub, torn at the perforation from the lefthand side of the scorecard. "Let's see if you have an invitation here," he says broadly. He checks for his team name, and the judging order. "That's right." Opening the pig-shaped mailbox, he says, "Let me feed Ms. Piggie here first so we can keep her happy and she's content. She squeals and hollers if we don't keep her happy."

Next door, John David takes his judge's stub and holds it in the air. "You know what this is?" he says. "This is the best thing that's happened to you today."

Down at Hawg Wild, Jeff Holmes is surprised when one of his judges hands him the entire scorecard, and not just the judges' evaluation stub torn from the left-hand side. *New judge*, he thinks.

"Welcome to Gwatney Company's Championship Barbecue Team," Al is saying after feeding the piggy mailbox. "Allow me to present our head cook, Mr. Rick Dalton."

"Terrie, welcome," Rick says as he invites Terrie up the two steps to his main rig. Rick's trailer houses the hog cooker at the back, two Backwoods cookers at the front, and a small kitchen arrangement with sinks and cabinets running the sides between. Rick ushers Terrie to the hog cooker and begins his presentation. He speaks directly and quickly, and—especially in presentations to barbecue judges—puts the brakes on certain words for emphasis. "Have yourself a seat, stand up, we're going to stay right up here, sit on the counter if you want to, it doesn't matter. This is relaxing, it's fun—if it's not, I know you're not going to do it and we're not either."

It may be relaxing, it may be fun, but you can't immediately tell that by the formality of all the team members not directly involved with the presentation. Wearing the team colors—usually polo shirts with team member name and team name and/or logo embroidered on it—the non-talking team members stand watching the judge and the presenter, often at parade rest. The first time Annie Sisson judged on-site, the members of the Coors barbecue team were in this sort of respectfully quiet lineup. This made Annie a bit nervous, and she mentioned that. At the presenter's instruction, the team members turned around, and, still in line, still at parade rest, looked away as she ate.

Not all team members are present upfront. Work for upcoming categories continues apace throughout the presentation. Most of that work takes place behind the scenes, but occasionally it peeks out from behind the tent wall. While John David presents the hog, Birm opens up the Big Show to baste shoulders.

John David tells judge Arthur that Grillers use charcoal laced with small chunks of hickory. "Along with that we want something a little sweeter so we come back with nice, sweet apple wood."

Next door, Rick sidles up to the hog cooker. "You have to have a grill to cook," he says. "Two smoke stacks. You've got a dense piece of meat in the ham, you've got a dense piece of meat in the shoulder, the ham being the densest. Two vents on each door. If we're behind on our ham temperature, to get it moved up to where we need it, we can dampen it and raise this end twenty to twenty-five degrees. On that end, that would have overcooked the shoulder. When we first put our hog on, Terrie, we put it on at 180 degrees. It's a cold smoke. The hog has pores on its skin like we do. We put it on 240 or whatever on your temperature, you're going to seal it, it's not going to take any smoke flavor. We use a lot of hickory sawdust."

Down at Sweet Swine, Pat Rooney says to his judge, "People go 'Oh, hickory, it can be a little bit overpowering at times.' Well, to me it's gotta have hickory to be true southern barbecue." Sweet Swine don't do that true Grayson County barbecue. A couple of weeks before the competition began, Judy and Tom Barr were discussing the event with Leesa Morris. "Tom was telling me," Judy said, "about a gentleman who was invited to cater with a smoker. And the guy that was catering evidently didn't know squat and he put pine in there."

"He thought softwood was wood," Tom Barr said.

Judy said, "And the meat tasted like a Christmas tree."

Soft wood creates sticky, resinous smoke, which in turn creates sticky, resinous meat. Yes, the primary crop in Grayson County, Virginia, may be the Christmas tree, but barbecuers don't need to smoke any more of them into existence. And even in Grayson County, the only thing that should taste like Christmas trees are Christmas trees. (Well, even they might not taste like Christmas trees. They might taste like chicken. Has anyone actually tried to taste a Christmas tree?)

"There's a way to use hickory and a way to overuse it," Pat says. "We understand that at times it's going to get overdone, so what we do to mellow it out at the finish, the last hour of cooking, we switch to apple for a mellow balance of flavor."

"Not just any apple wood—it's always center cut," John David says over in his booth.

"We have two sticks of hickory wood," Rick is saying at Gwatney. "Notice no bark. Bark has a tendency to be harsh, to be bitter. You don't like it, I don't like it and the hog doesn't either." (At a later competition, Rick will tell a judge he's familiar with, "The only person I know who eats bark off of wood is Al. He chews on it all the time.")

Hickory and apple are only two of the hardwoods used in smoking. Others include oak, cherry, alder, pear, pecan, peach, maple, plum…It's been reported that WCBCC rib champion Porkosaurus uses orange and lemon wood in their fires. Carbondale Eagles use a touch of sassafras. The choices depend on cooks' tastes and on, frankly, availability. The legendary Apple City team of Mike Mills and Pat Burke fame had, as the name "Apple City" might suggest, access to abundant supplies of applewood. Jack's Old South has similar access to peach.

Sometimes availability applies to charcoal, as well. Rib Ticklers out of Batesville, Arkansas, left for a competition without enough charcoal, and watched for a Sam's Club along the way where they could purchase in bulk. Twelve hours of driving later, and "we didn't see a Sam's," says David Wilkins.

"That's because you were driving too fast," says Tickler teammate John Harris.

(He had to drive fast, one might say, to live up to the slogan on the back of the Rib Ticklers trailer: "Haulin' Ash.")

They ended up buying small bags of charcoal at a local gas station.

The charcoals themselves vary. Lump or chunk charcoal (basically pieces of charred wood, unprocessed) vs. briquettes (charred wood compressed and held together with starches or other binding material). Lump leaves less ash and burns hotter (which can be an advantage or disadvantage, depending on the cooker). The binders in lower-quality briquettes can affect taste.

And type of charcoal can be dictated by sponsorships. If you land cash or charcoal itself from a sponsor, you'll happily use it. (Or display it proudly and use something else.)

"We cook him for twenty hours, two hundred and twenty degrees," John David is saying of his hog. "One-hundred-forty-seven-pound pig with the legs on—cut the legs off, and it's about 140 pounds like that. Cooked down to about 130, 125. And it is... *unreal.*"

At Gwatney, before opening the grill, Rick Dalton is saying, "This one's Sweet Cheeks, that's her name, 118th edition." Terrie chuckles; she's judged Rick before, and she knows that, as Rick explains, "We name every one of our hogs the same thing." Next door, Natural Born Grillers have named their hog "The Lovely Leesa." This appalls Leesa Morris, Galax Chamber President and inspiration of the name, until the Grillers explain that such naming is done in honor. It is, as Judy Brannock would say, a good thing. Yes, but not in *all* cases. As the story goes, one team named each of its hogs after team members' ex-wives, a practice that lasted until the ex-wives found out about this practice (or, likely, until they ran out of ex-wives, which may have covered hog-naming for a considerable number of competitions).

Hog-naming is another practice that seems to be fading. Says Gary Kerce, "I try not to name the pig. It's fun and all that, but I don't get personal with this thing you're fixin' to eat."

For some, the naming is very intentionally personal. Porky's Pride once named their hog Killer B. During prep, the portable workshop sawhorse that supported the hog collapsed on one side, allowing the tray underneath the hog to practically fall into Clara Scarritt's lap, scraping her thighs. "That bitch tried to kill me!" Clara said. Thus the name, and thusly they got even and dispatched Killer B.

Hawg Wild has done a little hawg-naming, itself. Jeff Holmes raises his own hogs, and one had a broken leg. As a joke he named it "I-Lean" when he decided to cook it. When at the competition he opened the grill for one of the hog judges, the judge said, "Did you name your hog?"

Jeff said, "Yeah, we named her I-Lean."

He got a noticeable reaction from…judge Eileen.

In the I-Lean spirit, he may well have called the hog he cooked previous to Galax "Harry." Jeff explains: "In D.C. I did something that's not been done before. I raise my own hogs, and I said, 'After we kill this hog, I'm not going to prep the head. I want the head just like it is.' So from behind the ears forward I left all the hair and everything on it. When the judge came on board I says, 'You're going to see something you probably haven't seen before; I like to do something a little bit different.' I raised that hood up and yeah, it was different. Lady judges. Ladies have better taste buds than men—sometimes they have more taste buds in their mouths. I like when they have some woman judges involved. But their perception of some things is different. They acted disgusted with the looks, so they dropped me. I got eleventh." He laughs. "But I thought it was something different."

Even something the same can cause some initial shocks. There's the story of the on-site whole hog judge coming to her first team. When the team opened the grill for the first category, the judge hesitated. "That's a pig," the judge finally forced out.

Surprise! A pig at a pig-cooking contest! In defense of this possibly apocryphal judge, this may have been her first competition, and there's a first-time pig-viewing for every judge.

At the 2005 judging seminar, Red Hot Smokers and Natural Born had done a mock presentation of shoulders. Afterward, during discussion of what they'd learned from the presentations, one of the students said, "I have never seen barbecue that color, that dark." He'd never seen bark on a cut of meat. "And when I first saw that, it looked like a little shriveled up piece of...something's dead."

"It *is* dead," Larry O replied. "He's not going to be asked back if it was otherwise."

In Galax, Rick Dalton is about to introduce to Terrie the also-dead but gorgeous *That's-a-pig!* named Sweet Cheeks, 118th edition, "decorated like none of the above, anywhere.... As seen on TV, here we go." He opens the grill to expose the cooked hog, a luscious mahogany color, lying on its back. "Good color, no burn-up, no nothin'." All evidence of the foil the hog has been wrapped in is gone. Green, white and red grapes fill the belly cavity; more lie upon leafy lettuce before the pig. Discreetly placed apples hide Sweet Cheeks's eyes. Pineapples flank the hog; a small American flag rises from behind it. One sawed-off leg sports a watch. Sweet Cheeks clutches the stem of a rose in its teeth, and jauntily wears strands of silver beads. "Been to Mardi Gras—we had to chase it down Bourbon Street to catch up with it. Tells time. Ever heard of a hog telling time? We got the rose in the mouth, what a darlin'."

The grapes, the apples, the pineapples—all represent a tradition of garnishing the grill, of framing the meat and trying to wow the judges. In a lull between presentations, Myron beckons Carlene and Larry into the Jack's Old South booth. "Come and look at this shoulder." He indicates the open shoulder grill. The competition shoulders are surrounded by greenery and peaches. Myron says, "y'all come and look at this. Nick is decorating this. Nick, you're scaring me."

"Stayed up too long," Nick says.

"Isn't that pretty? Did a good job, didn't he?"

"Where are the shoulders?" David says.

Myron laughs. "Behind that purple kale."

A few weeks later, Nick ends up utilizing the ultimate garnish when in Charlotte he lashes eight-foot branches from the fallen pecan tree onto the supports of the main awning of the Jack's booth.

Almost all the grill garnishes are fresh—but not Gwatney's. "We use all plastic fruit on our hog display," Rick says later. It was wife Kathy's idea. "Most of the good teams will spend seventy-five, a hundred an event to buy all those vegetables, especially if you do all three." Though Kathy hasn't traveled to Galax, her mark is there. "No one can decorate or set it up better. If the tablecloth is bent one-quarter of an inch somewhere, she's on it. Absolutely perfect."

Nonetheless, judges are trained to ignore the garnish. "It's not a fruit and vegetable contest," as is often heard. The garnish is for show, and not for eating (for which Gwatney judges can be thankful). It all kind of boils down to the KC Masterpiece barbecue sauce advertising slogan: "Broccoli would be better if it were made of meat and slathered in BBQ sauce."

Fifteen minutes.

Later that day, Cody Cline is spending a little too much time talking about his grill, and isn't allowing for enough time at the table. This is understandable. The grills are self-made; he's proud of them. He's also falling into a typical young-team trap. Judge Sharon Bassard forgives him, though.

Largely, Cody's presentation to Sharon (and all the presentations up and down team row) mirrors the way cooks—especially the Neandertalesque roast-with-fire cooks that competition barbecue ultimately evolved from—show off their skills (lacking the cave paintings, of course). Show fire. Talk about secret cook stuff. Show off food. Tear food apart proudly with hands and distribute to gathered hungry souls. There are some innovations—disposable rubber gloves, injection needles, in-cooker water pans, thermometers and aluminum foil. And innovations yet to come. Sharon Bassard has seen the future; like the Edsel, however, it's likely to be a future that won't catch on. "One team I went to in Memphis this year had a laptop," she says. The head cook led her over to it, clicked the mouse, and asked her to watch. "He actually did a little show of where the pig was raised, and the farm." Pork meets PowerPoint. At the time, Sharon was thinking, "This is taking this to a whole 'nother level."

If presentations reach that level, they'll likely sink back into the primordial barbecue sauce quickly enough. Gimmickry in on-site presentations comes and goes and mainly goes. It's the meat that counts. Teams have supplied live musical accompaniment for example, an accordionist at a competition in Knoxville. It's the meat. Teams have employed tuxedo-garbed greeters and head cooks with French chef accouterments. It's the meat. A team in St. Louis gave their presentation as a skit, portraying settlers who were about to pack up their gear and Go West, Young Man (the theme of that particular competition). Delightful stuff; it's the meat.

Part one of the presentation is done. Cooker described; hardwood identified; cooking time and temp detailed. It's time to eat. "Birmingham, you gonna bring us some while I tell him about our rubs and sauces? Come on over here to the table."

Up and down the midway, the meat is being served, the sauces are being described, the rubs defined. The meat is being sold, the cooks' preferred cooking processes are being sold, the teams themselves are being sold.

Overheard from cooks up and down the midway in presentations in Galax and on the competition circuit in general, in the whole hog category, the shoulder category, the ribs category:

"That's unbelievable, isn't it? That oughta be against the law."

"What I do is every two hours, I baste it with my secret whammy-jammy."

Some devotees of non-MBA circuits decry the presentation at MBA competitions. The decriers believe that judges can be bamboozled by facile gab and a slick line.

"And if I break into the meat here… Look at that. That is just beauteous the way it just comes apart like that. And that moisture is glistening. That is what we're looking for."

"I named that sauce after my wife. I call it my sweet goodness. She's got a little sweetness to her but she's got a little bite to her sometimes."

MBA adherents counter that the presentation is *not* ancillary, it is not supplemental, it is not garnish. Presentation is a category unto itself, scored separately. It's somewhat analogous to geometry tests; having the right answer is pretty important, but you're also graded on how you arrived at that answer.

It's the story of the grill: "It's the greatest cooker I've had," Chris Carter is explaining to a judge. "It holds temperature perfect, and—I don't know if you're familiar with the Jedmaster—the guy patented the design. It's a ring of fire in the firebox. It's a firebox that's portable—you pull it out—and it's got a trough about six inches wide and six inches deep, and it's in a circle. You can fill it with about forty-eight pounds of charcoal and wood. You light it on one end and it burns like a fuse, slowly all the way around. It can burn for eighteen hours. Never have to refill it."

Next door at Pure and Sinful: "This thing flies."

It's the story of the cooking: "The main thing we do about our ribs that's kind of different from what a lot of people do," Rick Dalton is saying, "we put them on at 240 degrees. That's what the thermometer says. Simple thing. Any time you open the door to a smoker, you're losing temperature. You're losing time. We cook fourteen, sixteen slabs of ribs to a contest. Takes us anywhere from three to five minutes to load them in there. We've lost twenty-five to thirty degrees, so we're at our 210 that we like to cook 'em at right then. You can't have your temperature going up and down on ribs. The meat will do funny things, without a shadow of a doubt."

It's the story of the rub: "I want you to try our 'Million-Dolla' rub," John David is saying at Natural Born. "We call it the Million-Dolla rub because that's how much it cost us to develop it." He puts a spoonful on the judge's plate to sample. He explains that this rub is good not only for pork, but for chicken and fish. And he touts it as being good in mashed potatoes, in popcorn and in eggs. "There's only one thing this rub isn't good in. Your eye." This is not entirely a joke. Once as John David sprinkled some of the rub, a breeze sent some into his eye. Million-Dolla has a touch of cayenne, and cayenne is not good in eyeballs.

Good flavoring is good flavoring. Jimmy Gevas once described the Carbondale Eagles rub to a judge: "It's a very versatile rub—we use it on all three of our pork products. I especially like it on egg sandwiches."

It's the story of the sauce: "You're saying, you're talking about a vinegar sauce, why are you pouring a tomato sauce?" Richard Lackie is saying at Sweet Swine. "Well, in order to glaze, you're not going to use a vinegar sauce. So what I decided to do was modify the vinegar sauce by turning it into tomato sauce. You know how you do that? You add ketchup...you also add a little bit of honey for sweetness and for texture so it's gonna stick, You also add a little bit of molasses for richness. So that's the finishing sauce. Now when you taste it, it's very balanced."

*It's the story of the **differences:*** "This is not a wet rib," Richard Lackie is saying. "It is not a dry rib. It's what we call a muddy rib. You get just dirty enough to know you're eating barbecue, but you can still go out and do something formal."

And, well, it's the fun. At the Tennessee Funfest and at other competitions, John David used his "ten" routine, saying to the judge: "I want you to note the *ten*derness." Ten. The top score a judge can give a team. Ranking a team at the top of every category is known as "giving them your tens." So John David's emphasis is a playful, self-conscious and not unsubtle request of the judge. "How do you spell 'ten'?" he says. "One zero." He goes on to point out that his team has *ten* members (well, maybe if you round down), and that they wear size *ten* shoes (again, in John David's case, if you round down). "And he's going to tell you a story about me and embarrass me," G.T. interrupts sheepishly, "so I'll embarrass myself. It took me *ten* tries to get out of the tenth grade . . ."

Now, as the tale goes, a KCBS cook and an MBA judge are talking. "What I don't understand," the cook says, "is how a judge coming into my tent and peering into my grill and checking to see how clean my tablecloth is makes my meat taste better."

The judge replies, "It makes your meat taste better...next time...after I come back and chat with you about what I tasted. With pure blind judging, you get scores. Not whys."

Clara Scarritt, the rib cook at Porky's Pride (the number eight team on the MBA circuit going into the weekend of

Galax), craves judges' feedback, craves the whys. "Whether they like the product or not, they give me constructive criticism. Whether it's negative or positive, I want it. You know, *It was a little too spicy, it wasn't spicy enough; a little too sweet, wasn't sweet enough.* And we can adjust, because you *have* to adjust to keep with the competition—you *have* to adjust." As an example, "When we first started, it took us two years to make sweet ribs."

"We did not like sweet ribs at all," teammate Boyce Winters says.

"But the judges said, you gotta cook sweet ribs because that's what the judges want. So we went to the candy-assed ribs. And that's what's winning. It might go backwards to the dry rib with the sauce again." And if it does, it will be judges' feedback that will allow Clara to track the trend.

"A hog will pick up three pounds a day eating."

"So will a barbecue judge."

Judges are instructed to make the feedback constructive and in the context of what the team did right. "You gotta remember," Larry says. "A cook is like an artist. They're sensitive, too. You don't go back and say, 'Well, I would do this...'" Offer praise first, and then..."say 'In my opinion, the piece that I had was too tender. I'm sure the rest of it was good, but what I had was too tender.'" Tell the team what you tasted; *don't* tell them how to cook. John David tells the story of a judge who gave him some cooking tips the day Grillers went on to take grand champion. "I was like, 'If we'd done that, we'd *really* have done good.'"

And don't, as one judge did, go back to a top-ten team and call them out on "a rookie mistake."

It helps if the feedback is the truth. Lisa Puryear was discussing judges Friday night in Galax. "We've had judges come back and say, I gave you a perfect score," she said. "And we get our scorecard, and it's not a perfect score."

"Well, that's fine," Dan said to her.

"They need to tell us the truth, so we can make our product better."

"Now wait a minute," Dan said. "Do you tell them the truth when we're doing our presentation?"

The pause was long. Lisa said, "That's part of presentation," and Dan ripped into a laugh.

For the good teams, the content of constructive criticism usually comes as no surprise. Judge Arthur once went back to Flying Pigs; head cook Chris Mills greeted him simply by saying, "Too dry." Cooks know their products. Skip Steele of Super Smokers once delivered a rack of ribs to judge Annie Sisson by suspending the rack on one upraised finger—a basketball without the spin—clearly communicating "they ain't done yet."

Jane Barber is one of those judges who makes a point to return to chat with teams. When judging was over in Galax, she visited Cody Cline at Nervous Wreck to talk shoulder. Cody would say later. "She said, everything was great, she said, first time, work on the presentation, she said, I know you get nervous. She said, you had a good product, she said it could be a tad more tender. That means it all to me there. It's about as good a compliment as you get. Because you know, people, if they think enough to come back and tell you this stuff, that's one hell of a compliment—that's my opinion."

Jane also judged John Bennett's ribs. "He told me to come back to critique him," she says. "I tried, but he had already packed up and left—a shame. He had a pretty good product, but it needed some tweaking."

"I've been a salesman all my life and I've always been told to keep your customer at eye level. I can't do it. I can't reach across the table and do it. I've got to stand up for that part."

"Wasn't that tender like a mama's love?"

And some say that the presentation helps the judges get better, that they learn what to look for from the cooks. At the very least, the cooks are getting the opportunity to point out areas of quality that the judge might have overlooked. Natural Born Grillers as an example takes that opportunity with their shoulder presentation: "You ever hear of the pearl of the shoulder? The pearl of the shoulder is the muscle right here. It's the densest piece of meat in the shoulder. It's closest to the middle of the shoulder, also. The reason it's called the pearl is because it's white as a pearl. Now here at Natural Born Grillers we call it the ruby. It's got a nice smoke ring all the way through it."

"Any questions so far? Except how did we get it so damn good?"

"The marbling in the meat makes it all moist and stuff and yummy and like that."

Like every other live performance, there's plenty of opportunity for the faux pas and the slip of the tongue. One team presenting shoulder at a different competition found themselves cringing shortly after the presenter spoke of "butt penetration." Judges are warned to turn their phones off; cooks' phones have gone off during their presentations. "We take this pig and we baste it every hour...two hours...shoot, I have my shoulders mixed up...we baste it every hour...we baste it every two hours..."

"Tenderize, flavorize, moisturize."

"This is our rub. Our head cook makes that. I know there are three or four types of pepper, Accent. We use sea salt; we don't use iodized salt anymore. We've gotten away from that. And we have paprika in there, some chili powder, and I betcha there are some other things in there that he's not telling me just to keep me on my toes."

And—well, sure—it *is* showmanship. During his shoulder

presentation, John David stands near the edge of the tarp that forms the back wall of the Grillers' judging area, hands behind his back. He talks about his charcoal, and produces a lump of charcoal from behind him. After the judge examines it, John David returns to his at-ease stance, hands behind his back, and talks about his hardwood. His hand returns, this time with a chunk of hickory in it. Back to at-ease, and he talks about cooking with onions, and produces an onion from behind him. The technique is not new. Pat Burke's Tower Rock team is famous for using it. John David only hopes that the behind-the-scenes person handing him the items isn't going to bring a Griller twist to the routine. Craig Wilkerson, he of goatee and glint of eye somewhere between Puckish and demonic, laughs when he tells of the time he handed John David a bottle of beer instead of the onion. Craig isn't in Galax this weekend; this may be a good thing for John David.

"And I think I've got all four corners covered. Any questions—anything I missed?"

"I appreciate the opportunity to serve you today. And if you've got the time, come back and offer your comments and criticisms. That's how our team grows. If we do something wrong, I want to know about it. I want to make sure that it doesn't happen again, because this experience is your experience as well as ours. We want to make it fun for you."

Applause breaks out down Main Street. Curious townspeople look in that direction. There is no reaction from the teams—they know exactly what the applause is all about. So do the judges. One looks at his watch in response to the clapping.

As the judges exit team areas after their allotted fifteen minutes, they are often given rounds of applause. "My favorite part is exiting the tent," says Terrie D'Amato. "I love the applause. 'Thank you for eating our food!'" It's all a part of the regal treatment that in part attracted Alex Brown to the circuit, and has attracted many others. When the judge leaves Natural Born Grillers, the Grillers clap, too, but they append a brief chant:

Natural!

Born!

Grillers!

(manly grunt:) Huoh!

Down Main Street, on the other side of Center, the Sweet Swine o' Mine team is applauding their judge, as well, and add either a tribute to or parody of Natural Born Grillers when they chant:

Sweet!

Swine!

o' Mine!

(manly grunt:) Huoh!

"Al's back there with the timer," Rick says to his judge after the meat is sampled. Fifteen minutes. "They're telling us our dance is about to end."

That particular dance couple breaks up and each moves to the next partner; the dancing continues.

Except for John David Wheeler. After the chant, John David sits. Winces. "I'm hurting," he says. "My back. Oh well, suck it up, gotta play hurt."

This cycle will repeat itself eight times during the preliminary competition. Three presentations per category. One blind-box scramble per category.

Then comes finals. Nine more on-site presentations, three for each category, from the top three teams in each category in the preliminary competition.

Mel and Ms. Piggie have their work cut out for them. No time for foolin' around.

26
T-MINUS PIGGY REVISITED: THE COUNTDOWN FROM 10 BEGINS

"It looks good, it tastes good, and you can dance to it. I give it a 10."

– Myron Mixon describing his rib to a judge visiting Jack's Old South

Saturday morning, July 16, about 11:00 am. When finished with her hog judging, Terrie D'Amato returns to the hospitality room to mark her scorecards. She has five criteria to consider and rate:

Area and Personal Appearance. "Is it clean, is it neat, do you want to eat there?", Larry had instructed at the judges briefing that morning. "It's not about the uniforms or ice-cream machines or money spent on the rigs or anything else. Are the cigarette butts picked up, are there beer cans laying around, are there open garbage containers? You're like the health inspector when it comes to this. Remember, you start with a 10, you're looking for reasons to count off. Are the teams neat? Are they wearing gloves when they handle the meat? Do they have a tire track running across their apron? Do they have grease dripping off their elbows?…Nobody wants to go into a restaurant and eat when the guys have grease all over them."

Presentation…"is the story of how they got that entry from the raw state to the table," Larry said in the briefing. "And it doesn't have to be true." He pointed to cook John Akins.

"Thank god for John. Because sometimes you just have to wink. They're going to tell you that whatever they serve today is exactly how they want it. If the meat falls off the bone on those ribs, they like it that way. If you have to chew, they like a little texture in that rib…. They're going to sell that meat. This is the fun part. You can learn some new lies."

So can the teams. "Whatever it is, you did it on purpose," Larry told grasshopper Cody on Friday night in Galax. When Larry was similarly instructing a new team in Butler, Alabama, he asked, "How big is your hog?"

"A hundred and six pounds."

"What's your ideal weight for a hog?"

"Oh, we'd like it to be about 125, 130 pounds, but . . ."

The interruption was immediate. "Wrong answer." The new team was confused. "Your ideal weight for a hog? A hundred and six pounds."

"But remember," Larry had said in the judges meeting, "when you get in blind, there's no one to sell you that piece of crap that they put in there. The meat stands on its own."

Appearance, "on the grill and on the table," Larry told his judges. "Remember we're not judging tableware, we're not judging fruits and vegetables. Does it look appetizing? Does it look fat, does it look burnt, does it look raw, does it look tasty?" (Probably not all at the same time.) "Does it look like something you want to eat?"

Tenderness. Judges seek a bit of resistance—"tug" or "pull" it has often been called; "integrity" as Bill Fromme of the Barnyard Roasters team phrases it. The meat should separate easily along the grain, yet have definition to it. When you pull it against the grain, it should fight a little but give way. The meat should "tear"; when explaining that criteria, Terry Black of Super Smokers had once picked up a paper towel and slowly tore off a corner—"Like that." Squeeze it; moisture should appear while the meat retains definition.

Reps in their briefings give more pithy ways of considering tenderness. "Does it stick to the roof of your mouth like peanut butter?" Randy McGee says. "Can you roll it up in a ball and bounce it like a basketball?"

"Do you get a hernia trying to pull those ribs apart?" Larry says. "I've seen shoulders that look great, but when you went to get it, it was like trying to grab CoolWhip."

On the initial test taken by trainees in the judging seminar, question #6 is "Tenderness in barbecue is best defined as:" Among the multiple-choice answers that follow is "B—The texture of warm butter."

B is the wrong answer.

Flavor. "Flavor is relative," Larry had told the judges in their briefing. "If it wasn't, we'd have one judge determine who won." Larry has actually experienced one-judge judging. One contest he repped held an ancillary dessert contest. "They had one entry," he says. "I ate it myself and declared it the winner." Galax was almost in the same situation with their Patio Porkers. In late June, Ron's cell rang while he was in the Smokehouse. After an exchange, Ron said to the caller, "I'm waiting for another week. If I don't have any other Patio Porkers—I've had several show interest, but no applications yet—if I don't have any more I'm going to have to move you up to the big dogs. You're the only Patio Porker at this moment. You could serve raw meat and win." (Ron ended up with four Patio teams and, at last report, no raw entries.)

"They have seven judges judging every entry today," Larry continued telling the judges Saturday morning. "Four in blind, three on-site. Every one of you is going to have a different opinion of taste. Some of you may detect the taste of lighter fluid. Some of you may *like* lighter fluid."

Rick Dalton is quick to halt any team gripes about judges' tastes by pointing out, "It's all subjective. Some people like crunchy peanut butter instead of smooth." He's speaking metaphorically, of course. Not many ribs are glazed with peanut butter, crunchy or no. One time Rick altered his analogy: "Say I had sardines on top of my ribs and somebody else had caviar. The judge might like sardines better than caviar. And he might not."

Lance Freemon paused as he considered this. "On the record," he said, "that's *sick*."

Overall impression. This is a category unto itself, using the same 10-point scoring as the others (though this is the only category where decimals are allowed). It is not a summary of the other scores on the card. "Overall impression is not an average of the scores," Larry said in his briefing. "It is not a total. We were at a contest, a judge turned in his scorecard: 36. Certified judge. Trained by Roy. Here's where we use that decimal point. It's very important." (Rep. Chuck Doan once received a scorecard where a judge took a bit of license with the decimal, and gave one team a 10.9.) "Overall impression is just that. It's your judging experience. Flavor, tenderness, certainly is part of it. Another one is their personality. We had a team in Memphis in May a few years back. The judge came in. The presenter came over with the ham, shoulder, and loin on the same plate. He said, 'You're the judge, you went to Roy and Jane's school, you tell me which is which.' He didn't get a 10 in overall impression." Larry paused, looked at Walt. "I hope you learned your lesson."

Ten is the top score in each criterion, and each criterion is weighted. So if a judge gives a team a 9 in area and personal appearance, the judge is not deducting one point from its final score. That judge is actually deducting one point times the criterion's multiplier. "So in each one of these criteria, it's based on the importance to barbecue," Larry O explains to judge trainees. "The flavor of the barbecue is a lot more important in the judging process than area and personal appearance." The more important the category, the higher the multiplier.

The Memphis Barbecue Association reps are cagey about the specific multipliers, especially with judges. Randy McGee tells the trainees, "The reason we have it set up the way we do with factors in the computer is to free you the judge to not worry about anything except that individual factor." They don't want the judges running a calculator through their heads while marking scorecards. The good teams know what the multipliers are, but they can't do anything with that information when it comes down to it. Get your flavor and your tenderness right, and you've won most of the battle. They concentrate on fighting that battle.

Scoring on the Memphis Barbecue Association circuit is on a 5 to 10 scale. However, half of those numbers—the lower half—are rarely used. Giving a team as low as a 7 communicates that eating their entry gave you stomach cramps, made your face break out, and likely would affect your ability to sire or bear children, depending on which ability you had in the first place. "If the team shows up at the contest," goes the rule of thumb, "they get a 5. If they cook, they get a 6. If you can put the entry in your mouth, they get a 7. They get an 8 if you can keep it there." So, in reality, MBA judges are declaring that, within each criterion, the sample is:

- 10, the best today (or close enough to the best sampled today to warrant a "tie" in that criterion)
- 9, good but definably inferior to the performance of the best sampled today
- an 8, plain ol' bad.

Continuing past reality, scores can be:

- 7, wretch-inducing or disease-inducing
- 6, an alert that this judge better get a new hobby

What confuses many judges is a conflicting concept: There should be at least one 10 in every criterion—after all, if you judge three flavors, for instance, one of the flavors will be the best. However…the judge is not forced to give a 10. As Larry said in the judges' briefing that morning, "I wouldn't expect you to give a 10 if every entry you had was burned, raw, or is a spitter—you can't keep it in your mouth. But if it's not burned, it's not raw, you can keep it in your mouth, if you can swallow it, the best you had today should get a 10."

KCBS scoring is on a 1-9 scale. 9 is excellent. 1 is bad. The lack of a 10 is unusual enough that the KCBS on-tape briefing specifically notes for MBA judges participating today that there is no 10 in scoring. The advantage of tenlessness is that it circumvents the perception, ingrained in us by its use in many scoring systems, that 10 means perfect. (See Bo Derek.)

In fact, the MBA judges' briefings stress that 10 does *not* mean perfect. It is "the best you've had today." MBA judges walk into the team booth assuming the team has tens down the board, and then count off from those tens as appropriate during judging. KCBS judges start with a 6 in mind, and adjust the score either up or down as they sample.

"The best you've had today" defines a major philosophical difference between Memphis Barbecue Association judging and judging on other circuits, particularly Kansas City Barbecue Association and the International Barbecue Association Circuit.

KCBS judges concentrate on one sample at a time, then score it only in the context of itself, yet based on outside standards. This is like Olympic gymnastics or ice-skating. The athlete performs her routine; the judges decide based on the performance itself and upon all performances, then hold up their scorecards. So it is with KCBS and rating the entries.

MBA judges, on the other hand, get to see all the gymnastics before making up their minds—at least all the gymnastics they're privy to during the judging of each criterion. MBA on-site judges visit three teams; blind judges weigh four to six samples in one sitting. (KCBS judges evaluate six.) MBA judges rate the teams against each other; "the best you've had today" (not yesterday and not what you cook at home and not what the team has cooked before and not the ambrosia of the gods) is the temporary and (for this contest) lasting standard.

Her decisions made, this Saturday morning, Terrie presents the cards to Walt, who examines them, looking for a clear overall winner, at least one 10 in each category, scores clearly marked, name on the card. If there is a low score—an 8 or lower—he'll ask about it. If the scores are too close together—say, one team gets all tens and another gets all tens except for a 9.9 in overall impression, he'll ask about that. Generally, review takes no more than ten seconds.

Walt has already input the blind scores into the computer. When all the on-site hog cards are turned in and approved, Larry will read the scores from each card to Walt as he keys in the numbers. Then, a couple of DOS prompts later, the computer prints two reports: an overall ranking showing all teams and their scores, and "the paper"—a printout of only the top three scorers and the times at which the finals judges will arrive at their front gates.

Walt takes three copies of the paper and a copy of the full scores and heads back through the bank to find Ron and Carlene, who will have the pleasure of handing a copy the paper to each of the finalists, and feel the pain of alerting the others that they had failed to make finals.

27

DON'T GRILL THE MESSENGER

"I'm going to take my first fiddle lessons."
– Tango of Natural Born Grillers after receiving word that his team
had made it into finals

Saturday morning, July 16, about 11:15 am. First stop on Ron
and Carlene's "paper" trail: Sweet Swine o' Mine. Yoga pig, he
of acupuncture and top-secret injections, has lotused his way
into the finals. There's just one hitch. No one is at home at the
Sweet Swine o' Mine booth.

Ron and Carlene don't have to go to the team's booth to
know this; Pat, Richard and Amy aren't cooking shoulders, and
this being shortly after 11:00 and therefore within the shoulder-
judging window, they're taking a break. The three of them chat
and check out the what's going on in the non-presentation
world during the judging time that would normally occupy
them, obsess them. They conduct their chat in the intersection
of Main and Grayson near the T-shirt gazebo—about ten feet
from Ron and Carlene as they're about to get into their golf cart
to deliver the announcements. About ten feet from Walt Brown,
who has emerged from his computer calculations-and-printings
to give the list of finalists to the contest organizers. Ron and
Carlene could, if they wanted to, just walk up and inform Sweet

Swine of their elevation to the next tier right there in the middle of the crowd, but this seems counter to the convention of approaching the booth with a big smile and finalist papers in hand and getting a whoop and a big smile and an excited handshake in return. Sometimes the team reaction is a grateful but knowing nod—those are the teams that expect "the paper."

Ron gauges Sweet Swine's obliviousness once more, then says to Carlene, "We'll go on to the next team," and they tool off toward Pig Pounda Kappa in the cart, negotiating the crowd of local folk that's strolling the northbound lane of Main Street.

Not a problem. There's no requirement in the order of announcing finalists. In fact, MBA rep Gary Countz tells the finals announcers at his competitions to "play" the announcements—purposefully drive the official golf cart past the finalists, go to the end of the park, drive past one of the finalists again, finally stop at another and make the announcement, keep 'em guessing, "play it." A few weeks after Galax, the judging chairperson of the Caruthersville Meat on the Mississippi competition took Gary's advice to heart, golf-carting past one of the ribs finalists, and a new team at that. The Goin' Hoggin' team had respectable showings in its early years, but had never made it to finals. When Ginny Braswell finally slowed down and stopped on her transit past Goin' Hoggin', she said to one of its members, "Got any samples?"

"Sure" was the hospitable response.

"Well, you better save them," Ginny said, handing him "the paper."

While the Galax paper makes its way north past the empty Sweet Swine booth, Walt Brown approaches Richard, Amy, and Pat. "You should maybe go back to your booth," he says to the three of them.

Sweet Swine is confused. They ask why.

"You should maybe go back to your booth," Walt persists.

It's like trying to guide the birthday boy—who wants to hit the town—to somewhere sedate where silly-hatted celebrants hide in dark couch shadows ready to yell *Surprise!*, without giving away said surprise.

Richard and Amy and Pat begin to comply, but are still confused. A rep suggesting return to the booth? Has some rule been violated? Some bit of etiquette, some sort of…

Oh.

They're not absolutely certain of Walt's intent as they head the twenty or so yards back to their cooksite, but they suspect. Happily, they suspect.

Up at the north end of the midway, Ron and Carlene wait in their idling golf cart. Pig Pounda is in the middle of its shoulder presentation. So is, one booth over, Natural Born Grillers, the third hog finalist. They don't want to interrupt. They don't know that competition etiquette allows them to approach one of the "guards" who is out of the judge's sight to present the paper. The guarding team member will nod, accept the paper with a quiet "thank you," wait until the judge clears the area, then take it on in to the head cook. But Ron and Carlene don't want to distract the presenter, when, in fact, the *only* distraction the presenter welcomes is a finalists announcement during his spiel. The savvy presenter will weave it in, sell it. "I see that we've just been informed that our whole hog has been judged to be worthy of the finals, and we're proud of that. I hope that the shoulder we've served you today will merit the scores that will earn us a second visit to the finals." Or some such salesmanship.

Ron and Carlene wait for breaks, for the judges' exit, for the team applause. The first break is at Pig Pounda Kappa. After Gary Kerce's judge clears the area, Ron approaches Gary with the news. Gary bursts into a smile, springs into a brief jig, and pantomimes playing a fiddle. Pig Pounda rings the bell.

It's a tradition for Pig Pounda, giving a little clang to a black

The Gwatney Championship Barbecue team receives word from contest officials that they've earned a finals berth.

bell, betopped with a pig silhouette, mounted on a piece of their wrought-iron fencing when they make finals. It's fiddle time; it's reinvigoration time. All the work is paying off. And the work is exhausting. "Especially if you do finals," Miss Pat has said, "because it's just nonstop. Start in the morning at 7 o'clock and you don't stop until whatever time, and then you got all that cleanup and all that. Physically, you get tired. It's just a fast pace going through all three categories. You hope and pray you get in the finals, and then you hope and pray you don't….But when we hear the bell, our energy level just shoots right up. But if anybody asks us before that, Can you keep going…?"

Pig Pounda keeps going.

So does Natural Born Grillers, who get the word about finals next door. No bell.

Another team on the circuit used to ring a bell in their tent, far more frequently and with far different purpose. On Friday night, when a pretty girl walked by, they'd clang so that the girl would stop and look to see what was going on and the team could get a better look.

But then there's the gloom ride—stopping by each team that *didn't* hit finals, and telling them who did.

On the gloom ride, Ron gets another exposure to barbecue reality, when one of the team members quietly slides into a couple of choice words not chosen carefully when he learns that his entry didn't make finals. Most teams just nod, say "thanks for letting us know," that sort of thing. At another booth, Danny Sneed reassures Ron that it's OK that Kings didn't make finals. Don't worry, we'll be back.

Meantime, the shoulder judging goes on, working toward determining the paper the next round.

Judge Sharon Bassard sits at Jack's Old South's serving table while Myron serves up his presentation and his shoulder. Myron is quiet during stretches as he pulls meat from the shoulder. He identifies where he's pulling from—"Down into our Boston butt..." pulls the meat, serves it. "Going into our midsection..." Despite David Hair's wind-up-the-automaton joke, and despite Myron's reputation of precise, well-rehearsed presentations, judges in Galax note a more relaxed, off-the-clockwork presentation. Says one, "He dropped his canned speech and seemed to be having more fun."

Sharon's chair is situated so that she faces away from the street, a calculated positioning made by many teams so that the judge isn't distracted by outside activity. This barbecue feng shui isn't working quite as well today, however. Sharon senses something. She asks Myron, "Are there people behind me?"

"It's more like a large crowd watching us," Myron says.

Alex Brown feels it, too. As he says, later, "You could feel the eyeballs beating you in the back of your head and hear 'I want that job.'" What goes around…

The crowd has gathered to view barbecue in general and the teams that Judy Brannock refers to as her "media darlin's" specifically. A number of teams, including Jack's, Gwatney, Grillers and Pig Pounda, should have one of those "As Seen on TV!" starbursts mounted on the upper lefthand corner of their rigs. They've appeared on the Food Network, on A&E, on Turner South, on the Outdoor Life Network.

When Terrie D'Amato visits Jack's Old South as one of his on-site judges, about twenty-five onlookers have gathered. They watch as Myron shows Terrie the cooker, then puts, as Terrie phrases it, "about four pounds of meat on the plate," and walks her to the feng shui seat. "Then I had something happen that never happened before," Terrie says. "One of the men watching told me that he would give me $100 for my seat, then that seems to have given all the spectators permission to start asking Myron questions, as he is trying to continue his presentation. Myron was gracious and answered him, but I never had that happen before. I think the town was very taken away with the whole event and the teams were very relaxed but it was weird. I think that they were really excited to have us there. Barbecue is about fun and friends—I shouldn't complain—it was just something that I wasn't used to."

And in fact the public in Galax are a gentler sort than is found at some competitions. On Friday night, Pure and Sinful were relaxing when a passerby stopped by their tent entrance. "Are y'all barbecuin' or just sittin' around?" she said.

Dan replied from the comfort of his folding chair, "We're just sittin' around chewing the fat."

"Y'all doing ribs?"

Dan said, "Just doing ribs. Put 'em on 5 o'clock in the morning."

"Five o'clock *this* morning?"

"*Nooo*. Tomorrow morning."

"Y'all need some help?"

"No, no, we're good."

"I can volunteer some time. I can tell you my secrets, what *I* got. You need me to win."

"Well, then," Dan said, "you need to be in competition."

"Yessir."

"Yes you do."

"We've only been here three weeks, so next year, watch out."

"You never know."

Teams are usually gracious with the general public, in part because the teams are usually nice folk, but in part because they're also politically savvy. It's a variation of the "next year, watch out" from local folk. Myron will say later, "Whether it's here, whether it's in Vienna, there's a relationship between the contest and the local folks. If the local folks become disenchanted and disgruntled with it, they're going to bitch to the city council people, they're going to bitch to the powers that be, they're going to bitch to the chamber, the people who put this on, and you ain't gonna have it no more. So it's a circle. So if a team acts ugly to a chamber of commerce member out here and don't really know it, or some local folks and they get into church and complain about it, it all started with the team acting ugly to the passerby. You gotta think about that. Because I love this. I don't want it to go away. And all these things, like getting drunk and showing your butt, and doing all that, that ain't good. You got some black eyes on the sport we call barbecue, it ain't good for what we're trying to do here, what I'm trying to do here." As has been said by Kell Phelps, himself a pretty close observer of barbecue as publisher of *The National Barbecue News*, "I've never seen a competition where the town gets behind it fail."

Occasionally, public participation is a bit more formalized.

Memphis in May recently instituted a "Hog Crawl"; people who sign up are given tours to meet participating competition teams.

Not formal but *planned* was the Gummersall public participation. Sara Gummersall from the Chicago area in 2004 decided to give her barbecue-fanatic husband Matthew a special birthday present—a trip to a barbecue competition. She emailed several competitions, and was shocked when Terry Black, head of Super Smokers and co-organizer of the St. Louis Barbecue Fest, emailed with not only an invitation to come to the Fest, but also an idea that allowed Sara to doctor a St. Lewis tourism magazine to include a mock ad that personally invited Matthew to come to the competition as an honorary sauce judge. At the event, Matthew indeed participated as an ancillary sauce contest judge and got to observe whole hog judging. Terry then employed both Matthew and Sara as ambassadors, and they got to follow shoulder judges to the teams—and enjoy samples themselves. "After we were done with the shoulder," Matthew says, "I was so full that I thought that I would sit out the rib competition. Well, the Man in me overrode that idea quite quickly and I buddied up with another official judge."

"We met loads of fun people," says Sara, "all very serious about the task at hand, but all were friendly and eager to share stories."

"A wonderful gift, indeed," Matthew says.

On rare occasions, the roles are reversed. The *public* commands *team* attention and *team* participation. At a cook in Alabama, a local man driving into the contest site managed to get his pickup truck stranded on a nearby railroad track. "This is a railroad that's being used," says Walt, who was repping the contest with Larry—the first contest they had ever repped. "Every twenty minutes a train comes roaring through." A group of contest participants, including Larry and members of Natural Born Grillers, went to help.

Larry says, "We actually lifted that thing to get the frame off the tracks before the train come by."

Walt says, "Didn't miss by much."

In Galax during Saturday's judging, standing outside the Nervous Wreck Cook'n Crew's booth is a bystander who should not be standing by. She should be inside the booth. Jane Barber looks at her watch. She is Cody Cline's second judge, and she should be in the area by now. The first judge is still inside, running late. "That first judge has been in there a long time," she says, but then it becomes clear to her what's going on. She's seen it dozens of times before—recall that she herself with husband Roy have judged, have organized contests, have been Memphis in May reps, have trained judges to *not* do exactly what Judge Order 3 has just done at Team Order 2.

It's not the first judge running late in Cody Cline's cooksite. It's the *third* judge running *early*, leaving judge 2 outside with plenty of time to hunt down rep Larry O to let him know what has happened. Dominoes are falling, or worse yet are *not* falling, as a result of the single judge visiting teams out of sequence.

On-site judges get three cards, each carrying a team name, in the order in which the teams are to be visited. Judges then sign the cards. Sign the top one, move it to the back of the stack. Sign the next top one, move it to the back of the stack. Sign the next top one, chat about the weather with the judge next to you, leaving card 3 on top. Or accidentally drop the cards, pick them up, fail to check the their proper order has been retained. So the judge then goes first to the team he or she should be visiting third. This upsets flow, it upsets timing, it upsets the laws of the barbecue universe. Forcibly thrown out of order, other judges have to adjust. When Jane Barber finally meets with Cody to be what in reality is his third judge, she then has to scoot over to another team to be *their* third judge (potentially their *late* third judge, unfortunately). Imagine "Row Row Row Your Boat" with one of the singers *beginning* merrily merrily.

For this to happen, three people have to fail at their mission. The judge, who was to have checked the teams and the team order. The judge's assistant, who was to have checked the teams and the team order. The team's greeter, who was to have checked the judge and the judge order.

One of the teams likely didn't pick up on the problem because this is his first contest. It is Cody Cline's first experience with accepting the judges' stubs, and with all the effort in living up to the Nervous Wreck in his team name, he likely failed to notice that Judge Order 3 has appeared when Judge Order 2 is soon to be hovering at his figurative doorstep. He should have pointed out that "You're early; please return to visit as Judge 3," and then waited until Jane (Will the real Judge #2 please stand up?) arrived in proper order.

Larry O finds the errant judge and pulls her aside. He alerts her to what she has done—and she's embarrassed and appalled to realize that she's made the mistake that's warned against sternly in every judges' briefing she's ever attended, and she's attended quite a few. She's also scared. She's made The Blunder. Will she be asked back to judge again? Larry is calming. He assures her that it's not that serious. "This isn't brain surgery," he says. "No one's going to die from it. It's barbecue—it's supposed to be fun."

And that story is true.

Not all of them are.

28 SEX, LIES AND VIDEOTAPE (LACKING THE SEX AND THE VIDEOTAPE)

"Stories are built out so much that you hear stories about you and you don't even know it."
– Merrill Fuller of the Tower Rock BBQ team

September 18, 1773. Consider the size of George Washington's backyard when he, as noted in his diary 9/18/1773, "Went to a Barbecue of my own giving at Accatinck." He made a great President, George did, but it's unlikely that he would make it on today's barbecue competition circuit. Harry S Truman might have done OK—after all, he's the one who said, "No man should be allowed to be President who does not understand hogs"—but the cannot-tell-a-lie boy would never be comfortable with an important barbecue convention: the barbecue tall tale.

July, 2005. Saturday morning, Larry O makes a point in the judges briefing, the same point that has been noted in earnest and in jest and in point of fact in hundreds of judges briefings and thousands of other times out on the circuit itself: "The cooks have to tell you the story of their barbecue. Sometimes it's true." Larry O looks up, considers. "Well, I don't think it's ever been true. Besides, it's more interesting if it isn't."

On Friday night, while coaching newbie Cody on presentation, Larry performs an off-the-cuff sauce presentation for his student. "'I'd like you to taste our sauce,' he says in the role of presenter. 'It's grandma's recipe from the Civil War.'"

In the background as Larry tells this story, the Embers play "Stir It Up."

"'It's actually made from ground-up galax leaves. We found this in grandma's recipe book. She'd been cooking for the county fair growing up. She died, and in her belongings we found this old cookbook, and this recipe fell out.'" Larry quickly adds, "Doesn't have to be true."

Barbecue people have all heard their share of almost-truths, damned lies and statistics. At the July judging seminar, Larry and fellow rep/trainer Randy McGee jump into a kind of whoppertopper contest.

"I had a team one time," Randy says, "who said, 'Of course, pigs can't talk to each other, but they have a way of communication.' This team has a deal with their processing plant, that they always get one of the first five pigs that go through the slaughter line, because of the way that pigs can communicate kind of like ESP, and after the first five pigs go through the line, the rest of the pigs realize what's happening and their endorphin levels will be pumped up."

"It really spoils the meat," a cook who's taking the class intones dryly.

Larry counters Randy's whopper with "My team always cuts our firewood with a pocket knife. We don't want to use a chainsaw because it's got oil on the blade and we don't want that to impart a flavor in the cooking process."

"That," Randy says, "and they always get wood from the outside of the forest. You don't want to get wood from the inside of the forest where the trees have to fight each other for water and sunlight....If they tell you that story to your face, you just smile and say, 'That is amazing. I didn't realize that.'"

"If you convince them that you believe them, under comments, 'Would you want this judge again?'...'Yes!'"

Says barbecue cookbook writer Steven Raichlen, "I love the tall tales that get told: 'Well, now this pig, we're serving you from its right side because obviously it laid on its left side so the right part is more tender . . .' I love all that stuff. That ties in in a funny way to a tradition in American literature, the Paul Bunyan story. Think of it as sort of vernacular homegrown literature or the oral poetry of the American backwoods or whatever you want to call it. It's fun."

Oral poetry or bald-faced lying, tales are told about everything taleworthy. There are whoppers about cooking. Whoppers about judges. Whoppers about teams.

And sometimes whoppers about whoppers. At a recent cook, Jim Johnson of Mile High Barbecue had just concluded a story about taking a prize using, as a last resort, ribs prepared on Friday for the Friday night guests.

"And Jim hasn't embellished that story," Walt Brown said.

"This just happened," Jim said. "I haven't had time to embellish it."

Perhaps the most common whopper in the context of this discussion is Presentations Are Dominated By Whoppers. By and large, the stories of cooking processes told during presentations are true. Perhaps not as detailed or complete as they might be, but true.

"If you don't tell the truth," says Keith "George Washington" Roberts, "it will come back to bite you." Perhaps an odd statement from someone who has been bitten by the truth itself. At a recent competition, a shoulder judge asked him, "Do you inject your shoulders?"

Keith explained that he does not.

The judge seemed doubtful as he sampled the meat.

Later, when the judge came back to talk to Pigs in Paradise, Keith said, "I had the feeling you didn't believe me."

"I didn't," the judge said. "You don't get pork this juicy without injecting."

"Yes you do," Keith said.

Success had backfired. The judge was ignoring the juicy meat and probably giving suppressed scores because he didn't believe the story of the cooking process.

But, *it doesn't have to be the truth*. The rule is core to barbecue, and even to the very word *barbecue*. The word, you see, comes from the fact that this style of cooked meat was served in drinking establishments, particularly those with billiards facilities. Smoked meat was well at home with in bars with beer and pool cues…bar-beer-cue. Thus the word.

Barbeercue. It doesn't have to be the truth, says Larry O, and there's no truth in this fanciful explanation.

The word, you see, comes from the French. *Barbe* means "beard," and *queue* means "tail." One cooks the whole hog, from "beard to tail," from barbe a queue. Thus the word.

Barbequeue. It doesn't have to be the truth, says Larry O, and this etymology is also hogsh…hogwash. Ever see a pig with a beard? Even a French pig? Little goatee, curling handlebar mustache? Soo-*oui-oui!*?

And then there's the tale that a Texan was so proud of his "Q" that he named his ranch the Bar B Q. Might as well claim that the word came about because Ken first met Barbie at an outdoor cookout, grilling pork steaks, and Ken said, "Hey, Barbie's cute!" (If you see this explanation circulating on the internet soon, you'll know where it came from.)

Another hogwash tale is that Spanish explorers coming to the Americas encountered Haitian and Guianan natives drying meats on raised platforms the Haitians called "barbacoa" (from a word in the Arawak tongue Taino) and the Guianans called a "barbicot." The Spanish adopted the Haitian word, which eventually was picked up with different spelling in English. It doesn't have to be the truth, says Larry O, who continues, "but sometimes it is." This etymology, in fact, is the correct one (though there's some argument that the word more precisely comes from *barabicu*, a Taino word meaning "sacred fire pit"—either way, we're still grillin' in the Caribbean). A back-yard grill is to this day known as a barbacoa in Spanish.

Word authority WordOrigins.com (yes, you occasionally find truth on the internet) notes that "The original sense of bar-becue is that of a raised, wooden (later metal) framework used for either sleeping upon or curing meats." Hopefully not at the same time.

The Haitians also roasted meat over these frameworks, basting them in wine. The word came to be applied to the meat, and eventually to the party accompanying the roast itself.

The "whoppers" now heard at that party are often either exaggerations in fun or a bit of salesmanship, usually told with a figurative wink. In his rib presentation, Rick Dalton of Gwatney has been known to say, "You need to get some ribs first. We used to raise our own. And what we did, we cloned the hog. And we kept reproducing the same rib with good quality." One response prompted by that line: "Your eyes gotta be brown, honey"—appropriate considering that the full text of Harry Truman's quote reads "No man should be allowed to be President who does not understand hogs, or hasn't been around a manure pile." And in fact, shortly after he uses the we-cloned-the-hog line, Rick spells out exactly what real-life farm provides his ribs, through exactly which real-life meat-packing house. "I've got no secrets," Rick says frequently during the Galax cook and other cooks as well. "If you want to know what's in my rub," he tells one judge, "I'll send you the recipe."

But overall, Mr. President, what's a little fibbing among

friends? Larry O tells of a night at a contest some years back, where he and others partied on Friday with a team called The Parrothead Porkers until 2 a.m. The next morning, Larry received his judging assignments. Among his rib teams…Parrothead Porkers. That contest used judges' ambassadors, and Larry teamed up with an ambassador who also had been in the Parrothead tent until 2 that morning.

When Larry was served the ribs—by one of the gents he had been late-night drinking with—the presenter told the story of how the team together. With a face much straighter than he'd been the night before, he explained to Larry that the team met in church, and that they never partied or anything like that.

The ambassador looked at Larry, gave him the *did-you-catch-that?* look.

The presenter said, "After you're done judging, come on back and we'll share a soft drink."

After they left the Parrothead tent, the ambassador tugged on Larry's sleeve. "He lied to you. He lied to you."

Larry cocked his head, looked at the ambassador quizzically. The grandfather-gotcha look. "Really?"

Incidentally, Ron Passmore's 3 Pigs and a Lady all knew each other from church.

And Ron claims that that's true. *It doesn't have to be the truth. But sometimes it is.*

29 JUDGING HOW THE JUDGES ARE JUDGED

"Superjudge! Able to leap tall tales in a single bound!"
— No one actually said that, but someone should have

Saturday, May 14, 2005, Memphis. "I'm going to stick my arm in your grill."

Clara Scarritt, rib cook for Porky's Pride, out of Tuscaloosa Alabama, listens to this announcement as she presents her ribs at the 2005 Memphis in May World Championship Barbecue Cooking Contest. She looks at her open grill, looks back at the judge. "That's fine, but I wouldn't recommend it."

"Well," the judge says, "I'm going to."

"Can you tell me why?"

"I'll tell you when I come back. I'll come back afterwards."

Then he sticks his arm in the grill and waves it about some, while Clara maintains a straight face and thinks, "What the hell you doin', buddy?"

Buddy was looking, he explains later, for cold spots on the grill.

"Why?" Clara asks him.

Because he was taught that way.

For what purpose, Clara is stumped. You're not judging the

grill. You're judging what comes out of the grill. If he'd found a cold spot, would it click in a different set of taste buds? A good cook could theoretically smoke ribs with a candle inside a refrigerator.

Or maybe the judge was trying to determine whether the meat was actually cooked on this grill, or just presented there.

Again, stumped. The rules state that the judge must see the meat on the grill. The rules don't demand that the grill in question is actually the one used—the rules acknowledge that some teams use a "showcase" grill that's easier to keep clean for on-site presentations.

At 2005 WCBCC, Porky's Pride had just been visited by *Superjudge*.

That's what people on the circuit call the gentleman or the lady who knows more than the teams, who is more important than the teams, and who cooks a pretty tasty barbecue himself in his backyard, and wouldn't the head cook of a top-ten competition barbecue team just love to benefit from learning all about how he does it?

Superjudge's existence is the reason for the judges evaluation card. After the contest, the teams will judge the judges by filling out the stubs that are keeping Gwatney's Ms. Piggie happy and content.

The questions are these:

Was the judge knowledgeable? In many ways, this means, did the judge ask the right questions? Was the judge concerned about the appropriate elements of barbecue? Did the judge *know* the rules of barbecue?

One of the symptoms of superjudgery is judging based on your own rules (see "Does it taste good with beer?"). Buddy visiting Porky's Pride had some rule in his head that he wasn't revealing to anyone.

Pigs in Paradise once entertained a judge who returned

after the competition's completion, explaining why he had dinged the ribs on his scorecard. "Your ribs were pink, so I thought they weren't done."

Smoke ring. Pink. Smoke ring all the way through a thin cut of meat. Pink meat. (The first time Larry O cooked ribs, he says, "I cooked them for like an hour and a half direct on the grill, and it was still pink. I said, 'These aren't done,' so I went another hour and a half, and it was still pink. After about four hours over direct heat, I had pork jerky. And it was still pink.") The judge was not knowledgeable about barbecue. (On the other hand, Randy McGee cautions judge trainees, "If the smoke ring runs red liquid out of it, it's probably not a smoke ring. And if they tell you it's an injected sauce, I don't think I'd believe that.")

In Galax, when all the judges evaluations had been submitted by the teams, all on-site judges were rated "Good," except for one receiving a "Fair." Though "Fair" sounds OK, it's likely as damning to a judge as a 7 or an 8 is to a team.

Was the judge attentive? Linda Booth of Red Hot Smokers at the judging seminar told trainees, "We had one judge one time—we were in a college town—it was a gentleman—and all he did was watch the college girls go by. Now, this man"—she indicated husband Wayne—"has stayed up twenty-two hours cooking shoulders. That's a lot of work. And I was livid that he could not give me ten minutes of his focused attention after how much effort that was put into that shoulder that he was supposed to be trying. That was very disrespectful."

Standing next to Linda, seminar trainer Larry O bowed his head theatrically and said, "I don't do that anymore."

Judges are told at every briefing, as Larry has at the Galax briefing, "As a courtesy, no guests, no smoking, no beepers, no cell phones, no cameras, no sunglasses, no Girl Scout cookies. Leave all that with a friend, and leave the friend at home." And "no private agendas." Wayne Booth tells of a judge who made his own sauce, and was trying to sell it to Wayne during a presentation. And "no promoting your contest." Some judges are also organizers; the occasional organizer has been known to recruit on the team's time.

As Larry briefs the judges, "Their fifteen minutes of fame is your fifteen minutes for listening."

Again, all the Galax judges were rated by their teams as "Good," with one exception as "Fair."

Did the judge stay ten to fifteen minutes? Did he or she devote enough time to the team without running off schedule at the expense of the contest? The fifteen minutes begin when the greeter introduces himself to the judge. There are tales of greeters stepping outside the gate to unofficially begin their pitch, thinking that timing begins when the judge enters the gate. Judging begins then; timing begins with the handshake. Greeters and judges who know each other often kill a little time while the team finishes prep by engaging in relaxed "off-stage" banter, idle conversation, some gossip, and, on one occasion, a joke so off-color that the judge and team member found themselves laughingly announcing to each other "Judging begins *inside* the gate" in stereo).

The Galax teams reported that all judges stayed in their time frame.

Would you want this judge again? No team in Galax said no. In fact, the stories told here about less-than-satisfactory judges are the exceptions. And yes, there are grumblings about the judges biased by a team's previous success (or lack thereof), or judges with personal prejudices, and some of that can't be denied. But, "In general, the judges treat us well," says Porkosaurus's Guido. "It's amazing how many good judges you have who are just doing it for fun. It's all volunteer work. It's not like they get paid. You really can't gripe about someone who's doing something for nothing." (Nothing except for the occasional bass boat, that is . . .)

Comments: Despite urgings from Larry, Walt and Ron to be as detailed as possible, identifying the good and the problematic, the teams don't go into much detail about their judges. Says Carlene, "The comments were 'very nice,' 'excellent poker face,' very nice and helpful' and that's about it."

No team mentions a judge out of order. And there are no mentions of arms in the grill. This time.

30 DRESSED TO GRILL

"Our wives all have uniforms"..."Nurse's uniforms, school girl uniforms...oh! you're talking about barbecue!"
– anonymous team repartee

Saturday, September 24, Charlotte, North Carolina. Myron Mixon and David Hair are bantering while waiting. Sitting on chairs that'll soon to be occupied by finals judges, they chat with themselves and with a couple of other judges and a couple more onlookers standing just outside their cooksite. David complains about Myron calling him at home one day and interrupting his baking a cake. Myron carps at him, "We're working hard on our men in black image, and he's cooking a damn cake. Y'all are chapping my ass."

Black is indeed order of the day. Black short-sleeve dress shirts, black denim, black belt and shoes. The rig is black, the tent…

Saturday, July 16, Galax. Over at Gwatney, order of the day has changed to yellow shirts. During preliminary judging, they wore red polos, with "2005 MIM World Champions" embroidered in yellow just above the sleeve cuff. All wear black shorts, except for Rusty and Hal.

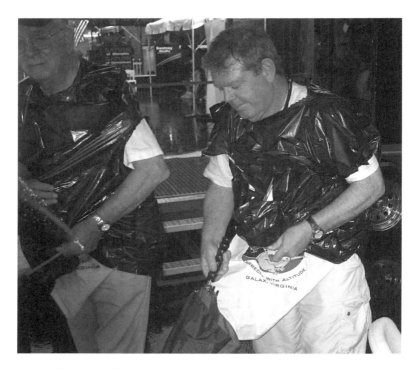

Finals judges Cliff Weddington and Skip Sawyer brace for more rain.

The teams are decked out in team colors, though the team colors can, as in the case of Gwatney and sometimes with Natural Born, change from category to category as they change to get into clean shirts, and to give themselves a fresh look for each round of finals judging. Most stick with barbecue style—polo shirts and sometimes T's with team name on one side of the collar, team member's name on the other. Smoked Encounters and Nervous Wreck top off the shirts with matching aprons (black and mottled orange, respectively).

Call it barbecue casual. As Rick Browne of PBS's *Barbecue America* once said, explaining his red-and-white checkered shirt and pants, "This ain't *GQ*, its barbecue." Only Hawg Wild varies much from the polo-esque. Jeff and the Hawg Wild crew wear black T-shirts with a splashy multi-colored Memphis in May applique on the front, equally colorful Hawg Wild logo applique on the back.

Down at Natural Born Grillers, in addition to black shirts and khaki shorts, the team wears its trademark red Nikes.

One team wears plastic garbage bags.

The team of four finals judges—and more on the garbage bags in a moment.

Friday night, July 15. Larry and Walt deliver passwords that allow entry into an exclusive social club. Not club 54. Club 4. The four who will judge finals. They approach Skip Sawyer of Raleigh, North Carolina; Cliff Weddington of Tullahoma, Tennessee; Sheila Davis, also of Tullahoma; and Wanda Barzizza of Germantown, Tennessee.

When selecting judges, experience and not taste in garbage bags is a factor. Cliff is a long-time cook. Sheila has been judging for years. Skip has a number of years of experience, both judging and cooking, as well, though this is only his second finals. Wanda was involved for several years with Memphis in May as a WCBCC volunteer, and now judges frequently

Yin/yang is a factor. Contests usually seek finals teams composed of two men and two women. Geographic diversity is considered, as well.

Availability is a factor. One aspect of availability is Are They Going to Be There? These judges have checked in Friday night and are sure to be available Saturday. Another aspect is Are They Allowed? MBA guidelines strongly recommend that no judge participate in more than two finals in a given season.

When these factors are considered and the invitations given and the four say "yes" to the invitation, Walt and Larry bring them together to meet, chat, and learn to be comfortable with each other.

Saturday morning. "If you've ever had the opportunity to

serve as a finals judge, you go in and you don't really know the other final judges," Larry says on Saturday at the judges' briefing. "It's sort of, to me, like going to a Japanese steak house and you're sitting down eating with people that you don't even know. You don't even talk to them for the first half hour. We've found that if the judges know each other when they go in there, they lighten up a little bit, have some fun, smile, instead of going in there like an accountant." He glances around the room, spots at least one judge with a financial vocation. "No offense to accountants."

At the later finals briefing, Larry says, "Go in there, they're your friends, they're feeding you. You wouldn't go to somebody's house as a guest and look down your nose at 'em. Be appreciative. They're giving you championship barbecue. You're going to have the best in the world here. So have fun, lighten up. It's OK to laugh, smile, joke with them. You'll find out that if you do, you'll relax them. Their presentation will be much better. You'll all have a lot more fun. That's why you came here."

Laugh, smile, joke: At one contest, rep Randy McGee was ushering a group of finals judges through the event. When they finished with one team, they were to walk down one row of teams and U-turn into the next row to a relatively new and completely nervous team. On the way, Randy stopped at a team that had dressed themselves as, of all things, clowns, and orchestrated a transfer. The finals judges gave their clipboards and scorecards to four of the clownly attired folk, who moved on to the next team to briefly pass themselves off as the judges. (All "How could the team tell the difference?" jibes will be cheerfully ignored.)

The finals judges' first trip together Saturday morning is not to the usual whole hog team, not even to the circus or a Japanese steak house, but to Mt. Airy, to do the Mayberry thing. Larry O has suggested that they spend some time together before the finals judging briefing at 1:00. So they become tourists, a half hour down to North Carolina, a visit to Floyd's barber shop and Goober's filling station and local shops and the mountain scenery that reminds judge Sheila of her middle Tennessee home.

Their second trip together is up to the first team to be judged in the final round: Natural Born Grillers at the north end of the contest site. Cliff, Wanda, Sheila and Skip walk from the bank building, arriving about five minutes before the 1:45 finals start time (fifteen minutes after the completion of rib preliminaries). They hang out a bit; they pose for pictures in the shade of the Farmer's Market. After a few moments, Wanda dons sunglasses.

Usually the judges have a ride from team to team—golf carts or Gators chauffeur them about. They don't even have to drive themselves—just sit on the back. At Columbus, Mississippi, the contest devoted a cart and a driver to each judge. Driving up to one of the hog teams a bit ahead of schedule, the four carts stopped in the midway, side by side by side by side. While they waited, another cart came up the midway from the opposite direction, stopped when the driver saw he was blocked. The blocked driver said, "You guys look like a Panzer division."

In Galax, though, the finals judges are cart-deprived. The teams are close to each other, covering just two blocks, making cartage unnecessary and even awkward, given the number of townspeople crowding the street. And, as it turns out, when all the finals announcements have been made, just one finalist sits in the south block. Three finalists sit side-by-side-by-side, with only two teams separating that grouping from the fifth finalist. The judges would walk further to get to and from the carts than they would to simply walk from team to team.

Finals judges visit the finalists in the same category order as the preliminaries: hog, then shoulder, then ribs. Within the categories, order is established by preliminary point total. The highest-scoring shoulder, for instance, goes first...*unless* a team has made finals twice, and this ordering would bring the judges back to back (for instance, third in preliminary hog and first in preliminary shoulder). Then the order would be altered.

Other than that, the preliminary scores are now meaningless to the finalists. Finals judging is a wipe-the-slate-clean new contest. A team that has scrabbled its way into rib finals by hundredths of a point over the fourth-place preliminary rib might now be head-to-head with a rib that managed a perfect score in prelim. Doesn't matter.

There's debate over what position is best to be in. First to see the judges? So that every sample that follows must be judged against the standard you have set? "I'd rather be the last one to go, myself," Larry O the cook says. "I want to make that last impression, because they're going to remember me more than they are their first hog."

"To me," Walt counters, "when you're hungry, stuff tastes better than when you're full."

And full the judges will be when they walk out of that last rib team. Nine samples, and three of those samples requiring tastes of three cuts of meat.

"Out of respect for the teams," Larry tells the judges in the 1:00 briefing, "you have to be just as enthusiastic when you go into that last rib team as you do that first hog team. You're pretty excited when you go in that first hog team because you haven't had any championship barbecue yet. So you have a tendency when you go in there and you're really enthusiastic, and you're going to be eating and stuffing yourself. If you don't pace yourself, by the time you get to that eighth team, you don't even want to smell barbecue. But you've got to pretend like you're enthused. So you're going to see me in your face about the seventh or eighth team if you're gonna be looking like this. All I'm going to say is 'Enthusiasm.' And that's when I want the big smile to come back." The Finals Judge's mantra: "Pace Yourself." The first time judge Annie Sisson did finals, she took the advice to pace herself so well that she paced herself into hunger. After the last award had been presented, Annie joined the contest's MBA reps and her husband at…a smorgasbord, where she continued to pace herself, this time on vegetables and fruit.

Team presentations for finals judges are usually altered only slightly, to account for more guests. More chairs, more place settings, more meat taken off the grill. Oh, and a little of "We're proud of having made it this far." There is one major change at Natural Born Grillers when the judging begins at 1:45. John David has found that he don't gotta play hurt. George Nicely fills in to make the whole hog presentation.

The trip from the judges' first team to their team takes a little less time than their jaunt down to Mt. Airy, considering that the second team, Pig Pounda, is right next door.

Then, down to the south block and Sweet Swine o' Mine, accompanied by a roll of thunder.

During Sweet Swine o' Mine's presentation at the cooker, Carlene is weather-watching. "I'll have to go in and get ponchos," she says to Larry.

Shortly after, Walt makes one of his rare appearances outside the reps' room. "They get to you with the last set of cards yet?" he says to Carlene. Walt's referring to the cards that list the three ribs finalists, one for each finals judge. "Ron's got 'em for you." The judges—who began the finals before the ribs finalists had been determined—will get the rib cards during the next break. MBA scorecards! Collect 'em all!

After the judges are seated at the serving table, Dr. Richard surveys his guests. "I definitely see some familiar faces here, so it's good to have everybody back. And if we haven't seen some-one before, welcome." A couple of minutes later, Dr. Richard is describing his sauce. "There's no fruit juice in that, but the essence of apricot is there. And once you get…"

The rains hit.

The rains come down heavy.

Richard gestures to Larry and Carlene. "You can come around if you like, bring it around, it doesn't bother me a bit." Larry and Carlene duck under the tent and stand close to the judges—unusual, since the people in their roles always stay out-side the judging area under normal circumstances. "Now," Richard says with barely a pause, "I want you to notice again the mahogany color. It's been on twenty-seven hours and I want you to notice. Look at the beautiful skin on the pig."

A few minutes later, Pat Rooney is distributing bark to the judges while Richard fields a question about flavors.

A snap of thunder makes Sheila jump in her chair, the only visible sign that the judges were at all paying attention to any-thing but the meat and the presentation. Pat doesn't flinch. "The tenderloin, the ham and the shoulder," he says. "This is the tenderloin off the top—has a kind of good bark…"

Focus. Underlined three times.

Birmingham of Natural Born tells a story of a contest in the rain where local police and firefighters ducked into their tent during presentation to get out of the rain. "Back when I first started cookin', that would get me…" Birm breaks into a mon-ster face and begins growling to imitate his back-then reaction.

"Part of doing business," John David says. "You just gotta get used to it."

"We've been through motorcycles, sirens," Birm says. Then, to John David, "One year a helicopter landed during your presentation, remember that?"

"We had it happen in Richmond, Virginia, the first year we

won it," John David says. "Had helicopter rides during presentation. Where we were, the only place it was, the helicopter took off and landed, and that damn dust and dirt." (On the other hand, Lubin Prevatt, one of Natural Born's Galax preliminary judges, expressed some surprise that the presenter looked up during his presentation and paused to admire a classic car from the nearby cruise-in cruising out.)

And whatever happens, roll with it. During a Grills Gone Wild presentation in Columbus, Georgia, a wind came up, lifted the front of the tent, and folded the tent in half over on itself. Peyton Turner missed only a beat or two. "Our meat is so pretty," he said to the judge, "we pulled the top back so you could see it better."

It's not the winds in Galax. It's the rains that continue to slop down through Sweet Swine's presentation. While Pat Rooney is saying "Look at that—look at the juices still in that hog," nature's juices outside the hog are flowing down Main Street.

Richard concludes, "It's been a pleasure having all of you. I hope you really enjoy yourself today. *Try* and stay dry." Larry beckons the judges across over to Carroll County across the street so they can jot notes under a store awning. The judges are given some make-do raingear, black plastic garbage bags. As they move back up the street to return to Natural Born Grillers, they are wearing the bags, toting umbrellas and looking like veteran trick-or-treaters. When they've cleared the area, Kell Phelps with *National Barbecue News* pops into the area to chat with the team. "Oh!" Amy says as something occurs to her. "I forgot the Wetnaps."

Kell says, "I think they have plenty of wet."

By shortly before 3:00, Larry and Carlene have delivered the finals judges to Gwatney for shoulder, and they move on down to Jack's to talk to Myron, where the Man in Black meets the Man in Black Garbage Bag. Larry hoists a black umbrella and himself wears the trendy plastic garbage fashion statement. Beside them, though Carlene's umbrella can't be all bad (it's purple, after all), it hasn't done much to keep her gray volunteer T-shirt dry. Carlene and Larry are here to tell Myron that the judges getting into their makeshift rain gear has thrown them a couple of minutes behind. "You're messing with my fine window of tenderness, which you may have heard about," Myron blusters. He's joking at his own expense, making light of the deeply memorized concluding remarks that he's made thousands of times and can recite at the snap of the fingers: "Judges, when you leave Jack's Old South, I want you to remember that indirect water cooking. Tenderizing while you're barbecuing. As I stated before, there's nothing in the world that tenderizes like boiling water and apple juice, and for the whole cooking time it's been laying there directly above it, tenderizing, steaming, gets tender for the whole process. Added in there that Georgia peachwood for that mild barbecue flavor, together judges, it makes an unbeatable combination."

The rains switch off and on through the rest of the judging, letting up by the time the finals judges arrive the predicted couple of minutes late at Jack's Old South for his shoulder, gearing up once more when they return to Grillers and to Gwatney for the ribs. Though there's not much more than a few inches of separation between the Gwatney rig and its main tent, the rains force Al and Lance to deploy umbrellas and escort the judges one by one to the table under the tent once Rick has finished explaining the cooker. Across the street, bystanders huddle beneath the shelter of the Farmer's Market, where the judges had started the afternoon huddling away from the sun, watching the two remaining teams present next door to each other, one after another. Sheila would later talk of the "very positive attitude of the teams we visited during the heaviest rainstorms. We were all laughing, although I can imagine what stress they were under." Ultimately, she says, "The rain was fun."

Almost on cue, the rain lets up when they leave Gwatney to head back to the First National Bank to mark their scores. There they scribble, ponder, erase, breathe, consult Larry's sample filled-out scorecard. Except for Larry offering additional explanation to Cliff, they work quietly. When Skip whispers, "Ah…shoulder…" it is almost a shout.

Larry and Walt ask their finals judges to make clear rankings of the nine entries in each judging category, so that no two teams receive, for instance, identical flavor scores from an individual judge. If the judge gives entry A a 9.9, he or she can't give entry C a 9.9, too. Walt and Larry will readily accept duplicate scores given in Area and Personal Appearance and in Presentation. "I would accept all these teams, if they made it into finals, they're doing something right." But…

"Now the work comes in," Larry had explained earlier in the finals judges briefing. "Appearance of entry. I want you to rate them one through nine, what looks the best. A rib isn't going to look the same as a hog or a shoulder. They're all going to look different. But the criteria you're using is, which one looked the most appetizing to you.…Now, tenderness the same way. It's hard because you're judging nine different entries. Rate it one through nine. Now you might get some and say, well, this was perfect for a rib. This guy's shoulder was perfect. They're different. It's tough. You've got to make a decision. You're judging nine pork entries." And on through the other categories.

Unsurprisingly, the finals judges, when they return to mark their scores and recall Larry's instructions, agree that *it's tough*. "Often, there is a very fine line between the quality of their product," Wanda says.

"All the teams that were in the finals are champions," says Sheila later, "and their barbecue on that particular day was as good as it gets. It was very difficult to decide which entry should get first place. My decision was based on small differences among the teams: my first place choice had a slightly better presentation and the flavor of the meat suited my taste just a little more than the others."

This one-through-nine criterion-by-criterion request is not made by other reps in finals, and Cliff is not used to the difference. Completing his scorecard requires further explanation from Larry; it subsequently requires more time, as well, pushing the event timetable back.

It's not the time taken in completing scorecards that threatens the 6:00 announcement time, however.

The power outage is already doing that.

TEN-POINT-OH, TEN-POINT-OH, AND THE RUSHIN' JUDGE GIVES IT A NINE-POINT-NINE

"You mark your scorecards in pen, then we can't cheat and change them."

– Larry O's joking response to a judging seminar participant's question, "Do you mark your scorecard in pen or pencil?"

Saturday, July 16, 2005, around 4:00. The power cuts out.

Lightning strikes an electrical line. Finals judging concludes during the outage, though neither teams nor judges are affected. Cooking by wood and charcoal. Judging by daylight. What little daylight the rains allow, anyway.

Still, the contest needs power. The problem isn't quite the hypothetical computer glitch that Walt had cited, in his conference call with Ron and Judy back in June, as a reason that 5:00 announcements were "pushing it." Yet, computer operation could be an obstacle; without electricity, unglitched computers run no better than glitched ones.

When the finals judges complete their scorecards, they do so in natural light from the windows in the unpowered bank building—ironically, in the area set aside for "blind" judging.

Shortly before the last of the scorecards is completed, power clicks back on. On one side of the street, anyway. The originally considered 5 o'clock announcement time is not far off.

Scorecards in hand, power back on, Larry feeds the scores to Walt and Walt feeds the scores to the computer and the computer feeds the results back. The results and a surprise.

The winner is . . .

A tie.

Walt and Larry are shocked. The finals scoring system is designed, with its decimals and rankings and category weighting, to prevent ties.

But there is a tie nonetheless.

Not for first place in any of the categories, fortunately. And not for grand champion. Those winners are clear and undisputed. But there, lurking in one of the categories, is a tie for second place.

Now, this isn't basketball; no overtime judges will be sent out. And it isn't football; the wild card won't be selected based on results of head-to-head competition or performance of other teams from the same state. No sudden death overtime, no 19th holes, no one-game division playoff, no quickie hamburger patty grill-off in front of Food Network cameras, no wheeled-cooker demolition derby of the barbecue rigs, second place to the last rig standing.

It's barbecue. And barbecue has its own tiebreaker. Walt and Larry go first to the teams' flavor scores. Of the two, which had the lowest score from the judges? That team loses the tie. If the flavor scores are tied, then tenderness scores are compared, and on through the categories until a winner is determined. But today there's a clear winner in the flavor tie-breaker, so they need go no further.

Walt and Larry don't like ties. A tie means consultation of the rule book. It means reinputting scores. That's a bit of a bother, certainly, but worse yet is that it's one more time-taker, one more element pushing the finalization of scores and the

Larry and Walt working scores in the rep room.

printing of those scores in various forms closer to the beginning of the awards ceremony. Kevin Weatherman, a Galax Chamber board member and keeper of the accounts, is waiting to fill in the names of the winners on the checks. He waits a bit longer to find out which name gets added to which check.

And 6:00 is looming.

Kevin already has some work taken care of—the winners of the Friday ancillary contests have been determined. But he needs one of the several reports Walt and Larry begin printing out after the tie has been handled—the report Ron Passmore will read from on the main stage (a report that serves, as well, as the official media statement). Among the other reports are the raw judging scores in both preliminaries and finals. These reports will be grouped by team, which sees only *their* raw scores, and distributed to the teams after announcement of grand champion. Each team sees what on-site Judge 1 gave them, criterion by criterion; what Judge 2 gave them, and so on. *But*: "A lot of teams think that they've got the system figured out," Chuck Doan tells judge trainees, "and we throw kind of a wrench in the system. They think it's judge one-two-three the way they came. When we put your scores in, we can put them in three-two-one, or two-three-one or whatever.... We mess with them. They're always trying to get these edges to figure out the system, and so we kind of mess with 'em."

Larry jokes, "We don't want them to slit your tires."

By quarter of 5, the paperwork is complete, and a few people inside the bank building know who's going to be celebrating. Judy Brannock writes the name of the grand champion on the big 4'x6' for-show check that will be handed out at the end. Her lettering is too big; she has to use the initial of the last word in the name. Larry cautions against anyone being able to see the for-show check ahead of time. Such sneak peaks have prematurely "announced" winners a couple of times at other contests.

"We're gonna get a little cover," Judy says.

"OK. A garbage bag or something?" (Why not? Worked for the finals judges.)

When all the paperwork is completed, and information is ready for the stage announcements, Larry says, "Piece of cake. Five minutes to spare."

"Oh lord!" Judy whispers in vociferous relief. "You're a darling, I'm telling you."

Outside, the Grayson Street emcee is apparently reading someone's mind. She's drumming up interest in the award ceremony, now just a few minutes away, by admiring the fiddle trophies on display on the stage.

"Make your way up to the stage, and check out the trophies that are going to be given out here in just a little while," she announces over the loudspeakers. "They were created by Barr's

Fiddle Shop specially for that. Those are *real* fiddles. They work, they're beautiful, they're absolutely gorgeous. Take pictures of them. They're one of the most unique trophies that have ever been given out at any barbecue competition. Y'all go up and take a gander at them before someone gets their hands on them and takes them back to…"

…she searches to think of a faraway place they might disappear to . . .

…"I don't know"…

…and then she pulls out of the air the state of origin of the just-calculated grand champion.

Reading someone's mind…

32

"IT JUST AIN'T THAT DAMN SERIOUS"

"This is barbecue."

—Heard over and over as another way of saying, "Don't worry; be happy"

Sunday, July 17, 2005. Looking ahead to next year, Larry Ohrberg has a suggestion for a better contest.

"Make sure you get some good reps next year," he tells Ron Passmore the morning after the competition.

Walt nods. "That's one way to improve things."

Especially because it's a joke, Ron will have nothing to do with that. "How do I guarantee that I get you guys back next year?" he has asked at least twice during the competition, mainly because he doesn't like the answer he first received: There is no guarantee.

Reps select the competitions, not vice versa. At the beginning of each half season, the seven sets of MBA reps meet to "draft" the events they will oversee in the next six months. There is no cook-off to determine ranking, no reppy sack race. Just names out of a hat to determine order. Some other rep team could very well select Galax before Walt and Larry get to choose. Ron's normally serious look goes grim.

"I think if we're spending the money with Memphis in

May and the reps don't object, they ought to honor our request. It's our money."

Larry says, "You should at least have the right of first refusal if there's some reps that you don't like."

"Well, how would I know that?"

"Wait till the contest is over," Larry says.

Walt nods. "We're not done yet."

But Ron *does* listen to the other suggestions. Early-morning Hank Williams, Jr./truck horn duets will lead to an enforced quiet time, probably starting at 11 p.m. "The only sounds you should hear at night," David Hair says, "is street-sweeping and cleaning the Porta Potties."

Long lines at both barbecue vendors will lead to additional vendors. As Brian Funk will report in *The Galax Gazette* on August 1, "The only squeal organizers heard was that there wasn't enough barbecue to eat." And the public's interest in the food will lead to installing a People's Choice. This is what the Kerces had recommended when they dropped off their rig back in late June; it's what David Hair had echoed after a brief exchange with a townswoman on Friday the 15th, while he worked to set up the Jack's Old South Booth. The local media had indeed been vigorous about declaring this a competition and not a festival. Ron Passmore made that point with Maurice Vaughan on WBRF; Austin Caviness had stated clearly in his Friday noon weathercast that "It's important to know that the folks here, they're serious about competition and we don't necessarily get to sample what they eat. In fact, if you want your own barbecue, there are plenty of vendors here offering that. But the teams don't want to be bothered by saying 'When can we have some, when can we have some.'" But if it looks like a festival, people think festival.

On that Friday, the townswoman asked David, "Are you giving out samples?"

David (thin David, bordering on gaunt, who looks like he could stand to eat a few more samples himself) responded politely, "No. These are competition teams." He gestured down to the next block. "They're vending barbecue on Grayson Street."

"Well, that's crazy."

"Health regulations."

"*Well!*" and she steamed off down the street.

Other changes for next year include service common at other competitions. At Galax, the teams are made responsible for taking out the trash. There are enough dumpsters, and they're not all that far away, but some competitions have regular trash pickup for the teams during Friday's prep. Teams will place trash-filled boxes and/or bags of garbage in front of their cooksite, and volunteers or paid event staff will swing by periodically to haul them away—despite the infrequent dangers. At one competition, Chris Mills of Flying Pigs received his blind box and, wanting to keep it from getting dirty, wrapped it in a pristine new garbage bag. A dutiful volunteer kept the garbage bag to its stated purpose, and threw the blind box away. (Chris sent a teammate to the judges' tent to explain what had happened and request another blind box. The contest organizer, well-schooled in the Crash Test Dummy Institute of Having Fun, responded by dispatching a volunteer to tell Chris simply that he was disqualified, then arriving a minute or two later with a replacement blind box.)

Looking ahead to next year, the future is looking good to most everybody concerned. A couple of teams warn that the travel time and cost of gas will dampen participation. On the other hand, two judges who have learned the distances involved later note that they will return—as cooks. Teams and judges alike praise the town, the scenery, the friendliness, the competition's attention to their needs, the trophies—always the trophies. They praise the hard work.

And they do this without seeing the members of the Galax Chamber of Commerce sweeping up on the Sunday after the event. Sweeping up, toting trash, wrapping up details. They do this without seeing Ron Passmore emerge from his upstairs apartment that noon, apologizing to co-organizer Judy Brannock, "I'm sorry…I'm so sorry…", simply because he'd overslept and hadn't arrived at 9 to help with the cleanup. After he'd gotten almost *no* sleep in the previous seventy-two hours while making sure things ran smoothly for the 24 part of 24/7.

In later weeks, as next year begins to approach more rapidly, Ron does not hear Larry Ohrberg briefings at later contests, does not hear about general speculations of barbecue futures that perhaps underlie some of his comments. In those briefings, Larry Ohrberg speaks of cycles. This is not Larry O the funster; this is not cook Larry #1 (or maybe Larry #2), that half or maybe this half of Two Fat Larrys; not even Larry the Crash Test Dummy MBA rep, though he is speaking as a rep at the Bowling Green, Kentucky, Balloons, Tunes and BBQ competition. Larry has added something to his judges briefing; something that didn't surface in his Galax briefings.

His specific topic is new teams. It's a topic that he speaks of often and passionately. New teams are the future of the circuit. Much was done in Galax to welcome and foster the two new teams there. The instructions to not feed the ambassadors were intended to take pressure off the newbies who probably didn't have enough food to feed both judges *and* ambassadors. Individual coaching sessions were staged for Nervous Wreck and So-Co. Judges were asked to be forgiving of lapses in new-team presentations or the amount of meat presented—as always, "We're not judging teams today. We're judging pork." But in Bowling Green, Larry has begun speaking not just of new teams rising but of old teams fading—implied in previous briefings but never specifically voiced. It's a six- to seven-year cycle for teams, he says. "They get burned out. They go broke. They become judges and they're delighted they don't have to clean up anymore." He says this lightheartedly, but he knows whereof he speaks.

And they become reps.

Teams dissolve because of cancer and staph infections and heart conditions. Teams split because of egos and internal battles and even domestic battles (including one married couple of cooks who walked out on each other right in the middle of a contest, leaving the other team members to scramble to fill their places.) The occasional briefing has begun after a moment of reflection on those judges and team members who have passed since the previous contest.

Roles erode, transpose, evolve. Cooks become judges, judges occasionally become cooks. Reps become organizers, organizers become reps. Old blood trickles away. New blood infuses itself. Teams wander to other circuits, to catering gigs, back to their own backyards. Teams come out of retirement.

When Larry Ohrberg speaks of cycles, one wonders if perhaps he is thinking of his own. He's been a cook, a judge, a rep. A rep who talks now about teams burning out…

Rick Dalton is talking about next year, too. Next year and next year and the year after that. "Hal Berry asked me four, five years ago, When does it end?" Rick says. "I ain't answered him yet. But I can tell you when it will end. When I quit having fun."

"Some people take it very seriously," Guido of Porkosaurus says, "but we gotta always remember, this is a barbecue contest, and the bottom line is, we're doing this for fun. And when we lose the fun, we've lost it all. When you lose the fun, you start to *find* bad judges, to *find* bad places, to *find* bad events. And that's what's not fun. If you keep it fun, and you emulate that through whatever you're doing, it's gonna happen."

AN ELEPHANT NEVER...UMM, HOW DOES THAT GO?...AN ELEPHANT IS NEVER FORGOTTEN...SOMETHING LIKE THAT

"Ninety-nine and a half percent of you are some of the finest people in the world, and we appreciate it."

— Roy Barber thanking participants in 2005's Tennessee Funfest barbecue competition

Saturday morning, July 16, 2005. Before the judges' briefing, Larry Ohrberg, Walt Brown, Ron Passmore and Carlene Poole are finishing up briefing the ambassadors who will assist the on-site judges.

"Ron," Larry says, "do you want to say anything to these ambassadors?"

"Thank you," Ron says. "Just thank you for being here."

"You know what you guys have done?" Larry says. "You've eaten an elephant."

One of the volunteers says, "We've eaten an elephant?"

Larry is referring neither to a meat selection in the Anything But contest nor to the amount of meat cooked and consumed at the competition, though the meat poundage is certainly elephantine.

For purposes of calculation, let's say the average hog cooked in Galax weighs 125 pounds, the average shoulder seventeen pounds, the average rack of ribs two and a half pounds. Eight hogs (six teams cooked one hog and Gwatney cooked two), seventy shoulders (for sake of argument, an average of seven shoulders for each of the ten shoulder teams), and 144 racks of rubs (again, for sake of argument, an average of twelve racks for each of the twelve ribs teams). That's 2,550 pounds—one and one quarter tons of meat, and that's just for a small competition.

Of course, the Galax judges don't eat all one and a quarter tons. The volunteers get their fair shot at the rest of it. (So, too, at competitions in general, do team members, local charities, and businesses.) As Carlene told volunteers on Saturday morning, "Your reward will be on the grazing table."

The previous Wednesday, at the end of his WBRF radio interview of Ron Passmore, Maurice Vaughan had said, "Finally, we want to wrap it up and tell you how you can be an important part of this—yes, you can do this as a volunteer. Ron, tell us about that."

"If you want to be able to eat all the barbecue that you can stomach, the best way to do that is to be a volunteer."

"Oh, you feed the volunteers?"

"The volunteers will be the only ones to actually be able to consume the competition product. Once the judging is complete, the judges take the box off the table and move it over to what we call the grazing table."

"Oh, the grazing...Mr. K," Maurice says to his producer, "you hear this—the grazing table, that's our type of pasture."

"And the volunteers can go there and just graze till they're sick. You get a T-shirt out of the deal and you get to eat all the professional barbecue competition barbecue you want to eat, and be a part of this first-year event. It's history in the making."

"Great great great."

When the first round of blind judging ends and the meat is

transferred out to the hospitality area, it quickly becomes clear that the Smoke on the Mountain volunteers have not yet learned the art of barbecue competition grazing. They line up politely at one end of the row of open blind boxes, and drift along the table, using forks to stab meat that they put on their plates. They exchange pleasantries and compliments about the food before them. This is the activity expected from courteous patrons of buffet restaurants. But a good barbecue graze rarely involves forks. And rarely anything as official as a line. And sometimes not even that courtesy thing. Cluster about. Grab a hunk, dunk it in some sauce. It doesn't even have to be the sauce intended for that meat. In fact, select the sauce the way you follow directions in the old joke: "Take a left where the old Whipple place used to be." In this case, use the sauce set down where the meat used to be. If it's good meat, with your luck it's gone by the time you get there. And if you graze your way to an empty blind box, at least you can comfort yourself with the possibility that the gone-gone meat's cook knew how to concoct a good sauce, too.

Plates? Occasionally. But not necessary. Yeah, get a paper napkin for wiping your fingers off, but that's about the only grazing accouterment you really need. Just like in judging. Compliments? Comment on how the meat looks, share your opinion with your neighbor. If it looks nasty, say so. If it tastes nasty, say so. If it tastes good, shut up or it won't be around long enough for you to get seconds.

"Remember," Larry O told the blind judges as they ate, scribbled, savored, pulled at the meat at a different competition, "the volunteers work for tips."

"The tip," said judge Marlene, "is 'Stay away from the full box.'"

"If the box is still full," Larry said, "there's a reason for it."

And it's not because the box is stuffed with elephant. That

beast has already been dispatched.

"You've eaten an elephant," Larry says shortly after Ron has thanked the Galax volunteers in person. The elephant is the considerable undertaking that a barbecue competition represents. "We said this last March, we said, 'This is like an elephant. You know how you eat an elephant? Everybody takes a little bite.' Everybody in Galax has been a part of this...."

THE GRILL OF VICTORY, THE AGONY OF DEFEAT

"You go home and wash those shorts, now."
— Brad Cheatham of Carbondale Eagles razzing a competitor who had just taken fifth place at a Missouri competition

Saturday evening, July 16, 2005. Walt Brown has allowed Sweet Swine o' Mine to come out of their booth for this announcement, the announcement of the Smoke on the Mountain Barbecue Championship winners. The clock is closing in on 6:00, and teams, judges, organizers, reps, numerous groups of local onlookers—all have gathered before the Grayson Street Stage.

The staff of the Galax Smokehouse sits at the very front. With the electricity still off over on the Carroll County side of Main, including the Smokehouse itself, staffers have closed down until power can be restored.

Contest officials—the ones not on stage for the announcements—stand off to the side. The Crash-Test Dummies keep perception in mind; they don't want anyone thinking there's any favoritism or secret signal involved should they stand with or near a team before the announcements. Carlene sits under the small sound equipment tent, similarly distanced from the

teams, and close to the Crash-Test Dummies she has so exuber-
antly named. Chief Clark and several officers and firefighters
stand offstage, stage left, to watch the ceremonies.

On the stage is a chorus of blue. Members of the Galax
Chamber of Commerce stand behind the row of fiddle trophies.

Jim is now properly attired. He wears the notorious pink
suspenders over his blue T-shirt.

In front of the row of fiddle trophies are Ron and Leesa,
who will be making announcements, including winners;
Elizabeth Roberts, Miss Virginia International, who will hand
trophies to the winners and smile big for the photo ops; Kevin
Weatherman, who will hand out the rarely declined prize
checks; and Tom Barr, who is scurrying about checking wires
and amplifiers and connections, trying to fix some pretty irri-
tating distortion that began when Ron took the microphone.
Unlike some of the Barr family endeavors, this is not an
acoustic performance. (Which is, as Judy might term it, "a
good thing," since competitions that try to get away without
PA equipment are consistently doomed to frustration.)

Awards ceremonies at barbecue competitions are rarely
extravagant affairs. Everyone involved is usually ready to Just
Get On With It. On the other hand, participants don't want
you to Rush Past It, either. One competition, apparently pres-
sured by the impatience of the crowd primarily assembled not
to watch cooks clutch hardware but to watch a country star,
began announcing winners without bothering to hand out trophies—and when they relented and began handing them out,
they did it so quickly that simply tossing them to the winning
teams wouldn't have been that much more efficient.

Often a band does indeed follow the awards, as is the case this
Saturday evening in Galax. But that's usually the extent of onstage
entertainment. In fact, awards ceremonies are sometimes held
indoors, depending on the weather. The Caruthersville heat had

Cody Cline of Nervous Wreck Cook'n Crew awaits the awards ceremony.

teams thankful for crowding into the judges' hospitality room…the *air-conditioned* judges' hospitality room.

One notable exception to Just Get On With It took place at the St. Louis Barbecue Fest, 2004, when organizer Terry Black brought in Leslie Johnson, a staffer for Missouri Senator Jim Talent, to sing the National Anthem. With a deeply felt, deeply resonant voice, Johnson tore out the hearts of the audience, musical syllable by strong musical syllable. At the anthem's conclusion: tears in listeners' eyes, emotional silence, many moments of emotional silence, before the audience broke into applause. The silence roared as ferociously as the sound of the F16s over the Barbecue Fest the year before. "The crickets, how dare you?" one judge later said.

Waiting for the awards ceremony to begin, the Galax

crowd is subdued, anticipatory. Sweet Swine o' Mine seems to be watching everything *but* the Grayson Street stage. Pat and Richard stand cross-armed, waiting for the proceedings to begin. They have one finals slot: whole hog.

Natural Born Grillers mill about the golf cart that John David sits in, a gravitational center. Mr. Bill leans into the cart, propping his arms on its top as he chats with John David. Grillers are in all three—whole hog, shoulder, ribs. The Natural Born Grillers vending booth has suspended operation for the time being; sales will resume after the awards.

Grillers' Tango, wearing loops of beads almost as festive as Sweet Cheeks's, is mingling, chatting up other teams, including the nearby group from Kings Cooking.

Pig Pounda Kappa team members, in back near the DJ stand, are a bit antsy. They round out the hog finalists, and are among the ribs finalists.

Jack's Old South team members are solemnly poker-faced. They finaled in shoulder only. This is rare for Myron and Jack's, to appear in only one finals category, but it can work to their advantage. If you have, say, a shoulder and a rib in finals, you're in actuality competing against yourself. Gwatney Championship Barbecue Team shares the Jack's Old South poker face. They missed only one finals category—hog. For them, too, missing a finals is rare.

Before the Grayson Street stage, Lisa and Dan and Debbie Martin of Pure and Sinful have brought in green canvas folding chairs. Dan stands behind Lisa and Debbie, joking about. Young Sean of Smoked Encounters sits pensively, cross-legged on the concrete, chin propped on folded hands, next to Debbie. His father and grandfather are in a rough line behind him, each striking a similar pose with their left hands in their pockets, as if they were real son and father, and not son and "just the father-in-law."

Mary Dyer fans herself. Her Pit Connection crew is standing next to the Natural Born cluster, and Cody Cline and several friends are grouped nearby.

Jeff Holmes isn't there. Some wonder if his absence is in protest of The Music. He explains later that he was simply exhausted, catching up on sleep. His kids sit cross-legged before the stage, representing Hawg Wild.

When wiring problems are solved and the presentation resumes about fifteen minutes past 6, Ron Passmore takes the microphone, and once again works his carefully prepared agenda. Item #1 this time is not "Thanks for participating" but "Welcome to the first annual Memphis Barbecue Association Smoke on the Mountain BBQ Championship." Ron dutifully thanks all the contributors, some by name and some by group, from the volunteers to the downtown merchants to the sponsors…to the teams, judges and MBA reps "for traveling the distance to participate."

And with little additional adieu, further or not, he makes the awards announcements.

First, the ancillaries:

A local business, Bearly a Memory, wins the Merchants Pig Decoration Award for its event-related window display. (And with its "Treasures and Treats From Fur-gotten Days" slogan, it should also get honorary membership in the National Pigpun Society, as soon as someone creates it.)

Smoked Encounters of the Third Swine takes second place for sauce, and Sweet Swine o' Mine, first. Both sauces feature unusual ingredients for sauce: raspberry and apricot, respectively. Sean accompanies his dad to the stage to accept the second-place plaque.

So-Co Smokers takes second for Anything But, and Hawg Wild, first. The labeling of the Anything But plaque follows through on Ron's spelling of the category, Anything Butt.

Local cooks Mike Stevens and Mark Fackrell—the Mountain Grillas—win the Patio Porker contest (as well as full membership in the National Pigpun Society).

Then, as Ron has called them so often, the Big Dogs start running.

When Ron reads the MBA category announcements, from the sheet that serves as both emcee script and, later, media handout, Larry reads along from his copy. He's double-checking that Ron gets the order right. Winners' names have infrequently been confused by emcees at previous contests, getting the wrong teams all excited.

Ron follows the script to the letter.

Fifth-Place Hog

Fifth place is an honor and it's often a trophy as it is today in Galax. That trophy has thrilled any number of newer teams, but established teams are not enamored with fifth place. Part of the disappointment is that taking fifth, like kissing your sister, involves no scoring. You *almost* placed high enough to nab that MBA point.

One point? What's one point? For two of teams that missed finals in the whole hog category, it's the difference between—at that brief moment, anyway, second and third place in the overall MBA standings. Recall that Jack's Old South and Gwatney Championship Barbecue entered the weekend in a tie for second, just two points behind Natural Born. There'll be considerable distribution of points as thirds and seconds and firsts are announced. But if you ain't in finals, maybe you can grab a fourth.

One point? What's one point? John Akins, Galax judge and head cook of the Huish Barbecue Team, knows well the power of one point. "We tripled in fourths a lot of times," he says—meaning taking fourth place in all three categories at a competition. "That will get as many points as a second." He tells the story of how Huish and Boggy Pond—another excellent team—were battling one year at the final competition of the year for the last spot in the MBA top ten. Tied in team points going in, Huish and Boggy Pond together nabbed the top two places in the shoulder and rib categories. Shoulder: first to Huish, second to Boggy Pond. Rib: the opposite. Points were a wash. But Huish cooked a hog, and Boggy Pond didn't. The Huish hog took fourth. One point. And finished out the year in the top ten. By one point. One hog point...that you won't get by placing fifth.

One point? What's one point?

Jack's Old South has kissed its sister. Not bad for a team that hit road problems and started out late. Myron is, in a sense, prepared for this. When he began cooking in Galax, later on Friday than he wanted, he decided to start work on the shoulders. By in a sense sacrificing the hog by delaying its prep even more, he could keep the shoulders closer to their ideal timetable. The other choice was to start work on the hog, which would push out the shoulder schedule.

Keeping the shoulder to its schedule worked; he made finals with it.

The hog, on the other hand: "It wasn't my best hog by far. Nowhere close. The hog—that just came up in the category of Not Enough Time. Hog would have been a lot better if Nick had been able to keep that fire up." It wasn't that Nick wasn't trying. "He was just trying to find the wood and get the heat up, and you can't jack the heat up like that with that wood—you gotta have something else that fuels it."

On stage, the team smiles big as they accept the intricately scroll-sawed fifth-place plaque. Ironically, David Hair pantomimes a kiss out to someone in the audience. It's doubtful that it's his sister.

Fourth-Place Hog

Saturday, September 3, Knoxville. A small crowd is clustered before a half-dozen or so video cameras on a terrace beside the University of Tennessee's Thompson-Boling Arena. It's after noon on Game Day. The football Vols are opening their season in Neyland Stadium, which provides a backdrop for the scene about to be videotaped. In front, to stage right, stands the Food Network's Bobby Flay and his team of UT frat rats nicknamed, for the purposes of this show, "The Boys." To stage left stands the Food Network's Paula Deen and her team of championship Memphis Barbecue Association grillers, nicknamed "The Men." Between Bobby and Paula, Kevin Moriarty of Al Roker Productions in black-and-white stripes—football ref garb—stares hard at an overhead jib camera, awaiting cue.

Behind the crowd, stage right, sits the "tricked-out" Airstream trailer the Food Network has constructed at a cost of six figures for this *Tricked Out Tailgating* special to be aired in October. Stage left sits the barbecue rig constructed years ago by The Men—the Gwatney Championship Barbecue Team. All stand at the 50-yard line of a green swath of outdoor carpeting painted with gridiron hash marks.

Bobby's Boys have just gone head-to-head on camera against The Lady and Men, iron-chefing a tailgate menu of burgers, hot wings, side dish and dessert.

On cue, Moriarty the chef-ref intones, "And the grand champion of the *Tricked Out Tailgating* competition…" He turns stage left, Gwatneyward, gives a first-down signal, and blurts…"The Men!"

Cheers, applause, whoopwhoop. Paula Deen high-fives the Gwatney crew, hugs Bobby Flay. Stage Manager Randy Beffrey gestures vigorously with his arms to keep crowd enthusiasm high. Thirty, forty seconds. Cheers, whoopwhoop.

When the hoopla dies down, when the tapes stop rolling,

Randy yells, "That was perfect! Let's do it again!"

He's referring to taping the grand-champion announcement, of course, but he's just shouted the secret of winning on the barbecue circuit week after week. Be perfect. Do it again.

"Consistency is key." Doesn't matter who said that—they've all said it.

Saturday, July 16, Galax, fourth-place hog. Rick Dalton didn't do perfect again, and he knows it. "It wasn't that the stuff wasn't done, we didn't get it as done as we usually get it done. The hog was off about six or eight degrees.

"My wife, she enters every score in the computer at home. When we go to the cooks' meeting, we put down every piece of information on a piece of paper she developed. How many is in hog, how many is in shoulder, how many is in ribs, what's the time, what's this, what's that, what's the events, what's thisthat. And what I'll do, too, is I'll write down what the temperatures are, is it raining, is it cold—she enters that in. We record what was the final meat temperature, what was this, what was that." Reviewing the this and that after Galax showed Rick that the temperatures he reached there weren't as high as those he'd recorded at more successful contests.

What else went into his notes? "Very very good contest. Nice weather conditions and so forth. Rain. Thank god we were on asphalt. Upset over the final judging. The hog went pretty much as I thought could happen to it. It happened. It was pretty much like Myron and I talked, two of us are going to get into this thing. And somebody's going to get in that normally does not. But that's fair. Don't get me wrong, that's fair. And it did happen pretty much like we thought it would. We didn't think that we'd be the two out, arguably the best two hog cookers in the country. But we can go to the next contest and have nothing get in."

As Myron and team descend the stage and retrace their

route back into the crowd, Rick and team are taking the same route toward their fourth-place plaque. The groups slow a bit in passing to exchange smiles and congrats and hefty hand-shakes. This exchange will be repeated by different teams ascending and descending with each announcement.

Third-Place Hog

Mission accomplished.

That's Richard Lackie's succinct assessment of his team's performance. Proud of the hog, proud to have beaten two of the best. But, most important, mission accomplished.

They came for the fiddle.

They got the fiddle.

Second-Place Hog

Members of the two remaining hog finalists tense up. Ron Passmore makes the announcement for second place. Natural Born Grillers breaks into a cheer. They're happy enough for Pig Pounda; happier still that Pig Pounda's second-place hog means first place for them.

Miss America. Miss Universe. You know the scene. The first runner-up, the should-Miss-America-not-be-able-to-fulfill-her-duties also-ran is announced. The last chick standing breaks into tears.

Natural Born Grillers is the last chick standing.

"We took second hog," says Gary Kerce. "I don't know why, but we did. What we do when we cook a hog to make sure we got a good one, I try to have that thing done about 5:30, 6 o'clock, because I want that hog to rest about three hours, three and a half hours. The more resting time, the better that thing gets. Matter of fact, there's been many times we've made finals in hog and on the back side of that hog that I haven't cut, it has rested five hours. And many times it gets ten times better if you get in finals. Because I know if I get in finals with a hog, when the finals judges come around, I know that hog's gonna be there because it's sitting there slowly bringing in everything."

First-Place Hog

Team members of Natural Born Grillers exchange congratulations with Pig Pounda as Gary and crew come down from the stage. The last team standing in the whole hog category gets to pose for pictures with a real last chick standing, Elizabeth Roberts, the one remaining in the Miss Virginia International 2005 competition.

Fifth-Place Shoulder

Though they'd been disappointed about not making finals, the team called first in the ascending order of the shoulder participants are "surprised and very excited." Pit Connection is called to the stage in their Galax Chamber costumes—their team T-shirts are the same color as the Chamber T's.

"We are fired up now," says Mary Dyer. "Winning now and then, even fourth or fifth place, gives you incentive to continue on. And we will be entering quite a few contests next season. The only way to go is *up!*"

Fourth-Place Shoulder

Says Gary Kerce later, "I thought we had a real good shoulder—I liked it, my judges liked it very well—but we ended up fourth on shoulder only by a hair." Though he's not totally surprised. "We used to be real strong on shoulder. . . a few years back we was cooking shoulders, they were strong shoulders—didn't know how to cook a hog or a rib." In perfecting the hog and the rib, he'd lost concentration on the shoulder. "We had a real strong shoulder then, so we're going to try to back up."

It may be fourth place, but before leaving the stage, Gary Kerce holds the Virginia-silhouette plaque high above his head like it was the Stanley Cup.

Third-Place Shoulder

"We didn't do our job in Galax," Rick Dalton will say later. "Nothing against Pig Pounda or Grillers, but we didn't do our job. If we do our job, it's not a struggle. We struggled like a sonofabitch in Galax. We struggled enough I cooked last weekend," the weekend after Galax, an "off" weekend on the circuit. Like his hog, his shoulder was, he says, off about six or eight degrees.

Second-Place Shoulder

"I wasn't sure of my hog," Myron Mixon had said Friday about how his late arrival affected his cooking strategy, "so I went to my shoulders—'cause I still had time to do my shoulders the normal way—and I did those first. I wasn't going to mess them up, too, because I was in the window there where I could get my shoulders on, and they'd be like they should be. Then I came back to the hog.

"Shoulders were good," he says, but he was not pleased when the finals judges arrived at his booth. "I look around, I see those Memphis-area judges," says the deep-south Georgian, "I start playing for second." Wanda is solidly Memphis area. Sheila and Cliff are, in the real estate parlance, Memphis-near at best (Tullahoma is closer to Nashville than Memphis). Skip Sawyer is currently out of Raleigh, North Carolina—he grew up in Virginia.

First-Place Shoulder

John David and Birm are liking their shoulder better than their first-place hog. John David thinks the hog wasn't quite there. But now with firsts in both categories, they have two chances at grand champion. If they take grand, neither will care which piece of meat did it for them.

There is only applause for them as they take the stage a second time. That's usually the case, but Birm has said with resignation that Grillers, like other consistent winners on the circuit, have heard the infrequent boo from within the crowd when they've won. Dissatisfied competitors grumble about contests being fixed, or about judges being biased by team reputation and previous success. While Ron Passmore was recruiting competitors for Smoke on the Mountain, one team leader told Ron that he would cook in Galax only if Jack's Old South was not there; he "knew" he couldn't beat Jack's because all the judges are wowed by his success. Birm at Natural Born answers such thoughts simply with "Good teams get good and stay good."

From the stage, John David works to mend fences. He'd already spoken to Jeff Holmes personally about The Music, and today he thanks all the teams for participating and singles out Hawg Wild: "You guys are great."

Fifth-Place Rib

"We were happy with our ribs," says Kings Cooking's Danny Sneed. "Wasn't too happy with the hog. What happened was we got too small of a hog. We cut our temperature down, backed our temperature off, and we shouldn't have done that.

"The judges were a little bit surprised that I was cooking the ribs direct, because they were cut on indirect wood. A lot of the judges are." Danny concedes that it's a regional factor. "We was brought up on direct heat. We won our first contest in '89 on direct heat. Burned hickory wood.

"We had the flavor on them. The moisture. They were surprised at that. They were surprised that they were as consistent as they were.... The key to it is moving them every thirty minutes. If you just let them lay there, you let them dry out. 'Don't you lose your heat?' Yeah, you do lose heat when you open the lid, but it recovers quickly on that cooker. It'll recover really quick."

Fourth-Place Rib

"Ribs were good," Myron says. "Not bad for a country boy with only one mama and one papa."

Third-Place Rib

"What people don't understand about this sport is the very similar parallels with NASCAR," Rick Dalton says. "It's a sport where you lose more than you win. And the ones who can accept losing and improve upon that are successful." Still, "Galax was a bitter pill to swallow." Just as he knew his hog and his shoulder didn't get the job done, Rick knew his rib was dead on. "That bad-ass rib shows up, it kills all the other cats on the island."

"Them ribs," says Al Norton, "was the best I've eaten in the last three contests."

"I know when it's good," Rick says. "I know when I need to increase my language to try to sell it. I didn't have to do that with the rib up there. I coulda just got up, walked off and said, 'There you go, do what you want with them at the table.'"

When Gwatney's third place is announced, Rick sees in the reaction of one of the finals judges remaining in the crowd that that judge agrees with his disappointment.

Second-Place Rib

About this time, a couple of teams are likely thinking "pass-down."

The grand champion of each MBA competition earns a bid to the World Championship Barbecue Cooking Competition in Memphis in May. A bid consists of a guaranteed invitation, and a paid entry. If the grand champion of any given competition has already earned a bid, the bid is "passed down" to the next-highest point-getter.

Three of the finalists have secured their 2006 bids long ago. Natural Born Grillers granded the first 2005 competition out of the chute—Batesville, Arkansas, in March. Gwatney granded in Jackson, Tennessee in early June (the second of three straight competitions they took grand champion, in each of the three categories). Jack's Old South earned its bid in Marianne, Florida in mid April in a fashion almost alien to them—they got the passdown. Sweet Swine and Pig Pounda have not snared their bids yet and are, therefore, "eligible" to receive passdown.

At this moment, Pig Pounda would prefer not receiving the passdown. Earning passdown would mean they stalled on (pun intended) second fiddle. They want the third fiddle. They want the grand championship and its bid to Memphis in May. Not that they'll turn down the passdown, of course.

If Natural Born Grillers is handed second-place, Pig Pounda takes one more step toward the grand championship. It also means that their rib has scored sufficiently high to make securing the passdown probable, should it come to that. Probable, but not guaranteed. Even though Sweet Swine's hog has taken a third place, this isn't a card game where king of one suit always beats jack of any other suit. First or second place in one category does not necessarily out-rank third in another. It's all points.

The finals judges, you see, are not tasked with ranking three hog entries among themselves one-two-three, then three shoulders, then three ribs. They have ranked nine entries, one through nine, regardless of category. In theory, the third-place hog could rank as high as third overall, and the first-place rib could rank as low as seventh overall. In theory.

Though Natural Born Grillers were concerned about the tenderness of their rib this day, the rib still made finals. The extra time allowed the remaining ribs to get tender; they have hopes for first place, which would also guarantee them the grand championship.

Ron Passmore intones the second-place winner.

Pig Pounda celebrates the hardest.

First-Place Rib

"The rib was on the money," says Pig Pounda's Gary. "I knew that going in. We know when we cook a rib whether it's there or not. Once I touch it…and I never taste my ribs. I don't eat no barbecue during the contest. When I touch it, 'Yeah, that's there!' I knew it was there. I knew it was a first-place rib."

He hopes it is a grand champion rib. He wants the third fiddle. He wants the Memphis in May bid clean.

Grand Champion

Friday, July 22, Memphis. One week after Galax, Wayne and Linda Booth of Red Hot Smokers have swapped cooker/cookee roles. *They* are the ones getting grilled. Gently. They and John David Wheeler of Natural Born are answering questions posed by students in the judges' seminar in Memphis. "What draws teams to a competition?" asks a student, herself an organizer.

"Free beer," John David deadpans.

Wayne asks where the competition is.

"Outside of Pensacola, Florida."

"Can I stay in your condo for a week?"

Following the jokes, Wayne, Linda and John David talk briefly and seriously about prize money. Expensive sport and all, and the bigger the purse, the more attractive the competition. John David says, "Yeah, we like the prize money, don't get me wrong, it takes a lot of money to do this. And [good prize money] really does bring a lot of teams. But we just went to Galax,

Virginia, which is, go to Tennessee until it runs out and take a left, and drive another two hours and you're there. Larry and Walt talked me into going up there and I'm glad I did. The reason I went is because they had real working fiddles for the trophies."

Saturday, July 16, Galax. Gary Kerce came for the trophies, as well. And as first-place rib winner, he is the only other candidate for grand champion after all the first places have been announced. Pig Pounda already has two fiddles. Taking grand champion would give him a coveted third—one for him, one for brother Roger, one for friend Ricky.

Nine-tenths of a point keeps the third fiddle away from him. Five hundred and sixty four point three points takes grand champion in Galax, Virginia, this July 16. Nine-tenths of a point, .16% of the total score, separates Pig Pounda's hog and the grand champion's hog. "That's why they call it competition," Gary says. Gary will accept the passdown.

On the flip side, just 3.6 points separate Pig Pounda's first-place ribs from second-place ribs. A couple of small scoring decisions made differently by the finals judges, and the team that took first-place hog and first-place shoulder might have also landed first-place rib and, by default, grand championship—achieving the sweep.

That's why they call it competition. Pig Pounda got the 3.6. The team from the state that the mind-reading emcee pulled out of the air when doing her come-gape-at-the-trophies-before-the-interlopers-hie-them-away schtick took the .9, and therefore the grand championship. The emcee had pulled Mississippi out of nowhere as an example of someplace far away. The only team from Mississippi would indeed be hauling 40% of the trophies far away. Two first places, one second place, and, as Ron Passmore announces from the Grayson Street Stage, one grand championship (and "yeah, we like the prize money"—a total of $2,850).

In Memphis, in remembering what they accomplished in Galax the weekend before, John David Wheeler of Natural Born Grillers says to the judges-in-training, "The reason I went is because they had real working fiddles for the trophies....Sometimes you get lucky, cook some good barbecue...

"We came back with a quartet."

John David Wheeler of Natural Born Grillers shows off his fiddle trophy, flanked by Leesa Morris, Janet Wheeler, Tango, Miss Virginia International Elizabeth Roberts, Miss June Wheeler, Ken Weatherman, Birm, and Ken Nottingham.

EPILOGUE

Wrapping up 2005:

Coming out of Galax, Natural Born Grillers led Gwatney by 11 points and Jack's Old South by 12. Through the rest of the year, Jack's Old South would participate in only two more MBA contests, taking grand champion in Charlotte and Vienna, Georgia. Gwatney shaved the lead to 5 points by Sept. 10, but a Natural Born sweep in Bowling Green, Kentucky on the 17th restored the lead to 11. The weekend of Oct. 1, Gwatney picked up 6 points on Natural Born in separate competitions. Lead back to 5. But then Natural Born hit stride. Another near-sweep (as in Galax, two firsts, one second and a grand) on the 8th returned the lead to 11, and another near-sweep on the 15th made it 21. By the full sweep on the 29th, Natural Born was ahead by on insurmountable 34 points. With only two weekends remaining, and 16 points being the most you can outscore an opponent in a given weekend, Natural Born had secured Team of the Year. They shut it down for the season. Gwatney cooked the final two weekends, reduced the overall point lead to 15, and overtook Natural Born as Shoulder Team of the Year. Gwatney also held Rib Team of the Year. Natural Born was Whole Hog Team of the Year.

John David Wheeler had a nerve block for his back pain on July 21, the day before doing the mock presentation at the MBA judges' seminar and the charity cook for the Southaven flood victims. He finally had his back surgery on August 8, the Monday after the Caruthersville cook. His wife had to convince him to not return to the circuit as early as the Butler competition Aug. 13. "I woke up from surgery, and the pain was *gone*." He returned to the circuit at the Greenville, Mississippi, contest Sept. 10. His absence in Butler was the first time no original members of the Natural Born Grillers were at a given cook.

Jim Davis was not quite as fortunate. As he says, "I am doing fine but my leg does not want to cooperate." A CT scan conducted around Christmastime revealed a seven-millimeter gap where the bone did not heal. At this writing, Jim is using a bone-growth stimulator, but surgery may still be in the offing.

John Akins, on Sept. 17, broke into the top MBA ten with two third places (hog and shoulder) in Bowling Green, Kentucky; he'd gotten the passdown Memphis in May bid the week before in Mt. Carmel, Illinois. His Huish team ended the year in the top five—fifth—with 50 points.

Pig Pounda Kappa was the year's last grand champion, of the Richland, Georgia, Pig Fest, with ribs. The victory launched Pig Pounda into the top ten with ninth place and 37 points.

Sweet Swine o' Mine nabbed their Memphis in May bid on Oct. 15, by granding the Covington, Tennessee, 32nd Annual World's Oldest BBQ Competition, with their shoulder. They ended up in the top twenty (tied for fourteenth with 27 points).

Porky's Pride finished in the top ten—sixth—with 48 points, and was the fourth whole hog category team with 19 hog points.

The Alleghany Lawnmower Racing Association season ended in North Wilkesboro, North Carolina, on Sept. 24. The final standings in its thirteen divisions are too lengthy to print here, but we must give a nod to Legends division winner Bill Rhoades, who ended the sevenrace season with 49 points.

Jeff Holmes officially protested to Memphis in May regarding noise after Galax and again after a competition in Bowling Green, Kentucky.

Galax became the only MBA sanctioned event in Virginia in 2005 when Fredericksburg chose to postpone their event until 2006.

Ron Passmore reported mission accomplished: "Over $950 was donated to the Foundation for Excellence in Education benefitting Galax area students with scholarships. The competition was a *huge* success in our community, and was a major profitable moneymaker for our Chamber. We made significant money on this first year event, when everyone told us we would lose money the first year."

Community support for the event was so strong that Smoke on the Mountain began arranging a trip to the Memphis in May World Championship Barbecue Cooking Contest so people could see their winners at the big show. Organizers first sought to fill a mini-van. Two busloads of participants quickly signed up.

The Bowie Duel in Vidalia, Louisiana, became one of the many victims of Hurricane Katrina. It was cancelled. The contest site was turned over to Katrina evacuees.

Pit Connection changed its name to JD's Smokin' Misfits.

Roger Kerce became the sole owner of Southern Welding and Fabrication on Sept. 30, the Friday of the Vienna, Georgia, Big Pig Jig.

Becky Guynn, creator of the Smoke on the Mountain logo, joined with three business partners to open City Gallery in Galax on Aug. 8.

The Chapters Bookstore met its "like Christmas" goal of book sales the weekend of Smoke on the Mountain: 73 copies of the latest *Potter*, and handful of barbecue books, and a surge of regional interest books.

At the time this book went to press, the galax leaves used as decorations in the bank-lobby hospitality room were starting to show a little brownish dessication around the edges, but were otherwise still green—demonstrating in the twenty-first century their nineteenth-century value as long-lasting decorative greenery in the days long before plastic and silk artificial foliage.

Jack's Old South finalized the designs on a new all-in-one rig to replace the cookers and trailers that had been giving the team so much road trouble. Myron also decided to paint his pickup truck black.

In October, Virginia Lt. Governor Tim Kaine presented the following proclamation during a campaign stop in Galax:

By Virtue of the Authority vested by the Constitution in the Governor of the Commonwealth of Virginia, there is hereby officially recognized:

SMOKE ON THE MOUNTAIN BARBECUE CONTEST

WHEREAS, During the weekend of July 15 & 16 2005, over 8000 people gathered in Galax for the Smoke on the Mountain BBQ Competition; and

WHEREAS, Twelve teams from around the United States competed in Smoke on the Mountain, with each team working for the chance to earn a spot in the 2006 (Memphis in May) World Championship BBQ Cooking Contest; and

WHEREAS, This year marks the first time that the Memphis Barbecue Association has ever sanctioned an event in Southwest Virginia; and

WHEREAS, The contest was a huge success due in large part to the hard work and dedication of the hosts and organizers of the contest, the Galax-Carroll-Grayson Chamber of Commerce and The Galax Smokehouse; and

WHEREAS, Smoke on the Mountain helped to raise thousands of dollars for the Chamber of Commerce while also creating a positive economic impact on the local economy, benefitting shops throughout the area;

NOW, THEREFORE, I Mark Warner, do hereby recognize the SMOKE ON THE MOUNTAIN BBQ CONTEST as the official BBQ Competition for the COMMONWEALTH OF VIRGINIA, and I call this observance to the attention of all our citizens.

Ron Passmore and 3 Pigs and a Lady began "lightly" investigating competition rigs.

At a black-tie awards dinner held in Galax on Dec. 9, Walt Brown and Larry Ohrberg, flown in by Smoke on the Mountain, were surprised when competition organizers awarded them two trophyesque fiddles. Larry O even took up the instrument. "I started playing 'Mary Had a Little Lamb' and it took my wife only five guesses to get it."

Ron Passmore got some sleep. We think.

Larry Ohrberg and Walt Brown meet Crash Test Dummies Larry and Vince distributing safety materials at the Bowling Green, Kentucky, Balloons, Tunes and BBQ competition.

APPENDIX

Get Yourself a Taste of Galax

Natural Born Grillers sells its Million-Dolla rub:
www.naturalborngrillers.net

Jack's Old South sells its sauces:
www.rdcss.com/samples/bbq/public_html/sauce.html#mixon

To listen to **Steve Barr** play:
Bluegrass Lullaby, by No Speed Limit
The album includes a cut called "Stevie's Breakdown," an
instrumental that hints at "Foggy Mountain Breakdown" but
is a bangup tune all its own. (The album includes "The
Hometown")
www.countysales.com/php-bin/ecomm4/products.php?prod-
uct_id=4376

Roger Kerce builds grills for sale:
www.pigpoundakappa.com/
And the Kerces have a video:
www.barbecue-store.com/howtobarbecuewholehog.htm

Associated restaurants:
Galax Smokehouse
101 N. Main St.
Galax VA 24333
276-236-1000

Boulevard Wood Grill
2901 Wilson Blvd.
Arlington VA 22201
703-875-9663

To Learn more about judging or cooking:
Memphis Barbecue Association
www.memphisinmay.org

Kansas City Barbecue Society
kcbs.us/

International Barbecue Cookers Association
www.ibcabbq.org/

A listing of more regional societies:
bbq.about.com/od/barbecuesocieties/

For updates on the barbecue competition world, and for links to great sauces, rubs and recipes:
www.TheGrillOfVictory.com

ABOUT THE AUTHOR

William Brohaugh has been judging barbecue competitions since 1990 and is certified as a judge on the Memphis in May circuit. He is a former editor of *Writer's Digest* magazine and former editorial director of *Writer's Digest* books. He is the author of *Write Tight* (ISI Books) and *Professional Etiquette for Writers* (Writer's Digest Books) and has written dozens of magazine nonfiction pieces. He lives in Union, Kentucky.

Bill Brohaugh (left) learns hands-on hog prep from Rick Dalton of Twatney Championship Barbecue in Butler, Alabama.
(Photo by Al Norton)